THE
WARRIOR
WITHIN

"Most people move from act to act without any struggle or thought. A hunter, on the contrary, assesses every act . . . he proceeds judiciously, as if every act were his last battle. . . . It's only natural that his last act on earth should be the best of himself."—Carlos Castaneda, *Journey to Ixtlan*

THE
WARRIOR WITHIN,

ACCESSING
THE KNIGHT IN THE
MALE PSYCHE

Robert Moore
and Douglas Gillette

WILLIAM MORROW AND COMPANY, INC.
NEW YORK

Library of Congress Cataloging-in-Publication Data

Moore, Robert L.
    The warrior within : accessing the knight in the male psyche / Robert Moore and Douglas Gillette.
        p.   cm.
    ISBN 0-688-09592-5
    1. Men—Psychology.   2. Masculinity (Psychology).   3. Archetype (Psychology).
    4. Machismo.   I. Gillette, Douglas.   II. Title.
    BF692.5.M66   1992
    155.3′32—dc20   92-9494
                                                                                        CIP

Printed in the United States of America

First Edition

1 2 3 4 5 6 7 8 9 10

BOOK DESIGN BY RICHARD ORIOLO

To the memory of Mohandas Gandhi and Martin Luther King, Jr.—and all the warriors who have risked their personal welfare and put their lives on the line for their loved ones and for their communities and, beyond a tribal vision, have fought for universal justice, for shalom, and for cosmos. And to all those men who have accessed the Warrior within themselves for fullness of life and self-affirmation—for themselves, for all those around them, and for the planet as a whole.

THE WARRIOR IN THE
MASCULINE SOUL

O FTEN DISPARAGED, SELDOM UNDERSTOOD, THE
Warrior is the most controversial of the archetypes.
Many feel the human race would do better without his
aggression and rage. And those who have been caught within
the Warrior's sadomasochistic shadow system have perpe-
trated the cruelest acts known to history. It is easy to see why
people fear this energy, and wish it away.

But archetypes may not be wished away. Among the
fundamental assumptions of the authors of these books is that
archetypes can never be expunged from the human psyche.
As we make plain in this series, each man carries a dynamic,

fourfold structure of archetypes—the King, Warrior, Magician, and Lover—within him. A woman has a corresponding system of Queen, Warrior, Magician, and Lover, but it is the male system we are particularly exploring. Each of these archetypes must be realistically appraised and managed. Those who try to banish an archetype from their psychic system endanger themselves, and those around them—because a banished archetype never goes away, only underground, into the unconscious.

Aggression is not, as some radical feminists would have it, limited to the male of the species. Both men and women have a Warrior to deal with (though, in terms of *physical* acting out, it does seem to be true that many men have more difficulty managing theirs). There is no way to socialize aggression away. The Warrior archetype is hard-wired into our brain structure. Socialization means repression, which only keeps aggressiveness in an all the more volatile, compressed, and explosive form. But aggression is not, in and of itself, a bad thing. In many ways legitimate aggression contributes vitally to our lives. In aggression we find our drives for life, career, social contact, self-definition, and service. Perseverance and fidelity are products of the Warrior's determination. Though the Lover initiates a relationship, it is the Warrior who maintains it—without the Warrior the Lover is merely promiscuous. The answer then is not to banish any of the archetypes, but to work on achieving the maturity necessary to manage them.

With a growing sense of what masculinity entails, many men today are claiming their birthright Warrior energy, empowering themselves and offering a plan for personal empowerment to others. As with the Knights of the Round Table, today's male warriors are pledging their fealty to metapersonal concerns: their workplaces, communities, and families. They are stepping forward as stewards of human community. From a position at the center of the psyche, the Knight within encourages every man to take up his sword and fight to preserve, to provide for, and to extend the things he believes in and the people he cares for.

Those readers who are new to this series will find in Chapters 1 and 2 a basic grounding in the Jungian concepts we have extended in this series. In the three appendices we expand, for the interested reader, on some intriguing structural aspects of the psyche that lend support to our work. These two chapters and the three appendices are common to all four books in this series, so the new reader can find all the basic information he needs in any single book. Thus the reader familiar with another book in the series may choose to turn straight to Chapter 3. Taken together the four books are an integrated "male quartet," and offer a balanced vision of responsible stewardship of the four masculine "horses of power." *If we, like knights of old, learn to ride such spirited steeds, perhaps the "four horsemen of the apocalypse" will take on a new, more hopeful, meaning.*

ACKNOWLEDGMENTS

T HE AUTHORS WISH TO THANK GRACIELA INFANTE for her careful reading of the manuscript. Doug especially wishes to express his appreciation for her ongoing support, encouragement, and many helpful suggestions during the long times of intensive work on the manuscript.

Robert wants to express especial appreciation to Margaret Shanahan for her inspiration and encouragement since the days when many of these ideas were being formulated initially as lectures. Since 1985 her ongoing companionship and support have not only stimulated his work but deeply enriched his life and his understanding of the four powers of the psyche.

Both authors wish to thank Patrick Nugent and Angela Smith for their transcriptions of Robert Moore's lecture tapes, Noel Kaufmann for his location of research sources, Max Havlick for his work on permissions and bibliography, and Rudy Vetter for his excellent photography.

Especial thanks go to Maria Guarnaschelli (vice president and senior editor at William Morrow) for her innovative vision for this series and for her intensive and superlative editorial work. Katharina Buck has been tireless in her ongoing liaison work and in her commitment to effective coordination and getting all the details together for preparation of the manuscript. Kathy Antrim has been very helpful in the editorial process at Morrow. Kurt Aldeg has given his insights into how best to communicate the ideas in this book to the widest audience. These and the other outstanding Morrow staff have made the success of this book possible.

In addition, the authors wish to acknowledge the many men, inside and outside of the men's movement, who have reflected on their personal experience as men and helped refine the understanding of the four powers and four masculine initiations presented in this series of books. With their continuing help, perhaps these masculine powers can be accessed in more helpful and generative ways to serve the human community.

CONTENTS

CONTENTS

"Be Glorious!"
The battle cry of the Knights Templar

PART 1

HARD WIRING: THE MASCULINE SOUL

1

GENDER IDENTITY, GENDER ASYMMETRY, AND THE SEXUAL IMBALANCE OF POWER

INCREASINGLY TODAY, MEN AND WOMEN ARE struggling to live in a twilight world of gender confusion. Anxiously they wonder what, if anything, constitutes their own unique sexual identity. Women don business suits and become bankers and lawyers. Men clean house and learn to change diapers. These shifts in traditional work roles may be all to the good. But are there any real differences between men and women? If not, what joy is left us in sexual union? Have we become interchangeable parts, androgynous to the core?

Some teach us to feel ashamed of our sex-specific differences. Supporters of radical androgyny go so far as to discourage research into the dissimilarities in brain structure, or in the chemical, hormonal, or instinctual configurations that may influence some culturally exaggerated scripts.[1]

Some theorists offer stereotyped ideals of "feminine" psychological characteristics, now alone deemed fully human.[2] Boys are said to be developmentally inferior to girls. Men are held to be biologically and emotionally inferior to women. Some radical feminists assert women would be better off without men entirely—or that male children should be genetically or socially engineered to eliminate "masculine aggressiveness."

This is not to say that all feminist criticism is invalid. The feminist critique of patriarchal societies makes a great deal of sense. Patriarchy *does* tend to institutionalize a particular kind of masculinity, prone to exploiting and oppressing other human beings, other species, and the environment. But oppressive, "macho" societies deny *men* their mature masculinity as certainly as they degrade women and feminine attributes. Typically a small minority of underdeveloped males at the top of the social pyramid will control power and wealth to the exclusion of all others, male and female. They rank these others in a descending order of usefulness to themselves and defend against them with all the force of their inflated self-regard. Patriarchy is therefore a manifestation of the infantile grandiosity suffered by its leaders.

Patriarchy is set up and run not for men as a gender or for masculinity in its fullness or in its mature expressions but rather by men who are fundamentally *immature*. It is really the rule of boys, often cruel and abusive boys. For the most part, we believe human societies have always consisted of boys and girls more or less unconsciously acting out their immature and grandiose fantasies. Our planetary home more often than not has resembled the island world in William Golding's *Lord of the Flies*. Thus our societies have, on the whole, opposed

4

the realization and expression of *both* mature feminine and masculine psyches.

Brutalized children—and for most children in most times and places brutality is a commonplace—become brutal adults. But they are not really adults. They can only pretend to be adults while they still operate on a level of childish self-aggrandizement. The developmental crippling that generates patriarchy is not however the sole responsibility of childish males. Immature males *and* females are unconscious partners in the socially sanctioned repression of children. A child's sense of self is distorted by a mother who fails to confront her own emotional issues, and her own unresolved needs for power and adulation. The therapist Alice Miller has written a pioneering series of books that addresses poisonous pedagogy,[3] as she calls this problem. Childish men and women never outgrow being self-interested and self-involved, and they pass their own wounds on to their children. Mature men and women find the ways to be selfless in their regard for others, even as they are manifestly self-caring.

In sum, we feel it is wrong to view patriarchy as the expression of a mature masculinity or of masculinity in its essence. Patriarchal societies are out of balance partly because at their helm are unbalanced men. And while we abhor the often horrific abuses of patriarchal systems, we also remember that males helped generate, from earlier urban neolithic cultures, all the higher civilizations we know from recorded history.[4] The efforts of dynamic, life-engendering men have left an astounding record of discovery and achievement. Clearly the energies of men, in partnership with women and their feminine energies, have fueled (and will continue to fuel) the significant advances of imagination and social organization that characterize our species. Men of the past, in every tribe and nation, have struggled to learn how to use their power to bless the human community. We continue to struggle today.

Lost in Childhood:
Failed Initiation (Egyptian figure of mourning)

Defining masculine and feminine characteristics has led
to much discussion. After years of research, depth psychologists and others argue that each sex carries both the psychological and physical traits of the other.[5] No man is purely
masculine, just as there is no purely feminine woman.[6] Jungian psychologists call the feminine characteristics of the male
psyche the Anima; the female psyche's masculine characteristics they call the Animus.

Both the Animus and the Anima develop in complex
fashion as the personality grows to maturity. Neither men nor
women can reach psychological maturity without integrating
their respective contrasexual other. A man's female elements
enhance his manhood, just as a woman's male aspects enhance
her womanhood. Typically masculine characteristics are dominant in a man, as are feminine characteristics in a woman. Of
course there are exceptions, but this is usually the case. Central to all these discussions is the question of whether masculinity is in its *essence* more coercive, more abusive of power,
more compulsively dominance-seeking than femininity. Many
have implied or argued that biological gender differences *ne-
cessitate* rigid sex-role differentiation and make masculine
dominance *inevitable*.

For example, the changing history of male and female
roles within the Israeli kibbutzim are presented as evidence of
innate masculine and feminine characteristics.[7] The kibbutzim were founded as farming communities in the late nine-
teenth century under the influence of Marxist ideals. Men and
women were viewed not only as equal, but as inherently the
same. In the fields, women worked the same long hours as the
men. In the kitchens, nurseries, and children's dormitories
men worked the same long hours as the women.

As the years passed, however, an unexpected development occurred. Slowly the women left the fields, the traditional areas of men's work. More and more they specialized in

the work of the kitchens, nurseries, and dormitories. Gradually, the men specialized in the field work. Against the enormous pressure of kibbutz ideology most men and women sorted themselves into "traditional" gender-specific roles. Was this the result of biology or immature manipulation of masculine power? According to sociobiology, primate ethology, and brain-structure/hormonal research, there *may* be instinctual biological roots for such tendencies in social behavior.[8] In addition, the anthropologist David Gilmore, in his *Manhood in the Making*—the first extensively documented cross-cultural examination of the "cult of manhood"—strongly indicates a widespread societal support for a division of social and work roles among men and women.[9]

Even if it could be proved, however, that some traditionally masculine or feminine *tendencies* may be inherited this would not be a basis for justifying the usual caricatures of these traits. Above all, it does not justify the assumption that men are inherently violent, inordinately aggressive, insensitive, and uninterested in intimate relationships, nor that women have a monopoly on gentle, nurturing, emotional, and intuitive behaviors. Probably the most accurate argument is that men are more "hard-wired" for some psychological tendencies and women for others. Unfortunately, historical cultures nearly always have amplified rather than helped us compensate for these tendencies.

Important as all these considerations may be, in this book our purpose is not to focus on gender difference. We intend rather to advance understanding of the deep masculine and the challenge of stewarding masculine power. *For whatever the source of masculine abuse of power, it is our responsibility as contemporary men to understand it and to develop the emotional and spiritual resources to end it.* We want to help men express what psychoanalyst Erik Erikson termed the "generative man" within themselves.[10] We will do this by exploring how masculinity is anchored in the place where body, instinct, mind, and soul arise in men.

Contrary to those thinkers who, with Reinhold Niebuhr, regard power itself as inevitably leading to evil,[11] we believe it is possible to steward power responsibly. The drive toward attaining personal and corporate empowerment is as much a part of our instinctual makeup as eating, sleeping, and procreating. We cannot wish away what psychologist Alfred Adler called the "will to power,"[12] the desire to overcome. "We shall overcome" is not just a civil-rights rallying cry—it is a human instinct to achieve efficacy and competence in adaptation. We cannot and should not raise our children to eschew this primal and ultimately life-enhancing instinct.[13] The issue should never be how to get rid of the urge for power, masculine or feminine. The real issue is how to steward it, and how to channel our other instincts along with it into life-giving and world-building activities.

THE PROBLEM OF THE MODERN
ATTACK ON MYTH AND RITUAL

The creative use of instinctual male energies, like the good use of any energy source, requires maturity. Human maturity has probably always been a rare commodity. But we believe it was, at least in some respects, more available in the past than it is today. It was more available even in patriarchal states, with all of their drawbacks, than it is in our modern societies. In the past there were powerful rites of initiation presided over by ritual elders to help boys and girls remake themselves into men and women capable of assuming their social responsibilities.[14] The scope of these premodern initiation rituals was often limited by inflexible cultural norms. But they did provide boys and girls with workable blueprints for achieving gender-specific maturity and were based on mythic visions of the tribe's view of the best in human nature—their normative vision of the possible human.

An apprentice electrician must be initiated by an experienced master into the mysteries of electricity's sources, methods of generation, and technologies of distribution. Whatever the apprentice does not take care to understand is a danger to him, because electricity carries force enough to kill him. In similar fashion all human beings need to be initiated into the wise and life-enhancing uses of human psychological resources. Where misunderstood, the energies of our psyches can wreak havoc upon our lives. Despite the elaborate training our modern society provides an individual mastering a trade, we do not think to offer anything similar to the man who wishes to master his own psyche. But our lack of teachers doesn't change our need to learn how to access the powerful energies of our deep souls.

Essentially, the process of initiation removes our Ego from the center of the universe. When a society abandons initiation rituals, individual Egos lose an appropriate means of learning this valuable lesson. Life circumstances will urge the same lesson upon the Ego eventually, but perhaps in a very painful, inopportune manner. But by far the most serious consequence of ceasing initiatory practices is the loss of a periodic social forum for considering the nature of maturity. A society has to know what maturity is before it can pass the knowledge on. It's as if we no longer have a map to get us to maturity. If you don't know where something is, and you don't have a map, how do you get there? A few will stumble across the destination. But most of us end up getting hopelessly lost. When people bemoan our culture's loss of values, in part they are missing the old transformative rituals—for rituals provide a structure within which social values can be recalled and reconsidered.

In many tribal societies initiation ceremonies are still given the prominence they deserve. Through ritual training and the special imparting of carefully stewarded wisdom, the Ego is displaced into an orbital position around a Transpersonal Other. The Ego may experience this Transpersonal Other as any kind of group or task to which the individual pledges his or her loyalties, best efforts, even his or her life. In premodern societies, such group tasks and loyalties are always themselves ultimately subordinate to and given meaning by a greater Transpersonal Other, which religions of the world call "God."

As a complete cultural system, modernity has largely turned its back on God, on effective processes of initiation, on ritual elders, and even on family, tribe, and nation. Consequently, an individual Ego can no longer reach the sober but joyous realization of its *non*central position in the psyche and in the wider universe. Nature fills the vacuum modernity has created with our modern Egos, which expand terrifically to fill the empty space. Where a powerful Transpersonal Other is missing, God is replaced by unconscious pretensions to godhood.

An individual psyche, bloated by dangerously distorted assessments of self and others around it—family, friends, lovers, company, nation, and perhaps the entire globe—must pay the price for its infantilism. Corrupt politicians, money-hungry yuppies, drug dealers, wife (and husband) abusers, and new racists are but a few examples of infantilism run amok. Petty dictators, self-styled fundamentalist "messiahs" and their terrorist henchmen, Khmer Rouge genocidal murderers, Chinese Communist-party bullies, irresponsible international oil company executives, among many others, cause the social and environmental devastation that always accompanies the

Ego inflation of the human psyche unchecked by a sense of limits grounded in a Transpersonal Other. These would-be men and women have failed to grasp a sufficiently wide and deep vision of the archetypal realities upon which our psyche is founded. It is time we look again to these deep structures and draw from them the psychic support our modern era so desperately needs.

2

DECODING THE MALE PSYCHE

C ARL GUSTAV JUNG FOUNDED THE SCHOOL OF
analytical or "depth" psychology that provides the over-
all framework of our work.[1] We rely heavily also on insights
from theorists of other schools such as Sigmund Freud, Erik
Erikson, D. W. Winnicott, Heinz Kohut, and Alice Miller. But
we believe Jung's approach is the only one to provide a truly
transcultural understanding of our human psyche. His is also
the only approach to adequately bridge the gap between modern science and the mythological and spiritual traditions of
our species.

Jungian depth psychology values the mysteries of the

human soul. Dreams, visions, symbols, images, and cultural achievements arise from those mysterious depths that the world's religions understand as the "spiritual dimension." Depth psychology embraces all human experience as authentic to the psyche. Consequently, phenomena such as the "soul," "demonic possession," "revelation," "prayer," or "god" are completely compatible with scientific truth. Because all experiences are psychological, all are real, no matter how strange.[2] Above all, *any* human experience is both *based on* and *perceived by* the deep psychological structures within us.[3]

Before we explore the deep structures of the male psyche, it will be helpful to define a few Jungian terms.

MYTH: For depth psychologists myth does not imply a naïve, untrue, prescientific tale about the origins of the world or humankind. Myths are true stories that describe the ways of the psyche and the means by which our psychological energies interact.[4] Myths project our inner dynamics onto the outer world and allow us to experience it through the filter of how we think and feel.[5]

Since in a real sense we *are* the universe and the universe is us, myths often accurately describe the workings of the larger universe by using anthropomorphic images. That is to say, we are products of the universe in the same way that galaxies, oceans, and trees are. It would be a very strange thing indeed if our psyche did not mirror the structures found outside in the cosmos. An immediate and intimate correspondence between *inner* and *outer* is fundamental to our nature as beings. If no such link existed, we would be unable to acquire any realistic or workable knowledge of the world. We would be unable to survive. Ultimately, it is possible that *inner* and *outer* are purely subjective, pragmatic distinctions made by our consciousness in order to navigate within a mystery it cannot fully fathom.

Creation myths illustrate this beautifully. In the Bible, the Hebrew God Yahweh creates the material world by speaking. He says, "Let there be such and such!" and there is such and such. Behind this concept of creation stands the idea that naming something brings it into existence. Of course, modern science maintains the world did not come into being through a divine uttering of words or the naming of material objects. The biblical account does not convey a scientific truth about the world's origin. The truth it speaks is psychological.

Human consciousness at its height is developed largely by the mastering of words. Arising from language, at the same time it gives rise *to* language, consciousness creates our experience as it defines creation. The words we use for things allow us to distinguish *this* from *that*. They also profoundly color how we think and feel about those things. What we cannot name is therefore not fully real or fully experienced for us. As far as our psyche is concerned, an unnamed thing is "uncreated."[6] Thus the biblical image of Yahweh creating the world by naming it is true to human psychological processes. At the same time, if we assume there is an intelligence behind the created world, it might be true that that intelligence manifested the universe through some process analogous to the human use of language. If this were so, the biblical story would be working both as a psychological parable and as a visionary expression of a process that really *is* occurring in the universe as a whole.

EGO: When Jungian psychoanalysts talk about the Ego, they usually mean the "I" we normally think of as ourselves.[7] The Ego is who we believe ourselves to be, the part of our psyche we identify with our name. When we say, "*I* feel this way about something," or "*I* think I'll do that," the Ego is probably speaking. Jungian theorists sometimes define the Ego as a *complex*. By this they mean a structural element of the total psyche that exhibits certain specific features. The Ego operates in what we imagine to be our capacity to think rationally, in our feelings, in our ability to will actions, remember the past, and create the future, and in our encounter with consciousness.

In reality, however, the question of the Ego is more complicated. Often "I" am not the one who is thinking, feeling, acting, willing, or deciding. Rather some *autonomous complex* other than the Ego may temporarily "possess" it and make it operate out of the complex's perspective. Since the Ego is largely unaware of these other complexes, it is tricked into the illusory feeling of holding a solitary place in the psyche, and into an accompanying illusion of its "free will." According to Jung, the other complexes operate largely from the personal unconscious, but may also be anchored in a transpersonal unconscious which exerts a deeper influence on the psyche.

CONSCIOUSNESS: Consciousness is not confined to the Ego. The *sub*conscious or *un*conscious is itself conscious. It is only unconscious—invisible and indistinct—from the *Ego*'s perspective.[8] Personal complexes other than the Ego, and the deeper transpersonal psychological structures of the unconscious, can be conscious of each other and of the Ego, and they operate out of their own agendas. The case of multiple-personality disorder demonstrates this clearly. Here highly activated complexes usurp the place of the Ego in the daily affairs of the afflicted person, causing him or her to behave in ways the Ego neither wishes nor sometimes even remembers afterward.

What is true for people who suffer multiple-personality disorder is true, though to a lesser extent, for all of us. We all at times act in ways contrary to how our Ego wills us to behave, perhaps through deep mood swings and emotionally violent outbursts of fear and rage. When we return to a state of Ego consciousness, we say such things as "I went out of my head" or "I don't know what came over me." What came over us, like a wave of energy that shifted our whole mode of perceiving, feeling, and acting, was an autonomous complex, another consciousness from within the total psychic system that is our Self.

Autonomous complexes are usually (though not always) organized around traumatic childhood experiences.[9] During early traumas, our emerging Egos split off and repressed aspects of the psyche that parents, siblings, or society found unacceptable. These split-off aspects could be thoughts, feelings, images, or associations. Often they are valuable and worth recall. They may carry hidden talents, intuitions, abilities, or accurate feelings that would make our personalities wiser and more complete if we could reintegrate them. Until reintegration can occur, our psyches are like the pieces of a broken mirror, which hold in fragments what was once a complete reflection. Through all our complexes, including the Ego, and the vast territory of the unconscious, consciousness pervades our psyche.

ARCHETYPES: Archetypes operate at a level of the psyche deeper than that of the personal unconscious with its autonomous complexes. They are the hard-wired components of our genetically transmitted psychic machine.[10] They are the bedrock structures that define the human psyche's own nature, and make it the same, regardless of the culture in which an individual lives. In this sense archetypes represent transpersonal human psychological characteristics. They are dynamic, energic elements in all of us. They well up and fall deep within our unconscious like tidal pulls. Our daily life is influenced by

17

these energies in ways we can never fully understand.

Jung declared that the archetypes are equivalent to the instincts of other animals. He located them in what he called the *collective unconscious*.[11] The existence of an unconscious, or what many called the subconscious, had been noted for some time. But Freud was the first to make it the focus of major psychological investigation. Before him, even where psychologists acknowledged the subconscious mind's existence, they usually dismissed it as an inert repository of forgotten or repressed experiences.

Freud's interest in the mind's possibilities had been aroused during his medical studies with the great Parisian hypnotist, Jean Martin Charcot. Charcot dismissed the results of his own experimental demonstrations as stemming from patient hysteria. Whatever their source, the hypnotic manifestations witnessed by the young Freud convinced him he'd found a rich field for further study.

Common to all of us, Freud's life work implied, was a subconscious deeper than a particular personal one. He called this instinctually based subconscious the *Id* (the Latin word for "it").[12] This wild, primitive Id was responsible for all kinds of enormously powerful and irrational impulses, especially aggressive sexuality.

Classic Freudians have tended to regard the subconscious as more or less unstructured. But a number of neo-Freudians maintain that the deep psyche, far from being chaotic, is characterized by structure. Erik Erikson talks about "instinctive structures" and "preformed action patterns," which, under appropriate circumstances, call up "drive energy for instantaneous, vigorous, and skillful release."[13] He proposes the existence of "a general psychic energy (instinctual force) which can be put to use by a variety of preformed and relatively autonomous instinctive patterns."[14] He also says, "the action patterns—the modes and modalities—are all present in

the ground plan from the beginning, yet they have their special time of ascending."[15] His thoughts come remarkably close
to the Jungian conception of time-and-circumstance-released
archetypal "action patterns" from the collective unconscious.

Jung pushed the exploration of the collective unconscious structures a step further. Stored within them, he
claimed, are both the human psyche's archetypal building
blocks and the accumulated collective memory of the entire
human race. He reached this conclusion because he discovered
that symbols, images, myths, and Gods from different cultures
and epochs bore striking resemblances to one another and also
to the images that appeared in his patients' dreams. According
to his conception, the collective unconscious is the source and
the limitless reservoir of all the images recorded in human art,
mythology, and religion. From it leap both the poet's song and
the scientist's insight. From it flow the signal dreams which
have implication often for an entire society as much as for
their dreamer.

The psyche's archetypal structures serve as conduits for
great charges of primal psychological energy. Because of their
own dynamic configuration, they mold this energy, imparting
to it their particular patterns. Psychologists call this life-force
in psychic form the *Libido*.[16] Freud believed that Libido is
fundamentally sexual. Any expression of the Libido redirected
into pursuits other than sexual ones he called "sublimations."
Jung, on the other hand, believed that the Libido is a general-
ized life-force that expresses itself through imaginal and spiritual impulses, as well as through sexuality.

For any individual the archetypes may be creative and
life-enhancing or destructive and death-dealing. The result
depends in part on how the Ego is able to relate to them based
on its own developmental history. Properly accessing and
using the Libido available to the psyche amount to a sort of
psychological technology. If we learn the technology and use

19

it properly, we can use the energy to make generative men and women of ourselves. But if we fail to learn how to use these vast energy resources, or misuse them, we will be courting our own destruction, and we may take others with us. If we try to ignore the archetypes, they exert their mighty influence upon us nonetheless. They bend us to their nonhuman, sometimes *in*human wills. We must therefore face the evidence depth psychology and other studies have provided us. We are not as free of instinct or unconscious content as we have been encouraged to believe. Genuine freedom for the Ego results from acknowledging and properly accessing the chemical fires that burn hot in our unconscious minds.

Some Jungian analysts romanticize the archetypes.[17] They encourage their patients to find and claim the particular archetype or myth that has organized their lives. Life then becomes a process of affirming and living out this myth. In our opinion our goal should not be to identify with an archetypal pattern, or to allow a mythic expression of it to make our lives what it will. We believe that when we romantically *identify* with any archetype we cease to be viable human beings moving toward wholeness. If we are drawn to an archetype by its seductive power, its promise that we can shirk our individual responsibilities and the pain involved in being a person with a personal Ego, we will be crushed by the sheer weight of unconscious compulsive impulses.

On the other hand, our goal is not to become *ordinary* in our quest for psychic health. We must not lose the vital connection with the libidinal energy the archetypes supply us so that we can live our lives fully, energetically, and creatively. Our goal is to learn how to *differentiate* ourselves from the archetypes without completely *disassociating* ourselves from them. If we learn to access them successfully, they become resources of energy both for our personal lives and for healing our planet—we become more radiant in every area of our lives.

More precisely stated, our objective is to develop mature Ego structures strong enough to channel useful libidinal energy into our daily lives. We can begin by making ourselves conscious of how archetypal energies already possess us. Only then can we begin to access them creatively, through a process that provides us with a greater sense of free will in the choices of our lives. The effort to achieve liberation for ourselves will in turn motivate us to help others do the same. Our renewed energies benefit ourselves and others on all the levels of our psychic organization: the personal, the familial, the communal, national, and global.

SHADOW: Jung himself occasionally identified the Shadow with the totality of the unconscious. But most depth psychologists view the Shadow as an individual, multifaceted contra-Ego, of the same sex as the Ego.[18] If the Ego is a photograph, the Shadow is its negative. Standing in direct opposition to the Ego, the Shadow is an autonomous complex, which holds opinions, expresses feelings, and generally wills an agenda radically different from the Ego's.

Like most autonomous complexes, the Shadow results from childhood trauma. Those qualities of a person's total psyche that are diametrically opposed to the emerging Ego, and that the Ego rejects because of the pressures of the childhood environment, coalesce in the unconscious. There they form a distinct, conscious, willing entity. Unless reintegrated later in life, they forever seek to sabotage the Ego's plans and behaviors.

We have all had the experience of willing one scenario and living quite another. For example, we intend to remain friendly while visiting our in-laws, but then find ourselves drawn irresistibly into arguments and confrontation. Our Egos want to maintain an image of family harmony. Our Shadows, unable to tolerate such hypocrisy, and feeling real animosity toward our in-laws, compel us to behave in a more honest, if more destructive, way.

The animosity we feel is ultimately toward ourselves, but it often takes a lot of work before we can realize this. The Shadow endorses this work because it longs for reintegration. It is the Shadow's method to lead us into holding our impossibly defensive, illogical positions—in order to confront us with whatever psychic complexes we would rather forget. Our "real world" hatreds are most usually against these inner complexes, and our Shadow works by *repetition compulsion* to call our attention to them.

Rather than face any rejected qualities, either positive or negative, within ourselves, we frequently deal with our Shadow by projecting those qualities onto others.[19] As an Ego, we don't project them. But our Shadow does so in order to focus our interest on its feelings, wishes, and agendas. Our Shadow induces us to see other people we disapprove of or dislike in colors that are perhaps only marginally like their "true" colors but which *are* colors that the Shadow itself possesses.

Jung believed withdrawing a projection of the Shadow and owning it as a part of ourselves requires enormous moral courage. He also believed that what we will not face within our psyche we will be forced to confront in the outer world. So, if we can claim our Shadow's qualities, and learn from them, we defuse much of the interpersonal conflict we would otherwise encounter. People who have served as the screens for our Shadow's projections become less odious, and more human. At the same time, we experience ourselves as richer, more complex, and more powerful individuals.

THE TRIANGULAR STRUCTURE
OF THE ARCHETYPES

In this book our definition of the Shadow includes this traditional Jungian understanding, but introduces another archetypal, transpersonal aspect to it as well. We believe masculine and feminine archetypes possess their own Shadows. The King, the Warrior, the Magician, and the Lover are the masculine archetypal structures we have undertaken to study in this series. In one sense these archetypes are operating at more primitive levels than the Ego accessing them, and each has its own Shadow.

In our extended definition, a Shadow always manifests where there is an immature, fragmentary psyche, because splitting is always a symptom of unintegrated development.[20] In the traditional Jungian view of maturity, wholeness is achieved largely to the degree that the split between the Ego and the Shadow is overcome. In large part, psychological maturity is a measure of how thoroughly the Ego is able to integrate the Shadow into its consciousness.

We maintain that the Ego/Shadow split represents a Shadow system in itself. The split actually involves the Ego in the *bipolar* Shadow of one or more archetypes. In this situation our Ego usually identifies with one pole of the archetypal Shadow and disassociates from the other. In our view, then, the Shadow can still be regarded in the traditional way as the psychic area from which the Ego is divided but, more fully, as a bipolar *system* characterized by splitting, repression, and projection *within* the energy field of an archetype.

For a long time psychologists associated "bipolar disorder" almost exclusively with the manic-depressive personality.[21]

Then, in his *Modern Psychopathology*, Theodore Millon extended the idea of bipolarity to include passive and active dimensions in all the major disorders of personality.[22] In a similar fashion, some Jungians have described a bipolar relationship between certain archetypes (though they are not in themselves personality disorders). That gave rise to such archetypal pairs as the senex-puer (old man–eternal boy), the domina-puella (old woman–eternal girl) and others.[23]

In the case of the Warrior archetype, for example, neither the Sadist nor the Masochist (the two poles of the Warrior's Shadow) represents personal growth or fulfillment. The full embodiment of the Warrior is to be found in a third transcending option that integrates the two poles into a creative psychological structure. Since they define psychic wholeness, archetypes always reconcile opposing forces in this way. Both of the opposing poles in the archetypal Shadow systems contain qualities essential for psychological health. But if left in their state of chronic tension, they will condemn the Ego to a fragmented and immature existence. Guided by the archetypes in their transcending fullness, a mature personality integrates these important qualities by reconciling the divisions in the archetypal Shadow.

Our refined understanding of how the archetypes work suggests interesting analogies with other schools of thought. The psychologist Alfred Adler, a contemporary of Freud and Jung, believed personality disorders appear both in active and passive modes in a way similar to our view of how archetypal Shadow systems work. The Christian theologian Paul Tillich grounded his thought with a belief in what he called the "ambiguities" of space and time in the created world. He believed that these ambiguities find their resolution in a third, higher reality "above" history.[24] The impulse to achieve this comes from the "Spirit." The German philosopher Hegel saw the forward movement of the universe as occurring through a

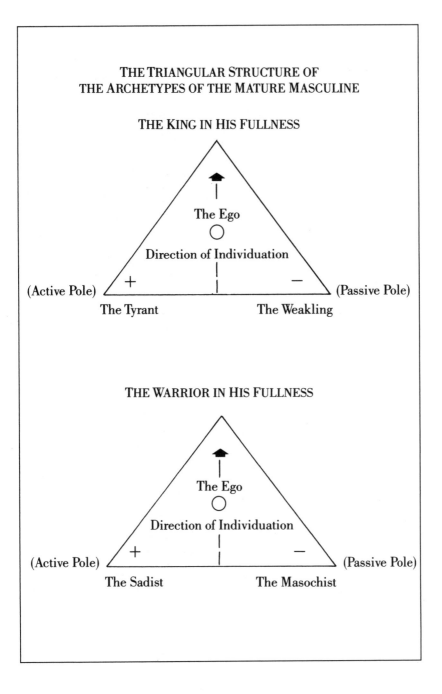

**THE TRIANGULAR STRUCTURE OF
THE ARCHETYPES OF THE MATURE MASCULINE**

THE KING IN HIS FULLNESS

The Ego

Direction of Individuation

(Active Pole) + − (Passive Pole)

The Tyrant   The Weakling

THE WARRIOR IN HIS FULLNESS

The Ego

Direction of Individuation

(Active Pole) + − (Passive Pole)

The Sadist   The Masochist

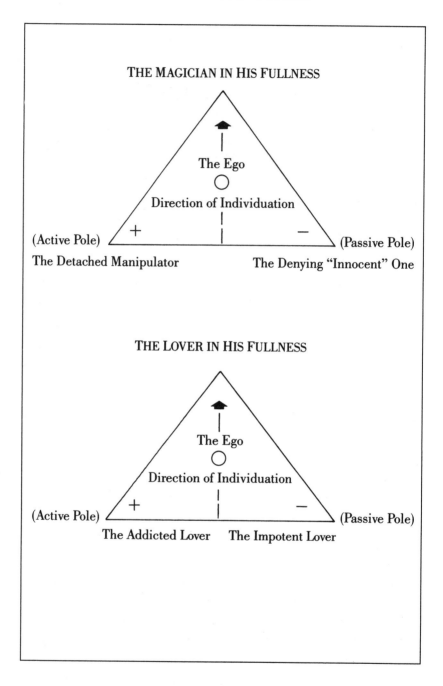

THE MAGICIAN IN HIS FULLNESS

The Ego

Direction of Individuation

(Active Pole)

(Passive Pole)

The Detached Manipulator

The Denying "Innocent" One

THE LOVER IN HIS FULLNESS

The Ego

Direction of Individuation

(Active Pole)

(Passive Pole)

The Addicted Lover   The Impotent Lover

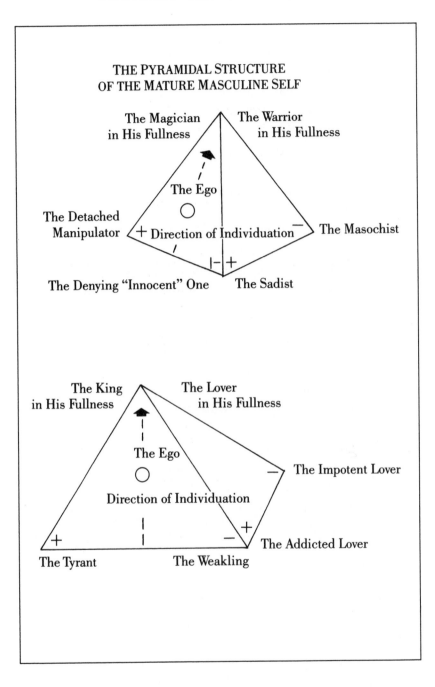

THE PYRAMIDAL STRUCTURE
OF THE MATURE MASCULINE SELF

The Magician
in His Fullness

The Warrior
in His Fullness

The Ego

The Detached
Manipulator

+ Direction of Individuation −

The Masochist

The Denying "Innocent" One   The Sadist

The King
in His Fullness

The Lover
in His Fullness

The Ego

Direction of Individuation

The Impotent Lover

The Addicted Lover

The Tyrant   The Weakling

"thesis, antithesis, synthesis" process in which each synthesis became a new thesis, and so on in a continual upward program of evolutionary complexity and integration.[25] Alfred North Whitehead, the great twentieth-century American philosopher, sees the whole "adventure of ideas," ideas that *create* the world, as a process by which God lures the created world forward in tiny increments, which he calls "occasions."[26] These occasions are like Hegel's theses, and God is the ever-changing antithesis. Whitehead calls this unceasing process "creative advance."

Similarly, Jung drew from his alchemical studies the idea of the *coniunctio oppositorum* ("union of opposites")[27] impelled by a "transcendent function"—the conceptual equivalent to Tillich's "Spirit" and Whitehead's "lure." Jung believed it is essential for the Ego to balance opposing images, feelings, and points of view without allowing either of the opposed sides to disappear into the unconscious. Eventually, when this struggle is consciously experienced with all the suffering it demands, our psyche can follow a transcendent third possibility into greater wholeness.

Jung's followers have largely neglected the Ego's vital role in determining how the archetypes will shape our everyday lives. With our model of the triangular structure of the archetypes, an individual can take care to see that the archetypes will manifest in their fullest form rather than in their Shadow structures. An Ego that does not properly *access* an archetype will be *possessed* by that archetype's Shadow, and left oscillating between the Shadow's two poles. At one the Ego will suffer *positive inflation* (explosion) and at the other *negative inflation* (implosion). Separated, the Shadow's two poles express a pathological darkness, which is only "enlightened" by polar integration into the transcendent third of the archetype. Their pathology is transformed by the Ego into a creative advance.

The action of the Ego is the key to this transformative experience. The Ego and the elements of the archetype exercise a kind of gravitational pull on each other. To allow transformation, the Ego must position itself "above" time and space, in the domain of the Spirit, or the collective unconscious. The Ego will serve ultimately as an occasion for the archetype's expression in time and space. Unless the Ego can work above the spatiotemporal dimension, the archetype will appear largely in its fragmented polar aspects, and the Ego will attract these to itself. In the Spirit's domain, the Ego can instead keep its proper fix on the lodestar the archetype's transcendent third represents.

The archetype's bipolar arrangement in time and space is portrayed in the mythic image of the Symplegades, the Clashing Rocks the Ego must pass between in pursuit of the archetype's transcendent third.[28] The Ego needs to be *lured* by this full expression of the archetype to experience creative advance on its own and in the world. And the archetype needs the Ego in order to experience itself in space and time, and to recover its lost Shadow fragments. The act of recovery empowers the archetype's ongoing creative action in the world.

According to our theory, there are four foundational archetypes of the mature masculine (as well as of the immature masculine). Each of these triangles—King, Warrior, Magician, and Lover—since they are interdependent aspects of the single masculine Self, fit together into a pyramidal form. The pyramid as it has appeared throughout the ages can be interpreted as a symbol for the masculine Self. Pyramids from Egypt to Mesoamerica, from Mesopotamia to Hawaii, are representations of the universe in miniature and often display a layered or stepped form. The layers of the pyramids nearly always stand for the layers of the universe, the different cosmic levels of reality. By ascending the pyramid, an individual climbed from the profane dimension to the sacred, from the less divine to the fullest manifestation of divinity.

This idea parallels ours about the "upward" direction of the Ego's individuation from a less integrated (profane) state to a fully integrated (sacred or "divine") state. A man's Ego must ascend the four faces of the stepped pyramid of the masculine Self, thereby overcoming the bipolar Shadow split at the base of each of the faces. The Ego must keep its eye on the capstone of the pyramid, which represents the fullest expression in an individual life of the four archetypes in perfect unity. This ascent of Ego-consciousness, according to Jung, is always a matter of reconciling opposites and of integrating split psychic materials. As a man's Ego ascends through each of the triangular structures of the archetypes, he becomes more integrated and whole. And he is better and better able to access the archetypes in their fullness at the top of the pyramid. On the King side, he integrates the Tyrant and the Weakling. On the Warrior face, he integrates the Sadist and the Masochist. On the Magician surface, he integrates the Detached Manipulator and the Denying "Innocent" One. And on the Lover side, he integrates the Addicted Lover with the Impotent Lover. Each of the poles of the split Shadows of the four major archetypes possesses insights and strengths that, when the Ego integrates them, contribute to a consolidated sense of Self. Each of the bipolar opposites, when united, reveals the "transcendent third" of the archetype in its fullness. By overcoming the splitness in the bipolar archetypal Shadows, a man comes to feel inwardly empowered. And, in a sense, while he is *building* internal masculine structure he is also *discovering* the pyramid of the masculine Self, which has always been within him, at his core.

The "Mountain of God" at the Center of the Urban Complex
(The Temple Tower Esagila at Babylon: a reconstruction)

From Xibalba to the Skies
The Levels of Reality in the Maya Pyramid (Tikal)

Teotihucán:
Raising the King-Energy and Generating a World

Stairway to the Sky:
Khmer Temple-Mountain of Koh Ker (tenth century A.D.)

Pyramid Power:
Great Morai Pappara, Otaheite (Tahiti)

The Masculine Self on a Monumental Scale:
The Pyramid of Khufu (Giza)

THE ARCHETYPES AND BRAIN STRUCTURE

Startling resonances are being discovered between the fields of brain research and depth psychology. In his book *Archetypes: A Natural History of the Self,* the psychologist Anthony Stevens has extended the exploration of areas of the brain that may be the loci of archetypal forms.[29] He tries to explain Jung's theory of personality types in terms of brain structures. Jung's intuitive types, he speculates, might be using predominantly their Right Brains, and those who favor their Left Brains would correspond to Jung's thinking types.

Briefly, the Right Brain (the right hemisphere of the cerebral cortex) "thinks" in images and symbols, grasps situations and patterns as wholes, and is the primary center for the generation of dreams, visions, and fantasies. The Left Brain (the corresponding left hemisphere) thinks sequentially, analyzes situations and patterns logically, and uses language in its cognitive processes. Many locate the Ego entirely in the Left Brain. In contrast, Stevens proposes that while the Ego may function most of the time in the Left Brain, it also draws on the Right Brain. Consciousness, he says, is a pervasive function of the whole brain, though Right- and Left-Brain modes of consciousness are quite distinct. The personal unconscious and its various complexes seem to manifest in the Right Brain. By dreaming, the Right Brain communicates with the still primarily Left Brain–identified Ego.

Rather than locating the archetypes in the Right Brain, Stevens proposes that they arise in deeper, older layers of the brain, layers that, according to brain researcher Paul Mac-Lean, have remained largely unchanged for millions of years of animal evolution.[30] The dihemispheric cerebral cortex we think of as the human brain is only the most recently evolved

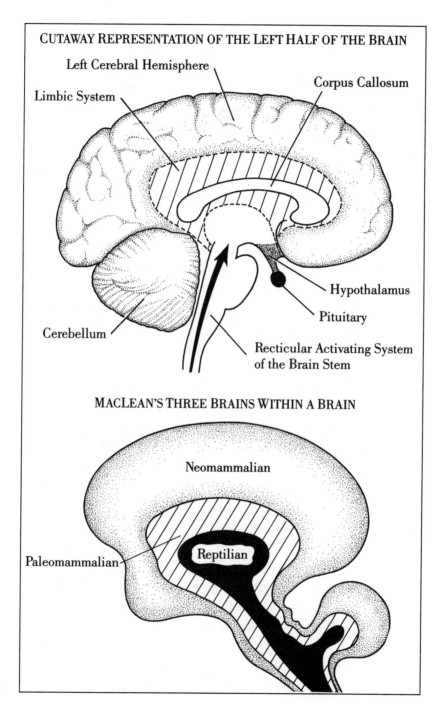

CUTAWAY REPRESENTATION OF THE LEFT HALF OF THE BRAIN

Left Cerebral Hemisphere

Corpus Callosum

Limbic System

Cerebellum

Hypothalamus

Pituitary

Recticular Activating System
of the Brain Stem

MACLEAN'S THREE BRAINS WITHIN A BRAIN

Neomammalian

Paleomammalian

Reptilian

element of three distinct neurological regions. Before it, in ascending order of antiquity, come the neocortex, or neomammalian brain, apparently responsible for cognition and sophisticated perception; the midbrain, or paleomammalian brain (limbic system), which seems to generate the basic emotions of fear and anger, affiliation, and maternity as well as species-characteristic individual and social behaviors; and the upward growth of the spinal cord, the reptilian brain, or R-complex, responsible for basic life activities, also probably the seat of our most basic instincts and our routine-driven behavior patterns. These three brains within a brain function relatively autonomously. Our process of psychological integration is, in part, an attempt to unify and synchronize these three regions of the brain.

If archetypes arise, as Jung believed, at a fundamentally instinctual level, then it could be that they originate in our most primitive region, the reptilian brain. Elaborated as they pass upward through the paleomammalian and neomammalian brains, the imagistic, intuitive structures of the archetypes would rise primarily into our Right Brains. But since our Ego's experience of the archetypes will also be mediated via the Left Brain, they will also be influenced by the linguistic and logical modes of thinking centered there. Archetypes hold a sense of otherness[31] perhaps because they originate in levels of the brain so much deeper than the source of Ego-consciousness, and then must be translated into terms that make sense especially to the Left Brain. Archetypes in their fullness involve *both* Left- and Right-Brain functions. This is clearly the case with the four foundational archetypes of the mature masculine, which we are outlining in this series. Certainly the rational, strategic, and emotionally detached modes of the Magician and the Warrior are characteristic of Left-Brain processes, although they seem to draw secondarily on Right-Brain functions, and the visually oriented, aesthetic, intuitive modes of the Lover are characteristic of Right-Brain functions, although the Lover also seems to draw on Left-Brain processes. We attempt a more thorough discussion of the origin of the four archetypes of mature masculinity and the brain's limbic system (paleomammalian brain) in Appendix B. This field of inquiry is wide open to exciting future research.

COVERGENCE OF THE MATURE MASCULINE ARCHETYPES

Depth psychologists often merge the mature masculine archetypes. Because only the most perfectly realized Ego apprehends an archetype's full expression, for most of us they retain a degree of mystery. The very images and symbols archetypes use to communicate to us refer beyond themselves to other images and symbols in an almost infinitely complex way. For example, the phallus, the cross, the tree, the *axis mundi*, the spine, the sacred mountain, and the pyramid can each be read symbolically as aspects of one another.[32] There are dangers, however, involved with overinterpretations. An individual can easily lose himself, as Yeats was warned in the course of his occult researches, along the Path of the Chameleon, a labyrinthine trail of correspondences. Besides this, the four basic archetypes that influence a mature man, the King, the Warrior, the Magician, and the Lover, are the fragments of a primevally whole Self, and complement each other to such a degree that no one of them receives its fullest expression without incorporating the others.

These archetypes have historically merged and diverged again in a bewildering variety of configurations. Rain magicians, for example, give rise to rain kings, who appoint priests to elect warrior kings, who commission other warriors to serve magicians who themselves become kings. A mortal king, to the extent that he fully expresses the archetypal King, is a warrior who enforces order within his kingdom and who may take military action to extend his kingdom. He is also a sacred king, the high-priest magician who mediates between the spiritual dimension and his people.[33] He is also a lover, of his people, and in a special sense of his sacred queen, since he cannot rule legitimately or effectively unless their union is fruitful.[34] Despite these uncertain boundaries, it is useful to distinguish masculine archetypes in order to enhance the Ego's capacity to access these psychic structures in all their richness and complexity. In this book we will be focusing on the warrior sector of the empowered masculine self.

THE ALPHA MALE AND HIS WARRIORS:
PRIMATE PREFIGURATIONS

Chimpanzees are our closest living animal relatives.[35] Their genetic profile is over 98 percent identical to ours.[36] Primate ethology research suggests close correspondences between their social structures and interpersonal behaviors and ours. It seems likely that similar psychological processes are at work.[37]

While of course we cannot *know* fully what other animals feel and think, in many ways we cannot be sure we *know* what another *human* feels or thinks. In either case we make judgments based on observable behaviors. Our great advantage in observing humans obviously is spoken language, but we still have the subjective task of interpreting linguistic signs. Chimpanzees, while they cannot speak, *can* communicate with us in sign language and through other quasi-verbal methods designed by researchers.[38] In addition, their complex range of body signals bears a striking resemblance to our own body

King, Warrior, Magician, Lover:
The Alpha Male "Displaying" (Figan as Alpha Male at Gombe)

language. It seems reasonably safe to assume that when chimpanzees *appear* to be fearful, wrathful, submissive, loving, or awed, they are in fact experiencing these emotions. Probably their emotional experience is less self-conscious and complicated than ours, but still it offers clues into primate psychology, including our own.

The hierarchical power blocs and coalitions of chimpanzee society center around a dominant adult male ethologists

The Alpha Male Defending His People (at Gombe)

call the *Alpha Male*.[39] Successful Alpha Males are usually mature and physically powerful. They display foresight, courage, and what can only be called "character." Alpha Males exhibit many behaviors common to the sacred king, the specific archetypally inspired figure we explored in *The King Within*.

Alpha Males surround themselves with male "knights" to help protect and defend their "realms." These warrior males exhibit characteristics of what David Gilmore calls the "cult of manhood" in human males. Like their human counterparts, chimpanzee males are protectors and providers for the females and the young of their societies.[40]

We believe the warrior males among chimpanzees, gorillas, and other primates are working out of archetypal structures similar to those of their human counterparts, albeit on a much more primitive level. They defend their community with great ferocity and at times pay for their efforts with their lives.[41]

Human males experience this warrior role in a significantly more elaborate form. In one sense the gap between other primates and the warriors of human history is an enormous one, millions of years long. In another sense, however, the gap is small. It fits within our skulls! If Stevens and others are right in their analysis of human brain structure, there is a warrior male within us. We must learn to steward his energies for the human community.

We offer this book and the series as a whole to the man who is looking for an operator's manual to the psyche, and to the woman who wants a guide to the hard wiring of men, and to her own inner masculine as well. Just as no jet pilot would try to fly a 747 without knowing its capabilities and instruments inside and out, the only way to "fly" successfully an immensely complicated male psyche is to know it inside and out, with a clear understanding of how to access its archetypal energy systems. The mindful use of this energy will bring a man safely into his mature manhood.

PART 2

IMAGES OF THE MASCULINE WARRIOR

3

THE KILLER APE

S HORTLY AFTER THE CHILDREN OF CLEVELAND
Elementary School in Stockton, California, throng into
the playground for a midday recess, a man ritually attired in
army fatigues opens fire with an AK-47 assault rifle. He targets
the children of recent Southeast Asian immigrants, who he
believes have taken jobs away from men like himself. Not a
veteran himself, he is fueled by the hatred his veteran friends
have for the "gooks." He kills five children and wounds thirty
others. He is Patrick Purdy, an alcoholic drifter who plays
with toy soldiers and imagines himself a guerrilla fighter. In an
act of vindictive triumph he finally shoots himself.

Hands Freed from Walking for Life-and Death Activities
(Faben brandishes a stick in Gombe)

A former employee charges into the offices of Standard Gravure in Louisville, Kentucky, and combs three floors of the building with bullets from another AK-47. In the midst of the carnage he encounters an old friend and says, "Hi, John. I told them I'd be back." After killing seven of his former co-workers and wounding thirteen, Joseph Wesbecker points his gun at his own temple and pulls the trigger.

These stories and others like them are all too familiar. Some of us cry out against the semiautomatic weapon; some look for psychiatric symptoms. Some of us shake our fists at the supposedly inherent violence of the male animal. All of us cry out against the long nightmare of human history, to date primarily a history of the violence of men, against other human beings, other species, and increasingly against the ecosystem as a whole.

Those men who act out their inner conflicts—in assaults on schoolchildren, in stockpiling nuclear weapons, in acts of terrorism, in holy wars, or even in toxic waste dumping—are really boys *pretending* to be men. They are trying with brutal desperation to find and affirm their masculinity, but they have no idea how to do either. We have had a long history of immature *Shadow* Warriors. Possessed by a blood thirst, maddened by rage, these "boys" seek absolute power over others. Their destructiveness attacks both themselves and others. Like a plague, their fury can sweep across entire continents; and like a plague, the fury ends by destroying its host. "Those who live by the sword die by the sword."

From the ancient Assyrians who flayed men alive for sport to the GIs in Vietnam who took Vietcong penises for trophies, the Shadow Warrior has terrorized the world for centuries. Understandably everyone fears power. We fear it in others, and we fear it in ourselves. If *possessed* by the aggressive might of the Warrior, we believe we will endanger the lives of our fellow human beings, and put at risk the well-being of the entire planet.

And yet there are examples of big-city cops who use their deadly force against violent criminals in an expression of controlled aggression, which protects the weak from the strong. There are wars waged to stop the insane and barbarous aspirations of Ego-inflated madmen. There are *just* revolutions waged by the oppressed against their oppressors. It's hard to remember that ultimately Martin Luther King, Jr.'s peace protests alone did *not* secure the freedom to vote for Southern blacks; federal troops did. Apparently there is such a thing as "might for right!"

In *African Genesis*, Robert Ardrey's thesis is that there is a "killer ape" inside us, inherited from our distant primate ancestors. According to Ardrey this instinctual killer was instrumental in assuring the survival of our species in the days when our ancestors had to contend against a number of predators and perhaps competing hominid species. While Ardrey's picture of the "killer ape" may be a bit simplistic as well as more than a little dismal, it is difficult to argue against the probability that our capacity for violence has had a major impact on the evolution of our species and has helped propel us to extraordinary success in the competition for life with other organisms.[1] The problem today is how to turn what was once a species-enhancing instinct into a beneficial rather than an endangering dynamic.

Some people choose not to believe human aggressiveness is innate. Others prefer to assign aggression exclusively to the male of the species. Various schemes have been proposed for eliminating the "killer ape" by these critics of so-called masculine aggressiveness. One would attempt to do away with aggression by a social engineering program, allowing boys to express only the so-called feminine virtues. Another would involve a pervasive drug regimen to inhibit aggression inducing hormones like testosterone.

The fact is that aggressiveness *is* an innate characteristic of our species. In the course of his work the psychologist Anthony Stevens has studied the bases of the archetypes in biochemistry and brain structure.[2] Specific neurological structures (primarily the hypothalamus and the pituitary gland, both found in the midbrain) do give rise to aggressive impulses. Other studies link various naturally produced chemicals, especially testosterone, to heightened levels of aggression. Agents such as the norepinephrine secreted by the adrenal glands may also be involved.

The archetypes are real dynamic structures and are not the dismissable fantasy figures some misinterpreters of Jung have made them out to be. Like the deep linguistic structures Noam Chomsky has identified, the archetypes shape our behaviors at such a fundamental level that we are often unconscious of their presence. And they are compulsive—a man possessed by one archetype or another is *compelled* to act out certain scripts, whatever his feeling of free will. An archetype is looking for a place to incarnate, and only a healthy Ego can channel archetypal energies without having them take over.

Women have essentially the same neurological structures as men.[3] The feminine hypothalamus and pituitary gland are the same rage center that they are for men. Testosterone is present too in women, though in much lower concentrations. During the course of a woman's menstrual cycle, furthermore, the drop in the production of the ovarian hormone estradiol and other hormones often produces violent and aggressive behavior. Any argument that there is no physical mechanism for aggression in women is simply false.

Women have been known to attack men and other women with a frenzy equal to that of men. Among counselors and school officials who deal on a daily basis with inner-city teens, it is common knowledge that teenaged girls are responsible for the *many* of the violent incidents in and around the schools. There is a rising tide of delinquent teenage girls convicted of the most brutal of crimes, including armed robbery and murder. The fantasy that the hard edge of male business management would be softened by the entry of women into the ranks has been belied by experiences with tyrannical and abusive female executives. And many tell us that most of the emotional or even physical brutality they suffered in school was administered by nuns or other female teachers!

Those who would eliminate aggressiveness by social engineering are pursuing a delusory goal. As Alice Miller and other developmental psychologists have demonstrated, infantile rage is to a significant degree a product of inadequate or actively hostile parenting.[4] When a child's primary narcissism and grandiosity are abruptly, repeatedly, or catastrophically challenged, a secondary narcissism will form in response. That secondary narcissism carries the rage. When this rage isn't transformed or modulated by subsequent life experience, it expresses itself through amazingly brutal behaviors even in what should be the adult stages of life. The inner Child manipulates the adult's feelings and life circumstances to conform to the trauma-rage-response scenario of infancy.

In *For Your Own Good* Miller compares the physical and emotional environment of young Hitler to the physical and psychological conditions of Nazi Germany as a whole, and of the concentration camps in particular. The match is a perfect one! In her view, Adolf Hitler reenacted his childhood rage and trauma, through repetition compulsion, on the stage of the world. He was saying essentially, "Look, this is what was done to me!" Presumably if his German contemporaries had had more Self-affirming childhoods, their desire to follow him would not have been so great.

It bears noting that aggressive behavior is *not* synonymous with rage or violence.[5] Rage and violence are expressions of overstimulated aggression. Aggressiveness, however, is necessary to the organism's struggle for life and for the development of the Self. Where threats to life or Self structures mount, so does the intensity of aggression in response, until the energy reaches a breaking point. After the break the personality may be possessed by a temporary insanity. Many human beings, both male and female, are caught in the grip of an insufficiently consolidated Ego structure, one overly susceptible to upwellings of infantile rage. Parental abuse is again a major culprit behind this susceptibility. As the British psychiatrist Anthony Storr points out in his book *Human Destructiveness,* if a person's need to affirm himself or herself through legitimate aggressiveness is thwarted, to the degree that it is thwarted, violence, fueled by narcissistic rage, often becomes the last resort. Storr adds to the perspective of developmental psychology the understanding that a person's ethnic and class origins also play a factor. The resort to violence is often seen among young men who have no chance to be self-affirming in the dominant culture.[6]

Aggression is an aspect of forceful Self expression, and as such it is a natural, healthy, and vital part of being human. Babies exhibit natural aggressiveness when they kick and scream in order to have their needs met. Toddlers need natural aggression to stay undaunted in their attempts to walk, no matter how many times they may fall. Young boys seem to be impelled by their natural aggressiveness to venture farther and more frequently from the mother's lap than young girls of the same age.[7] Aggression is behind the natural enthusiasm both sexes show in reaching for objects parents and other caregivers have repeatedly placed off limits.

Can social engineering of the infant's early environment eliminate aggression? No—at best it may minimize aggres-

sion's *rageful* expression. At worst it may force rage underground, if the child is taught (explicitly or implicitly) that
aggressive displays are unwanted. The child then represses the
rage to please the parent. In this case the child (and later the
adult) may appear to be overly passive, lackluster, and depressed. If the rage is ever given vent it will actually be
intensified by the years of repression. It seems unlikely then
that socializing aggression "away" will have any desirable effect. But if socialization is limited to providing *a positive
channel* for aggression, it might then be useful.

Only the most radical Behaviorists do not believe in some
innate form of "human nature." Although Freudians (and the
various schools descended from the Freudian milieu) have
tended to emphasize the importance of the early environment
over innate psychological structures in determining human
behaviors, even these schools of thought have made provision
for heritable psychological structures that shape human aggressiveness. Alfred Adler assumed the existence of what he
called the "power drive."[8] Erik Erikson wrote of "configurations" found in a psychological "ground plan" that includes
for boys an "intrusive" mode.[9] For Freud the Id is a vast
reservoir of unsocialized, aggressive "wishes."[10] The most fa-
mous of these is a boy's Oedipal "wish" to kill his father and
marry his mother. Jungians have elaborated the archetypal
dynamic within the unconscious psyche. Through an aggressive forward thrusting these dynamics move the personality
into progressively higher states of psychological integration.
According to these psychologies, then, aggression is not ex-
pungable. Whether it manifests in a pathological form or not
depends upon the severity of childhood trauma and the degree
of success of subsequent intervention.

The use of drugs to minimize aggression and anxiety can
be relatively effective. The results of such minor tranquilizers

as diazepam and lorazepam, a major tranquilizer like chlor-
pramazine, and the mood stabilizer lithium carbonate are well
documented. Of course no responsible psychiatrist advocates
widespread use of these drugs. All mood-altering drugs have
undesirable (sometimes unforeseeable) side effects and are
prescribed only for particular cases of psychological dysfunction.

Since human aggression *does* seem to be innate, it makes
no sense to try to eliminate it either through social engineering
or drug therapy. It seems aggression stems from the interaction of genetically inherited archetypal dynamics, neurological
structures, and chemical agents with forces in the environment. All we can do is modulate its expression and its intensity.

If there is a question that those who want to do away with
aggression would rather not face, probably it would be
whether aggressive human behaviors serve any healthy, generative function. We believe the answer is yes. Aggression would
never have retained such a prominent place in the human Self
unless it had an important contribution to make to the ad-
vancement of our species.

Aggressiveness gives rise to an impulse to *act* in order to
secure the resources an organism and its community need
to survive and flourish. Nature has especially equipped men to
carry out the essential aggressive tasks of our species. The
equipment includes a characteristically specialized male
brain,[11] our highly developed upper body musculature, our
greater size, and the added impulse of testosterone. (Young
men are flooded with twenty times the testosterone that young
women experience.[12]) Where the masculine aggressive drives
once served in our primate past to fight off predators, and
defend females and offspring, now they serve as a primary
impetus toward an increasingly fuller expression of the cre-

ative potentials of our species. It is this generative aspect of the Warrior energy we will explore in this book, along with his destructive potentials.

When a nation becomes mobilized for war, the Warrior raises the aggressive energy that inspires a whole people. In the presence of the archetypal Warrior, the feeling is that something momentous is about to happen. There is an upwelling of group pride and aspiration, and a sense of triumphal forward movement. Once the necessary emotional buttons are pushed we join ranks and march lockstep as one mighty collective Human Being, carrying the flags that designate our group identity.

Many men look back to the days of war with an intense longing. They miss a time in their lives when they felt on the edge, intensely alive, a time when life and love walked hand in hand with death and destruction. There is a fundamental mystery here. Why are men never so motivated to go beyond their individual Ego concerns as when they are going to war? What is it about war that men are so much in love with?

Whether in the guise of Rameses II swinging his mace over the rearing heads of his enemies, Douglas MacArthur striding ashore in the Philippines, or Arnold Schwarzenegger blazing a path of righteous destruction through a corrupt world, the archetypal Warrior has always gripped our imaginations. He has always quickened our heartbeats and stirred us to action. He awakens us and makes us long to fight life's battles. He makes us eager for challenges. Despite our post–Cold War age, we still spend billions annually on war. And think of the millions we spend on war movies! Add to this the *billions* we spend on athletic contests, tamed and ritualized substitutes for war, and the pervasive energy of the Warrior becomes apparent.

Archaelogical evidence from the earliest of human eras

Ramses II Making War on the "Demons" (Ramses II
destroying Libyans—Abu Simbel)

shows a fascination with the Hunter, a specialized face of the
Warrior,[13] whose aggressive action is directed against game
animals. We find beautifully executed spear points and ax
blades. Many of these spear points are far too large to have
been utilitarian. The mythologist Joseph Campbell notes that
these symbols of Warrior/Hunter energy are some of the earliest evidence we have of a sophisticated aesthetic development
and a spiritual dimension on the part of our ancestors.[14]

Certain caves in central and southern France appear to
have been dedicated by Cro-Magnon man to the mysteries of
the Hunter. Deep in the bowels of the earth, in secret recesses
and vast underground chambers, beautifully rendered game
animals are depicted along with the figures of shamans and
hunters. Scholars believe these caves were used during the

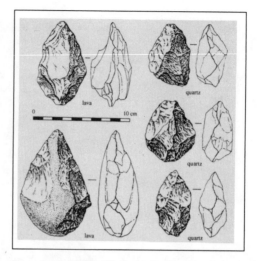

From Stone to Gold: The Tools of the Warrior: Bifaces from
Olduvai Gorge (redrawn after M. D. Leakey 1971, dated to
1.2 to 1.1 million years ago, Acheulean industrial tradition)

Our Hunter Forebears (Bushmen hunters in the Kalahari)

initiation of boys into manhood, and also for the practice of a kind of magic designed to make the animal whose image was captured submit to the will of its hunters. If these magic ceremonies were anything like primitive hunting rituals some peoples still practice, the animals were probably experienced as brothers and sisters.[15] The belief would have been that animals would only be lured onto the hunter's spear after prayer and supplication. The hunter would have asked the animals' forgiveness, and then explained why their flesh was so important to his people. He would finally have asked the animals to reincarnate themselves in order to return with the food, clothing, implements, and other benefits only they had the power to confer. In these ceremonies Cro-Magnon man very likely celebrated the mystical symbiotic union of man and beast, just as the poetry and art of his descendants would, thousands of years later.

Perhaps Cro-Magnon families lived in the large ventilated antechambers near the cave entrance. Long, narrow tunnels led from these chambers into deep interior galleries. Many of these tunnels were (and are) so narrow the only way to get through them is on hands and knees. Shrouded in inky blackness, ancient hand-held lamps must have thrown a flickering light over the rough rock walls of these chambers, making them seem alive with animal vitality.

Imagine the initiation rituals that may have taken place in these primeval cave sanctuaries. Boys are forcibly taken away from the "realm of the mothers" in the antechambers and led down long tunnels symbolic of the birth canal. Their release into the inner womb of Mother Earth, into some deep, nearly inaccessible gallery, signifies their gestation into the interior realm of masculinity. Here older men impart to the boys the myths of the Hunter, the myths of creation, the myths of the tribe and tribal technology. The central mystery of their traumatic experience is probably the revelation of the reality of their own deaths.

Almost certainly the boys are terrified by this dramatization of the death of their childhood and the birth of manhood. Now too is the time for the boys to learn what later cultures will call "the mystery of the sword," the symbol of phallic might that cuts both ways, making life for one by causing the death of another. Life feeds on itself, they are taught, and one life sacrifices itself for another. The many figurines of fecund Goddesses found in these caves probably are used to teach the boys about sexuality, its pleasures and its procreative intent. After gestating in this masculine womb the boys are finally released into the daylight world, reborn as men. Through these masculine rites of passage Cro-Magnon boys are turned into Generative Men, under the guise of the Hunter.

Evidently the Warrior has been with us for a long time. He is here to stay. We cannot wish him away. We should not alter our genetic code to erase all trace of him. We cannot neutralize him through social engineering, and if we tranquilize him we suffer a variety of attendant consequences. From the point of view of a depth psychologist, the question is not how to get rid of him. The questions are, how can we harness his aggressive potential for creative action? How can we avoid the brutal excesses of the *Shadow* Warrior? How can we wed might with right and power with goodness?

There are developmental and societal reasons why males of our species need a full complement of legitimate aggressiveness. Since boys must follow a different route than girls in their developmental journeys and dissociate from their mothers both as individuals *and* as males, a boy's maturation process is particularly gut-wrenching.[16] A unique gender-characteristic loneliness may set in when, at a certain point in the process, a boy finds himself in a wasteland midway between the feminine mode of relating he learned with his mother and the unknown, alien mode he needs to learn from men. At this point it is essential that a nurturing older man step in to alleviate this profound loneliness. Boys can learn from such men how to relate to feminine energy from a position of strength and confidence from the stance of a secure masculine identity. Even if all goes well, a separation from the mother is difficult. The separation from the "realm of the mothers" and the carefree dependency and passivity a mother offers, followed by the assuming of a forced identity of masculine prerogatives and responsibilities, has as its aim a masculine identity intimately involved with the world through traditional protector, provider, and procreator roles.

The problem of *our* culture is that so many boys are abandoned by their fathers specifically and by older men in general at this critical juncture. Consequently they feel inordinately susceptible to the passive allure of regressing to the protective feminine energies of the mother. Their choices are limited to living with an essentially feminine mode of relation, or an unbearable lifelong loneliness and isolation.

There is widespread agreement among depth psychologists and psychoanalytic theorists concerning the role of the father in this context.[17] If the father is not there, or the father is not assertive in moving in and claiming the son, the mother is put into a very bad position. Her son cannot help but experience her only as a tremendous source of power, and not as a human being. Through no fault of her own, the son has not been able to make the necessary connection to the masculine sphere that would help him separate from her without needing to "kill" her.

A man with a weak or an abusive father often ends up with fantasies of killing his mother. A lot of very violent men have been failed by the men in their lives. Any examination of the crack epidemic our society is currently facing will soon return to this—the young men and boys who are pushing and using the drug have simply not had contact with powerful, mature males. The only male power they see is manifested by the dealer who has the money to buy women and friends, and the guns to kill them.

Our society's astonishing impotence in the face of this and other epidemics that afflict young males stems from our inability to initiate our men into a sense of their proper responsibilities and power. The ancient Warrior/Hunter cultures had this institutionally incorporated advantage over us: Their men were available to assist boys with their traumatic developmental tasks.

With so little thought now given to what it means to be a man, and with women so far ahead of us of late in their work on innate feminine potentials, we face some particularly daunting problems in our culture. Men clearly need help coming into their own. Women would like to give their men this help; increasingly, though, they are intuiting that there are many things they cannot do, that much of the help can come only from other men. This can be a frustrating truth for both sexes to face.

Andrew Bard Schmookler argues that men, more than women, are the victims of what he calls the *mentality of scarcity*.[18] This he defines as the belief that there is never enough *good* to go around, and therefore that individuals and groups must compete for what little there is. Through their instinctual protector and provider roles men have been called upon to do most of the competing, often through warfare. Since their capacity to secure the good for their dependents often hangs upon these competitive successes, men are perpetually called upon to put their *souls* as well as their bodies to the test. A success is a *triumph*. But a failure brings, if not physical injury or death, *total humiliation*. Women have fared about the same, Schmookler argues, whether or not men succeed in protecting them from the depredations of other men. They have remained in a relatively helpless and vulnerable position, tied to the traditional physical and psychological state of affairs.

Men face the risk of being *unmanned* at any time. What is true of warfare is also true of the workplace. Men compete with other men for income and status, risking not physical injury or death (at least not in direct ways), but humiliation and dishonor.

Men must steer a course between the tendency to lie down and give up and the tendency to become sadistic and abusive. That is the bad news. The good news is that the Warrior, properly accessed, can do a great deal to empower us to live our lives, make our worlds, and protect, provide, and create a just order on a perilous planet. And the Warrior is within *every* man. We are *all* potentially capable of doing all these things.

4

HISTORICAL IMAGES
OF THE WARRIOR

I N AN AMAZING SEQUENCE OF SCENES, THE MOVIE *2001: A Space Odyssey* shows an early hominid discovering the first tool-weapon, a piece of shattered bone. He learns to use it to kill animals for food, and momentously finally uses it against a rival hominid "chief" during a border dispute. By doing so he assures the supremacy of his technologically advanced tribe. After pounding the carcass of his prey with his bone club, he hurls it into the air, where it soars high up into the sky. There it transforms into a spaceship. Kubrick manages a six-million-year transition with a single evocative cut. Through the rest of his movie, the Warrior is still on the

Short Bull: "Today Is a Good Day to Die!"

prowl, pushing back the frontiers of a peculiarly human cosmos, facing the darknesses of space with an enlightened mind.

Evolutionists have long thought that the human species shares the same primate ancestor as the great apes. Their thinking was that our species developed through the gradual enlargement of the cerebral cortex. Over the course of hundreds of thousands of years our brain case expanded to accommodate a much larger and more developed neocortex. But many early theorists believed that human behavioral changes were the *result* of this enlarged brain.[1] After their brains expanded, so the theories supposed, humans began to stand erect; with their hands then free, they began to fashion and wield weapons and tools. Their vocal apparatus evolved until speech became possible.

New discoveries of early hominid remains, and recent studies in primate ethology, are bringing startling revisions to this old view.[2] It is now apparent that we were fully erect *before* our brains began to enlarge. Therefore some environmental force selected freehanded standing hominids *long before greater intelligence was called for*. What does this imply? Very likely that the pressures of the time favored hominids who were capable of making and using tools and weapons.[3] Once we started down this evolutionary path, the inherent cultural significance of tool and weapon use applied a unique pressure toward the selection of intelligence.

Intelligence, in this scenario, allowed our ancestors to refine and develop their nascent technology. As in *2001: A Space Odyssey*, the team with the best weapons and tools won. Better weapons led to three successfully achieved goals: Predators were overcome, game animals were killed, and rival hominids were defeated. It seems quite probable then that the Warrior archetype was an important impetus for the development of human intelligence. The evolutionary selection for the Warrior's aggression and weapons manufacture is both a cause and a symptom of his presence in our hard wiring.

In a sense the science of primate ethology takes us even further back into our evolutionary past than does paleontology. Chimpanzees are our closest living relatives. Their genetic material is from 98 to 99 percent identical to ours.[4] We are not descended *from* chimpanzees (or from any other living primate) but chimps have a close relative, now extinct, in common with us. They are more similar to us than they are to gorillas, the next closest primate.[5]

Jane Goodall, building on the work of a handful of pioneers before her, began studying chimpanzees in the 1960s. Such studies have continued in even greater depth since then, in zoos and in the wild. This work leads to the unmistakable conclusion that our own instinctual, archetypal behaviors are governed by very similar biological and physical structures to those that govern the chimpanzees.[6]

Can we see evidence of the archetypal structures in our biological relatives? There is evidence of the archetypal King in the chimpanzee Alpha Male.[7] And the King has his retinue of Warriors. Chimpanzees are exceedingly aggressive, particularly the males. They play rough when little, and as they mature they engage in "bluffing" displays designed to intimidate each other. Part of the bluff is an enhanced impression of physical size achieved by making their hair stand on end. Plumes and epaulets serve a similar purpose for human soldiers. If bluffing doesn't settle the chimp conflict, growling, screeching, biting, and hitting soon follow. Enraged males will even pick up sticks or stones, raising them in clenched fists and hurling them at their opponents, though seldom with much accuracy.

Soon after these battles the antagonists make up through greeting, grooming, and presenting behaviors which signal good intentions and a desire for peace.[8] Despite these frequent conflicts (most usually a result of status struggles) males instantly band together when an outside danger threatens. Male bonding provides within the society a fraternity of warriors of the type the anthropologist David Gilmore has found within human groups. This fraternity provides the core structure of the community. At the apex of the power pyramid, the Alpha Male reigns (though not as an absolute monarch) and contains the aggressions of all the males and females in his charge.

Apparently primate males, including ourselves, have been assigned disciplinary and protective roles in the course of evolution. Male baboons are nearly twice the size of the females. The differences in size and musculature emphasize the male's aggressive role.[9] The size differential is lessened among human beings, but clearly we males have still been marked by nature for competition and warfare.

Battling chimpanzees seem absolutely possessed by a kind of war frenzy. They bare their teeth, clench their fists, rush their opponents flailing and screaming, and generally exhibit behaviors we label insane in a human context. Some scholars feel the origin of religion may be found in this altered state of Warrior possession.

For example, during a storm male chimpanzees will sometimes snatch up large branches, charge out into the wind and rain, and challenge the lightning bolts with weapons of their own. This behavior is exactly like their usual "display" behavior toward each other. Do they interpret this storm as the displaying of a "super chimp"?[10] If this is the case, this striking confrontation with the Great Chimp in the sky may lie behind the apprehension of the Warrior-God of sky and storm so ubiquitous in human patriarchal religions.[11] This is the dynamic underlying the psychic appeal of Lear's challenge to the tempest.[12] The same appeal is put to work in the movie *War Games*, when characters watch a map of the world light up with every apparent nuclear hit. The whole screen shines at last with an unearthly light. Awe and aggression seem to arise together during this type of traumatic, even spiritual, experience.

Battle frenzy is an irresistible emotional force. It takes over the whole person, physically and psychologically. At the same time the violent emotions are engaged, humane or tender feelings are cut off. It is an experience of *numinous* intensity. Scholars of religion use this word for the overwhelming sense of the divine presence. Rudolf Otto has called the experience of the numinous one of "holy dread." It makes the hair stand up on the back of our necks—remember the displays of the chimpanzees with their bristling hair? The numinous carries us forward on a superhuman surge of energy. It instills in us a sense of destiny that transcends narrow human concerns. The Irish celebrate the battle frenzy of their hero Cuchulain, who could expand his physical size at will to that of a giant. And the Bhaghavad-Gita, the Hindu "Song of God," celebrates the awful fury of Vishnu as he consumes the universe in his fiery wrath.

Many tribal societies valued this state of Warrior possession, especially in times of crisis. Yet they often feared it even in their own men. In *Totem and Taboo*, Freud notes that in tribal societies warriors returning from battle had to be separated from their communities in order to be ritually purified, a process that allowed them to come down from the high of archetypal possession. Only once normal Ego structures had been restored were the men allowed to rejoin the community.

Many of the well known difficulties faced by Vietnam vets upon their return home stemmed from a lack of respect for this necessary period of psychological adjustment. Instead of being mustered out over a period of weeks, as in other wars, somebody in the Pentagon decided the more humane approach would be to send the soldiers straight home. Many soldiers found themselves in their quiet hometowns less than seventy-two hours after leaving horrific combat situations.

God as the Great Warrior in the Sky (the Canaanite Ba'al
with weapon and lightning as a spear with branches, stela
from sanctuary near the Great Temple, Ras Shamra)

Add to this the indifference or active disrespect with which they were greeted, and their problems in adjusting are clear.

THE MENTALITY OF SCARCITY
AND PSEUDO-SPECIATION

Andrew Schmookler lays the blame for the mentality of scarcity squarely on the shoulders of higher civilization. In Freudian fashion he regards culture as fundamentally a narcissistically wounding enterprise. Schmookler believes cultural norms in themselves deprive people of the good things of life and so set up the conditions that motivate men to compete for them. His thinking seems to be that the drive for instant gratification, for pleasure, is culturally deflected into an acceptance of work-generated delayed gratification.[13] If this is true, we would certainly agree that civilization contributes to the arousal of competition and aggression among males. This is all the more true for underprivileged males whose competitive and aggressive drives are even more frustrated, eventuating in violent acting-out behaviors. However we believe Schmookler has succeeded only in giving a rather brilliant description of the *Shadow* Warrior (see Chapters 7 and 8 for an extensive treatment of the Warrior's Shadow). Schmookler has failed to account for the true historical origins of human aggression.

Aggression is not simply an anxious response to a narcissistically wounding culture. Furthermore the mentality of scarcity, which Schmookler calls paranoid, seems to us to be quite an accurate perception of the state of the world. The fact is that organisms *do* compete for survival. When one species carves out an ecological niche, quite often it does so at the expense of another. And not only does every organism aggressively pursue the good things available to it, it repels with equal aggression any organisms that threaten its survival.

Evidently all life operates according to a dynamic of scarcity. Take for example an apparently serene forest. Within it complementary species appear to manifest a principle of harmonious interaction, each contributing in its particular ways to the "balance of nature." But closely observed, the apparently peaceful trees are caught in a slow-motion life-and-death struggle for sunlight. This struggle is not only between rival species—but just as often between members of the same species, as the parent tree frequently suffocates the sapling. And all the associated species, the mosses, the fungi, the insects, and the birds who feed on them, compete with themselves as often as with one another for food sources that are either just barely sufficient, or failing.

Still, few animal species have been found to fight with their own kind as regularly and fiercely as do humans. Most real battles in the animal kingdom are *between* species.[14] This realization raises the peculiarly, but not exclusively, human phenomenon of *pseudo-speciation*.[15] All human beings alive on the planet for the last twenty-five thousand years belong to the same species.[16] By definition we are a group of organisms that can mate and produce fertile offspring, notwithstanding any minor physiological differences. Yet we make war on one another, contrary to the norm of most of the animal kingdom. By means of pseudo-speciation we claim other human beings are *not* human. The Spanish conquistadors believed the Native Americans they brutalized were extraordinary animals capable of mimicking human behavior. The Native Americans did some pseudo-speciating of their own, calling their particular tribe "the People" and viewing all the others as less than human. Dutch settlers in New Guinea hunted, killed, and ate the indigenous bushmen until they were finally convinced the natives were not a lesser species.

Though most of us now have at least an intellectual appreciation for the fact that we are all human beings, we continue to pseudo-speciate. At all levels of society, competitive behaviors based on racism, classism, sexism, nationalism, or differences between ethnic or religious groups are manifestations of pseudo-speciation. There are traces of it even in the violent outbreaks between players or fans of opposing teams at sporting events. What we would never dare do to a member of *our* group, we feel we have license to do to members of the *other* group.

In civilized societies even hardened criminals are given due process. Yet when we are at war we are encouraged to commit atrocities against innocent men, women, and children. Once we pseudo-speciate the "gooks," "gringos," "slopes," "kikes," "goyim," or "wetbacks," we feel we can brutalize them with impunity. Obviously pseudo-speciation has led to many of our individual and collective tragedies. It has made much of human history proceed like a nightmare. And as nuclear arsenals spread among tribalistic nations, pseudo-speciation threatens to extinguish us all.

It is interesting to consider how pseudo-speciation may have developed, and why it has become linked to the Warrior. Our Australopithecine ancestors almost certainly competed with other hominids in the East African environment of several million years ago.[17] These hominids may or may not have been discrete species. We have no way of knowing. What does seem likely is that the early hominids fought to maintain the integrity and purity of their respective gene pools. The instinct for pseudo-speciation would have arisen to protect these gene pools as well as to protect the societal cohesion and integrity of a particular pool.

Besides this likely biological basis, pseudo-speciation has been supported by an accident of culture. It seems certain that humankind spread gradually from East Africa into the vast

Early Warfare: The Violence of Pseudo-speciation (a group of
armed men, from Great Rock Shelter of Cuevas del Civil,
Castellón, Spain)

lands of Asia, Europe, the subcontinent of India, Australia, the islands of the Pacific, and finally into the Americas in small, isolated bands. Over thousands of years, these bands became increasingly cut off from one another. After losing all contact with other humans, each tribe quite sensibly called themselves "the People," assuming their unique cultural and racial characteristics were typical of all human beings. Once human populations had grown to the point at which they began bumping into each other again, they could not recognize each other as human! Whether or not there resided in the collective unconscious a racial memory of battles with other hominid species, these distinct human tribes began to engage in wars of mutual extermination. What had been a useful adaptation for ensuring interspecies survival became the plague of our single species. The Warrior worked to the advantage of the strongest groups even as it wreaked havoc on humanity as a whole.

Eventually human population reached sufficient density that interchanges, through war and trade, rendered pseudospeciation judgments less absolute. But they persisted in a different form. If other tribes were now recognized as *being* human, they still could be experienced as being *inferior* humans. Cultures, religions, customs, and physical characteristics could all be classified as inferior. At this stage of interaction (if not before) the psychological mechanism of Shadow projection began to occur. The "others" became "pagan," "heathen," or "unclean." This state of affairs is vividly depicted in the Judeo-Christian scriptures. "Unbelievers" are fair game for brutal depredations at the hands of the "chosen people." Along with other religious writings of the era, the biblical scriptures reworked older sacred writings that had shaped and responded to the emergence of advanced urban civilizations, especially in Egypt and Mesopotamia.

As Schmookler rightly demonstrates, it was in these cities

that the increasingly paranoid scramble for apparently scarce riches began. Here the Warrior takes on a more sinister aspect as exclusivist religions and accumulated urban wealth encouraged his tendency to lead men into interpersonal competition. In this intensely competitive world a warrior class of military elites arose. This often oppressive class dominated the social hierarchy and appropriated the wealth generated by the lower classes. But even given this oppression the archetypal Warrior's influence could be beneficial as well.

THE WARRIOR'S ROLE
IN MAKING WORLDS

After devastating earlier Neolithic cultures the warrior elites did much to organize, consolidate, and advance civilized urban societies.[18] In this sense the Warrior played a vital role in the creation of city civilizations, and the accompanying blossoming of art, science, trade, and commerce. Upper Egypt's military conquest of Lower Egypt propelled the high cultures of the Nile valley into civilization. In Mesopotamia the conquests of Sargon of Akkad stimulated a similar advance, not only between the Tigris and Euphrates, but as far afield as Syria and Palestine. Early civilizations in China, India, Persia, Greece, and Italy had a similar grounding in conquest.[19]

At this stage the capital city was believed to be the center of the universe.[20] Through it passed the *axis mundi*, a column of energy connecting the sacred dimension to the profane; the palace-temple complex served as a vast generating system, transforming and then transmitting this sacred energy into the created world. The sacred king accomplished this energic infusion, and the warriors of civilization fought and died in his service. These "divinely inspired" urban cultures had to be

King Narmer Defeating the Forces of Lower Egypt and
Founding a Nation (the Narmer palette from Hierakonpolis)

protected against human foes and demonic forces alike. Anyone who lived beyond the borders of the kingdom (hence outside of the created world) had to be either barbaric or demonic. The borders of the world had therefore to be extended in order to bring peace to all of creation.

For all the destruction they wrought these ancient civilizations did spread the benefits of high culture to outlying peoples. Under the warrior-supported rule of the sacred kings enormous cultural and intellectual advances were made.[21] With the Warrior's discipline, for the first time large-scale cultural projects were organized and undertaken for the benefit of society. Urban planning, construction and sanitation schemes, and public means for accessing environmental resources were introduced. People were given their first measures of security against disasters, with provisions stored against drought and famine years, and skilled military organizations trained to react against invasion. Of course many monumental construction projects were accomplished by using slave or forced labor, so these persons suffered unwillingly for scientific and technological advances. It is clear that the positive impact of warrior energy is limited by the morality of the vision that it serves.

The warriors who defended and extended the benefits of coordinated civilized life were often full-time members of the military. As often they were part-time citizen warriors, drafted in time of national emergency, or even (as in ancient Rome) conscripted for fixed-term mandatory stints. The Gods of choice for these men were fierce storm and battle Gods, and King-Gods of light and righteousness.[22]

Often these guardians of civilization consciously affirmed what they believed was a sacred duty to advance the work of creation which the Gods had begun in mythic time. The legionnaires of Rome brought order to a chaotic Mediterranean world and spread the adopted civilization of Hellenistic Greece

A Sumerian Phalanx (the standard of Ur, War Side, from the
Royal Cemetery at Ur, Early Dynastic III,
circa 2550 B.C.E.)

An Etruscan Warrior (small bronze votive figure of a warrior,
first half of the fifth century B.C.E.)

The Sword in India (memorial to a chieftan, Dumad, Baroda, C.E. 1298)

from the Caucasus to the Thames. In the process they fostered the most fertile exchange of ideas the world has known until modern times. For the first time a single world community was envisioned, made up of a unified whole respectful of all of its richly diversified parts. The Romans staved off the barbarians from the north long enough for these peoples to acquire some appreciation for higher civilization. The cultural embers smoldered so long that even a thousand years after Rome fell that ancient civilization's classical works kindled the European Renaissance.

Controversially crediting a military elite with developing the first differentiated self-conscious Ego structures, the scholar Julian Jaynes claims Assyrian warriors in the thirteenth century B.C. raised themselves above what was before them a largely unconscious psychic background.[23] Comparing particularly the Homeric epics with later Assyrian texts, Jaynes found there to be no trace of a conscious Ego in the

I Am Mighty! The Concious Ego Erupts into History
(King Ashurbanipal shooting at lions, Nineveh,
Palace of Ashurbanipal)

former, at least not in the earlier of the two epics, *The Iliad*.
The Gods who manipulated Achilles were unconscious forces,
driving him from one emotion or thought to another, whereas
the Assyrian heroes assumed *they* themselves were in charge
of their thoughts and actions.

If Jaynes is right, it would seem the razor-sharp clarity of
perception the archetypal Warrior stimulates inspired the psychological development of the Ego as we know it. Clear perceptions, coupled with strategic thinking, allow a man to
discriminate between possibilities in the world. As his dis-
criminatory abilities improve, a man will naturally be led to a
finer understanding of his differentiated *inner* world; and as
long as he can accept what he understands he will develop
stronger Ego structures. Once differentiated from a collective
background, the Ego can construct boundaries, protecting
itself from unwanted unconscious upwellings. In an axial relationship with the Ego, the archetypal Warrior *strengthens*

A Persian King Subduing the "Demons" (a Persian king
hunting wild boar, silver bowl, Freer Gallery of Art,
Washington, D.C.)

these boundaries and extends them in the course of Ego consolidation. With the Warrior to guide it, an Ego can no longer
truthfully claim, "The Gods made me do it."

HOLY WARS

While all wars have an unconscious "sacred" dimension to the
extent that they ritualize life and death in a fight between
"true" humans and demonic "others," the emergence of the
idea of "holy war" in ancient Persia profoundly altered the
mythology of conflict.[24] The Persian religion founded by
the prophet Zoroaster spread throughout the Mediterranean in
the several centuries before Christ. Its tenets were absorbed
into later Jewish, Gnostic, Manichaean, and Christian prac-

80

tices. Zoroastrianism is a religion of militant dualism. When misapplied, it leads to the most vicious form of religious intolerance. When its inherent dualism is correctly understood to be an inner *spiritual* struggle, however, it can yield a noble perspective on the state of the world, as expressed in terms of the archetypal Warrior.

Religions before Zoroastrianism tended to depict the opposites in creation (good and evil, for example, or light and darkness, creation and destruction, life and death) as necessary frictional partners in a harmonious universal balance. The new Persian religion, however, taught that good and evil were openly at war with each other. In the Zoroastrian myth, Ahura Mazda, the Creator, is a King-God who allowed the evil God Ahriman to have a hand in the creation. Since that time the two have been locked in a struggle for ascendancy. Human beings are called upon to side with Ahura Mazda, and to await his deliverance at the end of time. While they are waiting they are encouraged to purge the world of evil, in their own souls but especially among their "unrighteous" human neighbors. Battles on earth between the people of the "Good Religion" and the unrighteous are simply an expression of the struggle between Ahura Mazda and Ahriman. Eventually the myth teaches that Ahura Mazda will triumph and create a new world within which evil will have no part.

Mithraism was a potent offshoot of Zoroastrianism, and a particular favorite of the Roman legions, who spread it throughout the Empire.[25] It was Christianity's main rival religion for many years. Central to Mithraism was another myth of this Cosmic Combat. Mithra was the son of Ahura Mazda. The Roman soldiers who worshipped Mithra felt themselves to be fighting for his cause as they extended their empire. He was the savior come to show men how to become warriors of light. Mithraic services were exclusively male (one factor that assured its eventual decline) and were held in underground

Mithra Slaying the Cosmic Bull in Order to Create the World

grottoes. Central to the service was the well-known bull sacrifice, a reenactment of the original sacrifice of the Cosmic Bull by which Mithra had created the world through an act of violence. When the highest grade of initiate performed the sacrifice, he simultaneously renounced his physical passions and his material desires and placed his fate in the hands of Ahura Mazda.

When a militant, dualistic faith such as Mithraism is applied in a literalistic way, it encourages adherents to repress their own Shadows and to project them onto an outer "enemy." The authentic mythological dialectics the faith expresses are of *inner* psychic material, and *not* of outer contemporary "outer" events. When we project our demons onto others, we give ourselves a free hand to treat them with brutality. The horribly destructive holy wars of the Middle Ages in

A Proud Samurai

Europe and the Middle East were based on a profound misunderstanding of Mithraic mythology, which by then had been absorbed into the faiths followed by the combatants of each side. That mythology bolstered the scripturally sanctioned genocide already present in the Judeo-Christian and then Muslim traditions.

There were noble elements in the Mithraic-based Warrior traditions. The faith demanded relativization of the Ego, leading to self-sacrifice for a higher cause, enormous self-discipline, fidelity, faith in the future and in the ultimately benevolent purposes of God. These elements provided the inspiration for the knightly codes of honor of medieval civilization.

The samurai tradition is a similar expression of the archetypal Warrior, one that emerged in medieval Japan.[26] These professional warriors dedicated their lives to high ideals of conduct and inner spiritual discipline. Through exacting mental and physical disciplines they sought to channel the energy of the archetypal Warrior into world-making programs.

Of course the ideal samurai was as rare as the courteous knight. In both Europe and Japan a satiric literature chronicles the misdeeds of these "sacred" warriors. Sadistic cruelty, an exaggerated sense of personal honor, or just plain foolishness was the stuff of these satires. The last great character in this tradition is Don Quixote, a figure whose ludicrous failings were located in the very hubris the Warrior's mysteries were supposed to help a knight overcome.

THE WARRIOR IN MODERNITY

As bad as things were in some respects under the reign of the "sacred" warriors, worse was yet to come. During the French Enlightenment, rationalists steeped in the works of the pre-Socratic Greek philosophers moved the Ego to center stage in the human psyche.[27] Our culture of modernity is the psychological and spiritual heir to this "Enlightenment." Aspects of the movement were indeed enlightening, especially as far as they were empowering to the Ego. However, because the unconscious is devalued by rationalism, our source of life-giving Libido has become limited and despised.

Libido is supplied to us whether we want it or not. But when a culture holds the unconscious in disrepute, the way we receive Libido is altered. Many do everything in their conscious power to deny themselves Libido. The Libido then finds all kinds of indirect, unmanageable channels to manifest in our lives. When people blind themselves to their unconscious powers they leave themselves no means of control, and so their unconscious controls them.

In modernity it's as if the frontal lobe of the left cerebral cortex (the probable site of the rational Ego) has declared its independence from the rest of the brain. The volume of irrational events we've seen in the twentieth century proves what a failure this project has been. Jung criticized our modern culture for seeking to sever the rational from the suprarational mind, and the Ego from both the personal and the collective unconscious. The psychological split our culture fosters is extremely dangerous because rejected psychic contents do not die. They return in destructive form to haunt us.

Jung has pointed out that once you no longer have any archetypally sacred realm of Gods and Goddesses, all that energy collapses into the human realm—where people identify with it, and go crazy.[28] The Nazi movement drew on archetypal energy. Barbara Hannah, one of Jung's associates, describes driving across Germany in 1933 to meet Jung at a conference in Dahlem, near Berlin. She was struck by the hundreds of Germans wandering, on foot, from place to place in hopes of finding work, or a meal. They were possessed by Wotan, a warlike, wandering Germanic God. Here are Jung's impressions from the short time he spent lecturing in Germany:

National Socialism was one of those psychological mass phenomena, one of those outbreaks of the collective unconscious, about which I had been speaking for nearly twenty years. The driving forces of a psychological mass movement are essentially archetypal. Every archetype contains the lowest and highest, evil and good, and is therefore capable of producing diametrically opposite results . . . If an archetype is not brought into reality consciously, there is no guarantee whatever that it will be realized in its favorable form; on the contrary, there is all the more danger of a destructive regression. It seems as if the psyche were endowed with consciousness for the very purpose of preventing such destructive possibilities from happening.[29]

Thus individuation, the Ego's movement toward discriminating between itself and an archetype, was seen by Jung as a profoundly moral task. It is not merely a struggle of inner importance, but has a national and a planetary significance. Where there is a preponderance of individuated persons there can be no mass hysteria. The myths of human life are given the attention they require.

In modernity one myth the "enlightened" Ego rejected was that of the *eschaton*, the end of the world in a fiery deluge. Instead we embraced the idea that reason would prevail, leading us through an uninterrupted progress toward a kind of paradise on earth. But the eschaton is an important expression of the collective unconscious, full of important insights about the real nature of personal and collective growth. Progress is never uninterrupted but is a process of periodic trauma, recovery, death, and rebirth. The fires of the unconscious must be allowed to burn away the old before the new can arise from the ashes. The arena for this initiatory process is the soul. Therefore the real meaning of the myth of the eschaton is a *spiritual* one.

But because modernity has rejected the inner spiritual realm, most of us can read the myth only in an historical dimension. *Can* the earth end in a fiery deluge? The Ego's confident answer was *no*. So the unconscious *literalized* the potential for the eschaton when it delivered to the Ego the atomic bomb. To underline the lesson, the bomb itself is a product of the most advanced technology, itself generated by the empowered, rational Ego.[30] The dishonored Warrior has returned with a vengeance. When his cataclysmic outbursts in two world wars went disregarded, he invented a bomb that still threatens to actualize the final battle between the "sons of light" and the "sons of darkness," even in a post–Cold War age, one that is witnessing a greatly accelerated nuclear proliferation.

With the spiritual realm denied to it, the Ego has no means for realizing an Ego-Self axis. The Ego can no longer apprehend the magnitude and richness of a Transpersonal Other sufficient to bring about the condition of true humility. With the King exiled from the unconscious, the Warrior has no one to serve. The result for our times has been a breakdown of knightly initiation. The mysteries of the sword have been banished. The sacred code of service to the King and his forces of light has decayed into personal, political, racial, sexist, socioeconomic, or nationalistic triumphalism. We've invested lesser entities with the significance only the King (and beyond him the Self) can legitimately possess. Ego-aggrandizement and military careerism have always plagued spiritually impoverished warriors, but modernity has almost entirely handed over its affairs to infantile and grandiose individuals who know nothing about the true nature of the Warrior.

Many have remarked that the American Civil War marked the end of knightly ideals. Here the practice of "total war" was introduced. Mechanized masses of human cannon fodder were maneuvered against each other without regard for codes of honor. Sherman's March to the Sea was the epitome of the desacralization of ancient warrior codes. From this point on all American wars would increasingly lose touch with any noble purposes; general carnage obscured the view.

Japan's experience in the Second World War was similar. The ancient samurai devotion to spiritual ideals gave way to the sadistic crimes that were a regular feature of the Japanese P.O.W. camps, and the Bataan Death March. The Soviet Union saw its idealized quest to liberate the oppressed of the world dissolve into the cruelty of the war in Afghanistan.

War—within the psyche and in the outer world—is the paradoxically destructive and creative expression of the archetypal Warrior. Shorn of spiritual relevance, it becomes mere savagery. The world-making thrust of the fully expressed Warrior becomes lost in sadomasochistic extravagance and unredemptive suffering. A reappropriation of the repressed world of the archetypal Warrior is necessary if we are to escape the Warrior's Shadow and reinvest in an aggressive program of advancing civilization and establishing justice. For this is the original urge of the archetype.

MYTHIC IMAGES
OF THE WARRIOR:
THE COSMIC COMBAT

T HE CENTRAL MYTHIC EXPRESSION OF THE ARCHE-
typal Warrior is that of the cosmic combat.[1] In a world
that is demonstrably dualistic opposing forces contend with
one another in a never-ending quest for dominance. Complementary pairs of opposites achieve through conflict a rough
harmony, the means by which the frictional world transcends
itself in creative advance.

This creative cosmic dualism manifests in the human
imagination as the Warrior-Enemy polarity. Warrior and
Enemy are defined differently by every society, but the pattern
of dynamic interdependence between the two remains consis-

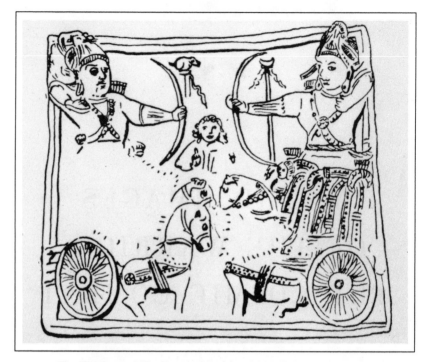

The Warrior and His Enemy (royal warriors, after a terra-cotta
plaque from Ahicchatra, U.P., circa sixth century C.E.)

tent. Our early hominid ancestors probably identified the
Enemy as both the predators that hunted them, and the other
competing hominid species or tribes. Competition among
males then as now would have been over territory, resources,
and women. Through the mechanism of pseudo-speciation
other beings of the same species, but with alien cultural traditions, became identified as the Enemy. Also, we can come to
regard any individual human being as an incarnation of the
Enemy. But behind all these perceived expressions of the
cosmic Enemy lies the Enemy itself, a mysterious force or
entity that seems to work against personal and collective ideas
of goodness, well-being, and the powers of life.[2]

The Warrior and the Enemy fight on the cosmic plane.

The mythological location of their combat is a kind of any-where and everywhere "theater of war." Since this drama is timeless and ubiquitous the cosmic combat has been experienced at all times in history. Whenever the profane dimension becomes transparent to the sacred dimension, what is eternal is at that moment perceived here and now—as temporal.[3] When conditions are right for it, the fabric between the worlds drops away, and we experience an archetypal moment.

One such archetypal moment is depicted in the movie *Patton*. While Patton crouches behind a sand dune scanning the North African desert for German tanks, his own corps lies in camouflage behind him. As the German Tigers rumble first into earshot and then into view, Patton gives the signal to open fire. His tanks roar out to engage the Germans. With the percussive tank missiles exploding against the sides of the Tigers, with the engines roaring, turrets swinging, and foot soldiers scrambling to get out of the way of the metal treads, it seems we are watching Armageddon.

In fact this is precisely how Patton views the battle. He believes he is a holy warrior on a sacred mission to destroy the Nazi forces of darkness. As he watches the battle through his binoculars, a smile spreads across his face as he realizes the Americans are winning. He throws back his head, laughs, and says "Rommel, you magnificent bastard, I read your book!" Patton believes he has engaged and defeated the legendary tank commander and strategist by using Rommel's own tac-tics. Patton feels a joyful kinship with his counterpart. The scene is archetypal: the Warrior and his Enemy locked in combat, deciding the future of the world!

When he later learns Rommel was *not* at the battle, Patton's joy in the archetypal moment evaporates. He stands that evening with one of his staff looking out at the desert sunset. He buttons his greatcoat against the wind, sighs, and says that the way the battle should have been fought is with

Rommel and himself each in a single tank, charging each other like medieval knights. A contest of champions—the Warrior and his Enemy—seems to Patton to be the best way to fight a war.

Ancient battles were often decided in this way. Patton's vision of the tank duel has its antecedents in the lists of the medieval knights. In these ceremonial tournaments two knights charged each other, each using a lance or sword to try to dismount the other. Though each contestant risked physical injury, the object was only to dismount, not to kill the other. Eventually some medieval disputes were decided in a real battle to the death between two "champions." In the Americas a Maya king fought personally with his opposite to determine the futures of their kingdoms.[4] Even in battles where single combat was not ritualized, the death of a commander frequently sealed the outcome. At the Battle of Otumba in Mexico, the Spanish were outnumbered by hundreds to one by an Aztec army, when Cortez charged the enemy general and killed him. Immediately the Aztec army dissolved, and Spain gained the victory through the death of one man![5]

In the movie *Robin and Marian* this type of duel is poignantly represented. Robin and the sheriff of Nottingham ride out from the ranks of their opposing armies, dismount, and then whack away at each other with spiked clubs and two-handed broadswords. The formidable weight of armor and weaponry soon exhausts the two combatants. They are fighting to the death, but when one stumbles and falls, the other helps him up. Even during their combat they maintain the Warrior's code of honor and the feeling ultimately of brotherhood.

The archetypal aspect of this type of combat is apparent in the duel between David and Goliath.[6] In ancient Egyptian myth, the eternal struggle between Osiris and Set is another figuring of this archetypal conflict.[7] Set is the jealous brother who murders Osiris. After Isis resurrects her dead husband, Osiris and Set engage in an eternal battle, which essentially represents the battle between light and darkness, good and evil. Both combatants were invoked in the pharaonic enthronement rituals; Warrior and Enemy are bound to each other forever. The Egyptians believed that without destruction there can be no creation. Both aspects of the universal dialectic are dependent upon their eternal conflict and ultimately their fight brings harmony. The Egyptians also believed this cosmic combat was waged within the bodies and souls of every human being, as well as in the phenomena of nature. If a man could place himself on the right side of the conflict he became a victor in the struggle between life and death.

In Mesopotamian myth the creation of the world was a direct result of the cosmic combat.[8] The hero God Marduk fashions the world from the dismembered corpses of his foes, Tiamat, the dragon of chaos, and her consort, Kingu. So we see the Warrior bringing order to the raw materials of chaos and destruction. A similar scenario is echoed in the mythologies of many people, from India to the New World.[9] Almost certainly it provides the basis for St. Paul's understanding of Christ as one who "swallows up" the last "enemy," Death, gaining "victory" over him.[10]

The mythic moment was always *present* for ancient peoples. The conflicts between Osiris and Set, Marduk and Tiamat or Christ and Death were waged in a sacred time that was eternally current.[11] The Babylonian conflict was dramatically portrayed every year by a group of actors, including the king, who played Marduk.[12] In the same way Easter is a highly symbolic reenactment of the most important event in the Christian calendar. These kinds of events and ceremonies allow people to participate intentionally in the eternal, archetypal presence of the cosmic combat.

Slaying the Dragon of Chaos: A Medieval Survival of the
Babylonian Myth of Creation (the Red Cross Knight from
Spenser's *Faerie Queene*)

As we have seen, the conflict Ahura Mazda and his son Mithra wage eternally against Ahriman is central to the Persian religions of Zoroastrianism and Mithraism. Many of the Greek philosophers, most notably Heraclitus, also saw conflict as being the essential dynamic of the world.[13] His opposing forces were light and darkness, cold and hot, and water and fire. He believed the history of the world moved in great cycles. At the end of one cycle the world ends in a watery deluge. After another, fire destroys everything. His thinking was gradually elaborated into an eschatological myth. According to such a myth, space and time move various elements of the cosmic combat inexorably toward a final war. Good will finally triumph over evil, and a totally new creation will emerge, one that has permanently transcended the duality of the present universe.[14]

Nowhere do we find this eschatological vision expressed more clearly than in the myths of the ancient Hebrews, Jews, Christians, and Muslims. Human life is seen in these traditions as the central battleground of the Warrior and his Enemy. According to these myths, many have fallen to the Enemy and become his servants. These individuals are the "sons of darkness," the unbelievers, the unrighteous, and the infidels. But those who are the saved, righteous adherents of the true religion will triumph in the final battle, to be fought at Armageddon, the "Hill of Megiddo" in Palestine. Here the genocidal fantasies of the ancient Hebrews, and their Christian and Muslim descendants, will reach their full and final expression. Whole nations of unbelievers will be slaughtered. The Book of Revelation pictures Christ engaging Satan in single combat and sending him forever into the flames of the Lake of Fire.[15]

Our modern, "rational" world still relies unconsciously on the myths of our cultural heritage. Look at the rhetoric of the two world wars. In the first, Americans fought to "make the world safe for democracy." In the second we waged war against the Nazi "terror" and the "evil empire" of Japan. Until very recently most Americans believed we were engaged in a life-and-death struggle with the "red hordes" of the Soviet Union and China. Many now have trouble letting go of an Enemy they have spent a lifetime hating. Many televangelists have built their considerable fortunes interpreting this former national struggle as the final enactment of the prophesied Christian version of the cosmic combat.

Science has provided us with an immediate means for realizing Armageddon. Tensions between East and West may no longer lead to this final battle, but nuclear proliferation ensures that now any number of countries can begin the enactment of their own versions of the eschatological myth. Ahura Mazda's lightning bolts are now in an increasing number of many human hands.

As a species we are still afflicted by the phenomena of projection and pseudo-speciation, which tempt us to experience others as the Enemy and ourselves as the righteous Warrior. When we project we make others bear our own Shadows. On the level of the collective unconscious, entire groups make other groups carry the archetypal Shadow. We make the "gooks" carry all our own unacknowledged cunning, deceitfulness, and cruelty. "Infidels" bear our own repressed doubts. We give Muslim terrorists, abusive police, or urban rioters all of our hidden sadism or fanaticism. Once we have externalized and projected these qualities, we give those who carry the projections no quarter, so desperate are we to maintain the illusion of our own innocence and righteousness.

Anyone who challenges these projections instantly makes an enemy *of himself* as well. The average man's thinking goes, "the man who attacks my prejudices must be hostile to them, and therefore hostile to me, and therefore he is my enemy." If a narcissistic pathology is operative, the intellectually honest man can even be promoted from a personal enemy to an enemy of the people. This mechanism was obviously in place in the Fascist and Communist states of the thirties and forties. The thinking is, "by insulting me, you insult the state." Because of Ego inflation, the individual party member sees himself as indistinguishable from the party as a whole; all undesirable qualities are projected onto those outside the party. Anyone who challenges his behaviors must automatically be a traitor.

The problem of projection is a serious one.[16] It is a symptom of the psychological division that has led us to the brink of collective suicide. But also it obscures the real enemies, who really *can* be "out there" in the world. Not all of our enemies are limited to the inner world. The cosmic combat *can* take place between individuals, and not just within souls. The danger of projection is that our focus is too often shifted away from the real enemies that face us, and the Real War we are now called upon to fight.

6

THE WAY OF
THE WARRIOR

A SOLDIER IS NOT NECESSARILY A WARRIOR. A soldier, whether he is an army regular or a soldier of fortune, is often primarily a mercenary. If he kills for pay and without caring who pays him he is a killing machine. A warrior *may* have to kill. But killing is the outcome of a warrior's commitments, his vision of world making, and his disciplined quest to serve a Transpersonal Other.

While capable of killing when necessary, a warrior knows the *real* war is within. A man who appropriately accesses the archetypal Warrior draws upon enormous resources that enable him to live an empowered life in the service of his fellow

Eternal Guardian of Civilization: A Toltec Warrior
(Tula, valley of Mexico)

creatures. He embodies the characteristics of the fully expressed Warrior. What are these characteristics?

The Warrior is alive, vivid, fairly crackling with energy from the sacred dimension! When the Warrior is on-line we feel a rush of blood and adrenaline, a quickening heartbeat, and a sense of something momentous about to happen. We feel mobilized for action, ready to charge forward to meet life head-on. Our daily concerns fall away from us and we are swept up into a kind of ecstasy in which we see ourselves and the world with a sharpened focus and clarity. Hidden rage is transmuted into energized courage. We come into touch with the great mystery of life and death, and we feel a strange sense of pleasure in the midst of pain.

When Patton, as portrayed in the movie, stands among the ruins of his tank corps after the Battle of Kassarine, he is caught up in this Warrior ecstasy. He is drunk with the sights and sounds of dead and dying men, burning tanks and barking dogs. He takes a deep breath, filling his lungs with the stench of gasoline and burned flesh. He stands tall, sighs, and says, "God help me! I do love it so!" In states of mind like this one, Patton wrote ecstatic poetry affirming his belief in reincarnation and his conviction that he had lived in many epochs and fought in the great battles of history. He seems to literally relive these battles and to see them through the eyes of the eternal Warrior.

Every man knows the ecstasy of the Warrior. Many of us have been in actual combat. We have spent sleepless nights on the eve of battle, filled with anxiety and anticipation. We think with nostalgia of our loved ones and our personal lives, now being swept aside by life-and-death events that call upon us to subordinate our Egos to a greater good, a higher cause. We have felt the rush of adrenaline and that strange mix of terror and eagerness that approaches awe. Whether or not we knew it we touched the "mystery of the sword" and were one with the initiates of the ancient cave sanctuaries.

With lesser intensity perhaps we have known the Warrior in more mundane circumstances: packing for the make-or-break business trip; preparing the keynote political address; driving the last bolt into the skyscraper's steel frame; proposing a marriage, or a divorce.

The Warrior is an energy resource, one that permits us to be assertive about our lives, goals, needs, and causes.[1] He gets us moving again after a period of stagnation. He supports us when we act from our real feelings and needs instead of from other people's expectations. Instead of our compulsively saying yes when we mean no, he directs us to responses that are in our strategic self-interest. If we say yes under the Warrior's aegis we mean it!

Self-psychologists talk about "false self organization,"[2] a concept similar to the Jungian persona. The false self or persona is the mask we wear in order to get along with others. Behind the mask we hide our "true self," the vulnerable core of our soul. A man develops a false self early in life after his true self is attacked or ridiculed. A false self conforms to what others want and expect, so he believes by adopting this mask he will get at least some of the love and approval he needs for survival. The problem is that the false self becomes an automaton. Although it may be strategically necessary to use a mask from time to time, perhaps especially in childhood and adolescence, by adulthood the mask takes on a life of its own. The Ego becomes its captive and loses touch with the true self which is buried ever more deeply in the unconscious. A man may forget who he really started out to be.

Life demands, sooner or later, that we regain contact with our true selves and begin to live out of them. If at this point a false self is too powerful and persuasive we may be unable to meet life's demands for growing authenticity. The persona gets tired though, and the mask slips, because it takes an enormous amount of energy to keep up false appearances. But the real person we've concealed beneath layers of false smiles, macho bluff, and histrionic affectations is reluctant to come out of hiding for fear of being attacked again as it was in childhood.

The Ego needs to call upon the Warrior in order to protect the true self's gradual emergence. The Warrior encourages the full expression of our total psychic system. He throws up a defensive shield to protect the consolidating identity. He puts a sword in the hand of the Self to enable the new psychic integrity to be aggressive about its legitimate need for power and affirmation.

The Warrior helps to provide us with firm boundaries. After enabling us to build Self-structures at the heart of our psychological territories, he helps us to control who and what will be permitted to influence the inner sanctum of the true self. He enforces a kind of camp perimeter and mans the boundaries of a cohesive psychological identity. He denies access to unauthorized, invasive, or hostile forces, whether they be other human beings or psychological entities from the inner world.

Men hear a lot of talk these days about their need to be vulnerable and their fear of intimate relationships. It is true that some men fear their own tenderness as well as their inner feminine, what Jung called the Anima,[3] which hinders them in their attempts to feel safe with women. But what most men fear *isn't* intimacy. They are starving for it. What they really fear is the destructive and hostile behaviors of others, which they have been taught are a part of intimate relationships. They fear being attacked for who they are. They fear sarcasm, ridicule, criticism, and depreciating remarks. Underlying these fears is the fear of being drawn back into a symbiotic merger with the all-powerful mother.

We are right to fear being attacked as persons and as

Protecting the Center, Serving the King: Warriors of the
Chin Dynasty (part of the vast underground tomb for the
Chinese emperor Qin Shi Huang, founder of the Chin Dynasty,
third century B.C.E.)

men. And we are correctly cautious about engaging in relationships that carry such a costly price tag. We are also appropriately wary of anything that smacks of regression into
childhood passivity and domination at the hands of an un-
equally powerful feminine.[4] We all begin quite literally at one
with the feminine and are completely dependent upon it for
our survival. Successfully achieving a masculine identity requires enormous work in terms of self-definition and boundary setting.

Part of that work involves a break with an overly empathetic tie to our mother and her ways of being and doing. It
includes a "phase-specific" rejection of feminine qualities.[5] It
necessitates the construction of defensive walls against an intimacy we have no choice but to associate with an inordinately
powerful woman. The heroic stage of boyhood engages us in
a titanic struggle to overcome the power of the mother, and,

at the same time, to discover the limits of our masculine powers. Without the Warrior it is doubtful that we can ever succeed in these tasks.

In adulthood a man continues to need a defensive perimeter. He should not surrender it under the misguided notion that he is safe without it. Because of his hard-fought struggle to become a man, a legitimately autonomous adult male, he must be careful to build his intimate relationships with women out of a consolidated masculine structure. With firm boundaries in place, no relationship will challenge his psychological integrity.

At the same time this boundary setting can be taken too far. We do not want to create or maintain an *impregnable* barrier between ourselves and others. We should not become prisoners behind our own walls. We need to feel safe enough to let others in when we would like to. The Warrior gives us the capacity to share our inner lives with those who merit our trust, and not with those who mean us harm. His perceptive acuity defends us against neurotic, merging bonds, relationships now popularly called *co-dependent*. By providing us with secure boundaries, the Warrior actually *enhances* our capacity for intimate relationships with women as well as with other males.

The Warrior also permits us the legitimate expression of controlled aggression. Many life situations *call* for aggressiveness. The business world, for example, abounds in such situations. Marketplace aggression is essential to the generation and distribution of wealth. But the aggression needs to be controlled. In recent years we have been reminded what financial burdens result from underhanded and duplicitous aggressive business practices. The insider-trading scandal on Wall Street, the corrupt practices at the Chicago Board of Trade, the S and L catastrophe, and the growing insolvency of major banks following get-rich-quick schemes all point to Warrior energy

running wild. Many of us have been the victims of false advertising, whether from the car dealer or the televangelist whose
aggressive impulses have far exceeded the natural control a
concern for the greater good imposes. Yet the Warrior's ambi-
tious acquisitiveness can generate goods and services that
make human life not only livable but also healthier, more
comfortable, and even psychologically and spiritually richer.

There is also a useful aggressiveness that seeks to make
our city streets safe. While there are unquestionably some
abuses of police authority, the reality is that most of the men
and women of our big-city police forces are dedicated and well
disciplined. Their expression of controlled force under often
dangerous circumstances contributes significantly to the welfare of our society.

We have all encountered situations in which we needed to
be aggressive. If the school bully pushed us, we needed to fight
back to stop his attacks and to experience our own power in
threatening situations. Even if we were beaten, a forceful
response built courage and self-confidence. Our work lives
frequently call upon our aggressive skills. A problem at a
construction site may need to be "attacked." A demanding
customer may need to be confronted. In academia another
may try to plagiarize our ideas, and we may need to take
self-assertive action in order to get our rightful acknowledgment. We may encounter chronic browbeating, ridicule, sarcasm, or dominating behavior from our wives or children. We
need to stand up for ourselves, firmly and resolutely.

Crippling and killing diseases, natural disasters, environmental decay, the catastrophic troubles of our inner cities,
corrupt social and political systems, injustice in the workplace, all call for an aggressive response from human beings
willing to be warriors. The oppression of one class by another,
of one race, one sex, one religion, one nation by another: These
things too require a compelling reaction. In the *Pirke Avot*, the

Jewish "Sayings of the Fathers," a peacable young man asks a rabbi, "Are we not to forswear anger and live peacefully with all men?" The rabbi answers, "My son, God made anger for a purpose. If He had not intended for us to use it He would not have put it in our souls. Only be careful how you spend your anger. There are many things we should not be angry about. We should save our anger for those things which *demand* it. We must be angry about these things if we are to do God's will!"[6]

The samurai held that a warrior's method is to attack and attack, always moving forward. He never gives up the vision of his mission. This defiant human quality is the essence of the human drive to conquer new frontiers. It is the Warrior's willingness to charge into the unknown that moves the mind and soul of our species forward, claiming new territories both mental and physical, and eventually perhaps even new planets for Homo sapiens to inhabit.

Without the Warrior none of us would plow through the mountains of paperwork on our desks. We would be unwilling to make present sacrifices for future goals. We would not rouse ourselves to community action for a noble cause. We would not make every effort to overcome diseases like cancer and AIDS. Were it not for the Warrior, though we would still dream our dreams, we would not have the will to make them come true!

The Warrior is the dynamic inspiration of the phallic thrust. A man who is appropriately accessing the Warrior is filled with a sense of adventure. Perhaps he climbs a rock face that has never before been climbed, or perhaps he finds a new way to scale a familiar cliff—like the paraplegic rock climber at Yosemite. Perhaps he finds adventure using his computer, brainstorming for new ways to manufacture a product. Or his own imagination might provide his experience, as he creates something new, useful, or beautiful. Perhaps he journeys into his inner landscape and explores the furthest reaches of his own mind.

Adventure is by definition perilous. During an adventure a man needs the courage the Warrior provides. He may come up against any number of obstacles: fear, depression, malaise, despair, and even the possibility of death. There is a wonderfully illustrative scene in the movie *Star Trek III: The Search for Spock* in which Captain Kirk is standing with Dr. McCoy and other crew members on a bluff overlooking an alien planet. Rescue is doubtful. Up in the sky they see their beloved starship, *Enterprise,* burning as it falls through the alien atmosphere. Kirk turns to McCoy and asks, "Bones, what have I done?" McCoy replies, "What you have always done. Take an impossible situation and turn it into a fighting chance to live!" This is the courage of the Warrior! He gives us a fighting chance, to live and to *flourish.* Men like Anwar Sadat and Mikhail Gorbachev called upon the Warrior (unconsciously or consciously) and found the courage to do the unthinkable. If we are to recover our world from the brink of destruction, millions of us will need to draw upon the same archetypal Warrior who inspired both of these leaders, as well as the fictional Captain Kirk.

The Warrior helps leaders develop their potentials. He is himself devoted to the archetypal King, and he recognizes men who similarly serve something greater than themselves. He provides energy reserves of determination, fidelity, courage, and self-discipline.

Unfortunately we do not have enough positive models of Warrior-inspired leadership in our society. In the absence of formal, ongoing initiation practices, modern men have very little help maturing once they've passed adolescence. A lucky few find a mentor to help guide their search for a way to live productively. Most don't look for, or never find a mentor, and as a result never learn to exercise responsible leadership either at home or in the workplace. The contemporary phenomenon of the "absent father" is well known. Increasingly fathers are unavailable to their children. The reasons are many; some fathers feel an emotional distance from their children, others are at a physical distance because of work demands, or separation or divorce. Some learned how to be an absentee parent from their own fathers, who used alcohol or the office to keep life's problems as well as the blessings of relatedness at a distance.

Similarly men in the business world often seem to be treading water, padding their résumés and looking for an out rather than working to improve products, services, or the quality of their leadership for their corporation and community. They are happy to enjoy the salaries and benefits their firms provide. They like their suspendered uniforms. But when they make decisions, increasingly the end results are short-term windfall profits, and not the long-term health and integrity of either company or community. If the Warrior is on-line at all in these circumstances he is only supporting personal gain. *And the men who are using his energy are merely mercenaries.*

What is true in the business world is true of other walks of life as well. Many school administrators have too long ignored the quality of education it is their responsibility to advance. They have not supported their teachers. They have caved into pressure from those parents who would rather lower academic standards than push their children to acheive. Despite graduate degrees in leadership, these administrators cannot seem to translate their training into courageous action.

Many politicians in this and other countries are afflicted by the same malaise. So many problems face our society, on local, state, national, and international levels, but as the media rightfully wonders, "Where is the leadership?" Perhaps the way our political system is set up and financed works against the possibility of finding the men and women we need to have social problems realistically addressed. One thing is clear: We need political warriors, willing to fight the good fight for our world! The East-West nuclear peril seems to have abated only to give rise to regional powers that have developed terrible arsenals of their own chemical, biological, and nuclear weapons. National, racial, and religious wars rage on. The world drug trade flourishes with only token opposition. Environmental pollution and global warming continue apace, bearing a potentially catastrophic array of consequences: the dislocation of millions by retreating shorelines, the reduction of arable land, mass starvation, and political instability. Where are the "armies of light, of the true king"? Evidently meaningful, effective leadership requires a strength few men—even those already in leadership positions—are able to access or steward responsibly.

The fully expressed Warrior has the capacity to anesthetize us against pain and suffering. His anesthetic enables a man to withstand tremendous suffering for the sake of achieving a goal. Witness the athlete who pushes himself beyond the normal limits of physical and mental endurance. Boot camps and astronaut training programs are Warrior schools. In even more grueling disciplines Native Americans suffered the rigors of the sun dance in order to learn how to access the Warrior's anesthetic. They found that there is a point of concentration beyond pain. Boys of almost every traditional society discover this point during the painful physical ordeals of the *rite de passage*.

Many are the life circumstances we face that require us to find this painless point of concentration. We use it when we are burning the midnight oil to finish a vital business report, write a final term paper, or see a child through a serious illness. With a goal firmly in sight, we can move heaven and earth without being unduly distracted by discomfort or even physical pain.

The Warrior has several means for demanding that we be goal-oriented. He gives to us a sense of Mission or "Calling," an awareness of being asked to transcend narrow Ego concerns by focusing on some special task. Leaders in any field—artists, musicians, reformers, teachers, doctors, ministers, fathers— are often *called* through the noble spirit of the Warrior. *He gives help setting goals and then gives us the energy we need to achieve them.*

Self-discipline is the hallmark of the Warrior. We are all familiar with the discipline of the body associated with train- ing for athletics or the martial arts. Men involved in these endeavors must discipline their bodies to endure pain, expand their capacities, and achieve skilled coordination of mind and muscle. The same degree of physical discipline is demon- strated by a fine artist's use of his materials, and the musi- cian's use of his instrument.

What we may not realize is that the Warrior's discipline is not limited to the physical arena. His will is applied even more fundamentally to the mind and the emotions. He offers us greatly heightened vigilance, sharpened perceptions, and the capacity to discriminate between friend and foe. These characteristics survive from a time when a snapping twig or a sudden hush had to be instantaneously interpreted as evidence of game or predator, or of an enemy best avoided—or immedi- ately confronted.

This split-second reaction to danger is not so alien now as it may seem. When we walk along a deserted street at night and we hear footsteps behind us, the Warrior immediately puts us on "yellow alert." If the footsteps quicken he moves us to "red alert," ready to take evasive action; we cross to the other side of the street or duck into a lighted entryway. If our

Wading into Battle: "Might for Right!"

accessing of this aspect of the Warrior energy is excessive, this heightened vigilance can become paranoia. In this state a man's perceptions are amplified like an overloaded electronic system. We start to short-circuit. We experience danger where there is none, or exaggerate present dangers. But adequate mental discipline will help us avoid these pitfalls of the Warrior's discipline.

The mental and emotional self-discipline that the archetypal Warrior inspires has been elaborated in many cultural traditions into a spiritual path. Some examples of this we have seen already—the knights of medieval Europe, the Japanese samurai, and the Warrior religions of Zoroastrianism and Mithraism. This same capacity for spiritual discipline has been exercised throughout history by practitioners of the world's contemporary religions as well. There were the "desert saints" of early Christianity who sat on pillars in the desert sun in order to subdue the temptations of the demonic. Jesuits subjected themselves to a harsh daily regimen of prayer and self-examination, even after posting themselves to the most forbidding parts of the world. Buddhist monks, Hindu yogis, the "whirling dervishes" among the Moslem Sufis, all strive for a spiritual discipline to defeat what they believed to be forces of evil within their own souls.

A Spiritual Warrior: The Amitabha Buddha
(Kamakura, Japan)

Frequently a religion's founder provides the model for understanding the Spiritual Warrior. Jesus struggled in the desert for forty days with his own inner demons. Buddha sat under the Bo Tree, determined to pierce through his own inner resistances and gaze upon the core of reality. Muhammad wrestled in a desert cave with the spirit of Allah, demanding a revelation. These men were Warriors in a depth dimension. Our best scholars, theoreticians, and researchers have similarly disciplined their minds in order to see more deeply into the hidden patterns and dynamics of things. Because of these inner-directed warriors the frontiers of human knowledge have been extended. These men and women have begun to map the outer world and our inner psychological space with impressive accuracy.

The Warrior imparts to a man the capacity to be faithful. The psychoanalyst Erik Erikson has shown that fidelity is possible only where there is sufficient psychological integrity.[7] Integrity comes from *integration.* Hence the consolidation of a personal identity, achieved by realizing an Ego-Self axis, is necessary to any abiding loyalty. As we actualize our Self, we acquire the ability to be faithful to the person we really are. As this happens we recognize our true values, goals, feelings, beliefs, and preferences, and this in itself furthers our consolidation. And as this occurs we find ourselves increasingly faithful to those who are important to us.

We also become more faithful to organizations that embody our own values, whether they are the companies we work for or voluntary organizations such as political parties, community action groups, masonic lodges, or churches. At the same time, we may find these organizations are so flawed, perhaps even corrupt or criminal, that they do not deserve our loyalty. In such cases the Warrior may call upon us to be "whistle blowers," or to change the organization from within, or to abandon it altogether.

The same process occurs in our personal relationships with other people. The Warrior enables us to moderate our own Ego needs and endure a significant amount of pain and personal hardship for the sake of an intimate relationship. He also helps us to break free of relationships that prove inordinately or chronically hurtful. Dysfunctional patterns, if unexamined, often influence destructive marital dynamics and combative relationships with children. Fidelity to a dysfunctional family pattern is the opposite of the generative loyalty of the Warrior.

Realizing this deepens our understanding of the ultimate nature of the Warrior's fealty. He serves a Transpersonal Other and encourages men to do the same.[8] The Transpersonal Other actually enhances the status of those relationships that are worthy of a man's faith. If we are not in a conscious and committed relationship with a divine Reality, we will tend to experience our parents, children, friends, lovers, and spouses in idolatrous ways.[9] Since no human organization or being can carry our projection of a God-image we are bound to be bitterly disappointed. But if we can withdraw our projection—and along with it our expectation that others will provide us with unlimited mirroring—and redirect our expansive longings to an adequate Transpersonal Other, then we can relieve others of the inordinate emotional burdens we have placed upon them. We will be free to experience them as the beautiful and wounded creatures they are. We are then free to love them realistically and to be faithful to them with all of our mutual limitations accepted.

This healthier relational dynamic stems too from the Warrior's power of purposeful detachment. This is not an uncaring rejection of involvement. Rather, the Warrior helps us to detach from behavior patterns of enmeshment, merger, or codependency. If caught in these neurotic patterns a man is overstimulated by the needs, moods, and expectations of others, to the detriment of his true self. The husband who gets hooked into his abandonment anxiety every time his wife goes into a rage, and so capitulates to her perhaps unrealistic demands; the therapist who loses his temper easily with a particularly irritating client, one he is experiencing as his own repressed Shadow; the minister who burns out on his parishioners' demands because he can't say no; the employee who panics whenever his boss expresses displeasure with him—all are failing to access the Warrior's centered, self-assured detachment.

This detachment is useful not only in distinguishing ourselves from others, but also in separating the deep Self from our Ego. We can detach from our Ego only to the extent we grasp the inevitability of our own deaths. The realization of mortality is an essential part of the mystery of the sword. All warrior traditions incorporate the painful truth of the transience of the Ego. A warrior's sense of urgency and intensified life comes from his realization that his days are numbered. When a veteran experiences nostalgia for his war years, most often what he misses is this heightened appreciation for life! Once he made every day and moment count. Knowing what little time he has, he opens himself to the noblest of human purposes and learns a deep commitment to a Transpersonal Other. Native Americans called the detached perspective achieved by a man on intimate terms with his own death his "long body." He can take a long view of his life as a whole, a life that transcends the individual moments of joy and pain.

There are murals preserved by volcanic ash at Pompeii depicting the Dionysian mysteries.[10] In one panel we see a young male initiate gazing with shock and horror into a bowl filled with water. Behind him a man holds up the contorted mask of Old Age. The bowl is held at such an angle that the boy sees the mask reflected, in place of his own face. We can suppose the intended effect was to tear the boy away from illusions of immortality and set him firmly into the world of mature masculine responsibilities.

In a similar vein, Carlos Castaneda writes in *Journey to Ixtlan* of the advice of the old Yaqui Indian sorcerer Don Juan:

> Use it [*the knowledge of your own death*]. Focus your attention on the link between you and your death, without remorse or sadness or worrying. Focus your attention on the fact you don't have time and let your acts flow accordingly. Let each of your acts be your last battle on earth. Only under those conditions will your acts have their rightful power. Otherwise they will be, for as long as you live, the acts of a timid man . . . It isn't [*so terrible to be a timid man*] if you are going to be immortal, but if you are going to die there is no time for timidity . . . Being timid prevents us from examining and exploiting our lot as men . . . Most people move from act to act without any struggle or thought. A hunter, on the contrary, assesses every act; and since he has an intimate knowledge of his death, he proceeds judiciously, as if every act were his last battle. Only a fool would fail to notice the advantage a hunter has over his fellow men. A hunter gives his last battle its due respect. It's only natural that his last act on earth should be the best of himself.[11]

The Warrior is a destroyer. He destroys the enemies of the true Self. He attacks whatever is wounding and damaging, whatever causes despair, depression, injustice, oppression, whatever is cruel or discouraging or making demands that are abusive. The Warrior's destruction clears a space for renewal and a new, more just order.[12]

Each of the fully expressed archetypes of mature masculinity must be balanced by and incorporate influences from the

The Sword in Service of the King (Otto I, Saxon king of the
Germans with his loyal knights)

other three. The Warrior integrate the dynamic structures of
the King, Magician, and Lover; together the quadrated structures of the masculine Self make a complex whole. The cohesive masculine Self is composed of these four archetypes, but
transcends them. The four archetypes interact in a mutually
enriching and regulating way.

The Warrior serves the King. The King is the Warrior's
Transpersonal Other, the focus for his loyalty, the source for
his causes. The Magician gives the Warrior aid in reflecting on
his commitments. The Magician enhances the clarity of the
Warrior's thought processes and strategies, and provides
the Warrior with inventive technologies. The Lover helps keep
the Warrior humane and compassionate. In conjunction with
these other archetypes the Warrior becomes an essential com-
ponent of the Generative Man in his empowered wholeness.

PART 3

THE UNINITIATED WARRIOR: MALFUNCTIONS AND SHADOW FORMS

The Dying Gaul: A Warrior Cut Off from His Power
(the *Dying Gaul*, a copy of the bronze statue erected by
Attalos I of Pergamon in the third century B.C.E. after his
triumph over the Galatians of Asia Minor)

THE MASOCHIST:
A DISHONEST WARRIOR

MPOTENT MEN ARE GRIEVING. THEY ARE HURT AND in pain. Self-emasculated by their own impotent rage, they have underdeveloped Ego structures and inadequate Ego-archetypal axes. Consequently they fall under the power of the bipolar archetypal Shadow systems. For the Warrior the two poles of the Shadow are the Sadist and the Masochist.

The tendency to split into opposite, mutually compensating aspects appears to be endemic to all psychic material.[1] Personal or group trauma fragments the psyche along the "fault lines" of the underlying archetypal structures, just as a crystal, met with a hammer blow, splits along the lines of its inherent facets. Often after trauma a psyche fractures into Ego-identified and Shadow-engaged features. Like a house divided against itself, the divided psyche cannot stand. The psychological opposites become mutually antagonistic. Their conflict is the only way they can continue to experience each other. And they *do* continue to experience each other, seeking (however inappropriately) some eventual means of reconciliation.

The Shadow Warrior splits into the Sadist and Masochist just as the Shadow of the King divides into Tyrant and Weakling poles. The man caught within a bipolar Shadow system must find a way to integrate the polar opposites if he is to achieve psychological maturity. The Ego plays a critical role in achieving this integration since it is in a position to learn the activities of these hidden forces and has the means available for containing, merging, and transcending them. Through painstaking and often frustrating work the Ego can secure a thorough enough reconciliation between the Shadow poles to effectively move out of the Shadow system. As this happens the Ego is able to develop an Ego-Warrior axis that opens up access to the full expression of the archetype. The fully expressed Warrior incorporates both the Sadist and the Masochist, but in a fully integrated condition that is cohesive and much more than the sum of its parts.

The man whose Ego is more closely identified with the Masochist brings sadists into his life.[2] He has a wound exactly the size and shape of the Sadist's sword. He projects his repressed Sadist onto those people in the outer world who are, in fact, sufficiently sadistic to attract and hold his projections. Similarly, the man with a Sadist-identified Ego ensures that there are masochists available for him to torture. In this way each pole of the Shadow keeps the complementary half of the psyche within its sphere of influence. But the relation is fundamentally dishonest since neither pole recognizes the other's presence within the same psychic system, or that each needs characteristics of the other.

The man possessed by the Masochist is dishonest about his passion, aggression, and rage. The man possessed by the Sadist cannot acknowledge his fear, tenderness, or vulnerability. An impotent masochist is grieving the loss of his masculine power to an inner Sadist, who continues to wound him to remind him of his incomplete identity. The sadist's rage covers his grief over the loss of his humanity. His inner Masochist wounds him by pricking his conscience over cruel behaviors and reminding him of his poorly hidden weaknesses.

While the Ego is primarily identified with one pole or another, sudden shifts in polarity do occur. For example, the masochist (often unconsciously) invites an attack from his mate and takes enormous abuse in the process. Finally he snaps. His repressed Sadist roars forth to devastate his mate and place her at the masochistic pole of the spectrum.

We can look to Germany in the last months of World War II for an example of a sudden reversal in polarity on a national scale. Many German generals urged their leaders to open peace talks once it became clear that the war was lost. But instead they were told to "honor the Reich" and go down fighting. One of history's most protracted episodes of sadism ended in abject masochism.

What are the characteristics and dynamics of the masochist? He often tries hard to be the "nice guy." He is the man who is afraid to make a pass at his date for fear she will think he "only wants one thing." Often enough he *does* want to be sexual, and she may well reciprocate his desires; but without broaching the subject, neither is satisfied. He misses the point that by pursuing physical intimacy he may be mirroring and supporting her own wishes. What really stops him is a fear of the repressed force of his own passion and the consuming hungers of his instincts.

If he receives a token pay raise after five years of unrewarded loyalty to his company, the nice guy demonstrates gratitude! What he is really doing, beneath his repression barrier, is seething with rage. He has to be obsequious to compensate for his hidden rage. The degree to which he bows and scrapes is an accurate indicator of the intensity of his rage.

There is an interesting episode in the television series *Star Trek* that illustrates this. In it Captain Kirk is split into "good" and "evil" halves. The good half becomes physically and mentally weak; the force of his once-whole personality has evaporated; he is unable to make decisions or *will* anything to happen. All his Libido, his energy, physical strength, and decisiveness have been captured by the "bad" half. But without the "nice guy," the bad Kirk is brutal, abusive, and given to throwing childish temper tantrums. When the two halves are eventually reunited, Kirk is restored to his normal "good" but powerful self. The lesson is that nice guys who have no vital connection to their instinctive energy (the very energy they fear so much) become listless and ineffectual.

A similar split is the basic premise of the Superman character, from comic books to movies. Much of our pleasure comes from knowing that "mild-mannered" Clark Kent is secretly a "man of steel." We are frustrated when he does not reveal his true identity. In the movie *Superman II*, the duality between Clark Kent and Superman is brought to its logical conclusion. Superman has renounced his Clark Kent aspect and become sadistic and destructive. He has gone to work for an evil "super yuppie" whose goal is to take over the world. He meets with Kent in a junkyard after having gleefully ripped a hole in an oil tanker to pollute the ocean. When Kent tries to reason with the "evil" Superman, Superman decides to get rid of Kent once and for all. He bashes the wimpy Kent into jagged piles of wreckage. He hurls Kent against walls of rusting cars. He even puts Kent through a huge trash compactor.

The strange thing is that Kent does not die! In fact, with every blow he becomes *stronger,* until finally he punches his way out of the trash compactor, his strength now equal to Superman's. From that moment on he fights as an equal. In the course of the fight he forces a reintegration of the composite character. The reborn Superman, we can safely imagine, is a much better integrated, and hence an even stronger version of the old split Superman. The Kent side of the equation will no longer be an inept weakling in Superman's eyes. And the Superman side, with a greatly strengthened Kent beside him, will never fall prey to his sadistic rage again.

The Masochist exhibits many of the characteristics of the classically defined "dependent personality disorder."[3] The hallmark of a person afflicted with this disorder is that he is deathly afraid of self-affirming behaviors. He has an infantile need for people to like him, no matter the cost to his own self-esteem or authentic identity. The dependent personality is willing to conform to whatever others want him to be so long as he can remain in a passive relationship to them. He depends entirely on others for his meager sense of self-worth.

This is the man who slavishly tries to please his ill-behaved teenage children. His attempts to be firm with them are doomed to failure by his more urgent need to be "liked" by them. The children then generally institute a "reign of terror" in the household, coming and going as they see fit, demanding and getting their way, and controlling their parents by playing on parental guilt and fear.

This man lets his wife or lover lead him around by the nose, finding it nearly impossible to stand up firmly to temper tantrums or sadistic outbursts. This man will often wonder, "What have I done to make her or him angry? Whatever it is,

I deserve to be punished." And he takes the sword and plunges it into his own chest!

Such a relationship always involves an implied contract—"hurt me, darling, then I'll have an excuse to leave you, since I never trusted you in the first place." Often the first thing a battered man needs to learn is to be appropriately careful. When he sees his wife walk through the door with a sword in hand, he doesn't have to offer her a target. We're often told to be more vulnerable in our relationships. But when we're faced with extreme anger and aggression, sometimes the best response is to button up—until the rage transforms into something that can be worked with.

Often a couple fights only to bring some archetypal energy back into the relationship. And often they'll make love right after the fight because they've broken through the chill. The masochist may bring his world down around him, only to experience the short-lived but "justifiable" sadistic rage that results.

Another example is the executive who speaks excitedly at the board meeting about his great new idea. When he is met by cold stares from his peers, he smiles ingratiatingly and retreats. He cannot stand up for his own ideas and risk others disliking him. The unconscious fantasy that drives a dependent man is that nobody could possibly like him for who he really is. And the infantile fear behind the fantasy (which may be based in reality, as the sad facts of child abuse testify) is that if he is self-assertive he will be abandoned, beaten, or killed by his parents.

The masochist is naïve in proportion to the "thickness" of his repression barrier. He is the cheerful guy who tries to befriend everyone, who looks for the bright side of everything, and who glibly recommends ineffectual philosophies like "the power of positive thinking." This man cannot deal with the forces of evil that undermine his business life, his friendships, or his family. Fearful of acknowledging his own rage and sadism, he cannot face the reality of rage and sadism in others. He is often either an armchair philosopher, believing in easily achieved utopias, or a pacifist.

In keeping with his dependent personality, the masochist *is* largely passive. He is quiet and "patient" with others, even when they are aggressive toward him. He is the minister who accepts the complaints and criticisms of his congregation, no matter how unfounded and childish they may be, and never raises a hand in protest. He prefers to be a "nice boy," and nice boys accept their beatings. And nice Christians turn the other cheek, absorbing the poison that others dish out. They naïvely expect not to be crucified despite their role model's example!

In many other ways the masochist allows himself to be victimized. Some victims evoke the victimizer latent in others. If we bare our necks, we will find somebody to bite us. The masochist will put up with abuse from others far beyond the limits of healthy human endurance. He will do this because he feels he cannot afford to release his pent-up demands for self-expression. *If he were to do so, his aggressive self-expression might burst forth in an explosion of rage.* The victim is thus afraid of his own repressed vengeful impulses. He is afraid what his hostility might mean about *him,* and his attempt to masquerade as a saint. Also he is afraid what his rage might mean for others—at the very least, it may drive them away, and at worst, it may destroy them. Since he has no idea how to express his rage, he tries to avoid it by denying it.

It takes a tremendous amount of energy to keep rage repressed, especially under the impact of repeated blows from the outer world. This spent psychological energy leads to another common characteristic of the man possessed by the Masochist: chronic depression. We can see behind the ingratiating smile of a masochistic man, beneath his flatness and lethargy, his tears of hurt, fear, and anger. His body is also expressive of his lack of energy and enthusiasm. His posture, his gait, his gestures, and his halting speech patterns all communicate signs of fatigue and despair. When he seeks out counseling, he does so out of a sense of profound malaise.

One counselee, in his late twenties, began analytic work because he couldn't finish his workday. He was so de-energized and depressed after just three or four hours of calling upon his sales customers that he would take off work early. He would go home to his apartment and down one beer after another. He reported fantasies of buying a gun and going on a killing binge. He would often ask in his sessions, "Where is my energy? I just don't understand it!" The answer was that his Libido was locked up behind his repression barrier. Without a healthy means of expression, his Libido generated the sadistic fantasies that so distressed him.

Many psychologists believe that depression is a "bad" thing. Certainly it can have debilitating effects. But depression can serve a positive function in the psyche as well. It may keep a man from acting out his repressed hostility. The repression barrier needs to remain intact until there is a supportive, therapeutic environment available. Then the unacknowledged hostility can gradually be faced, and the swamp of anger behind it can be drained. Anna Freud called the core of this swamp of rage "secondary narcissism." The extent of this rage can be calculated from the depth of the depression that covers it. Men who are depressed are, temporarily at least, healthier than men who act out their rage in acts of rape, domestic violence, murder, and other forms of carnage.

Another hallmark of the masochist is his passive/aggressive behavior.[4] He is a man who is habitually late for his appointments, who meets enthusiasm with feigned indifference, who drops "innocent" remarks about others that are really designed to run them down and call their efforts into question.

The mature man, appropriately accessing the Warrior, wears his "sword" for all to see. The passive/aggressive man carries a hidden dagger. He conveys the impression that he intends us no harm, that he is unarmed and defenseless. Yet we experience uneasiness and discomfort in his company; somehow we are aware that he is inflicting a series of minor wounds upon us despite his pretense of friendliness. He starts rumors at the office. He sets up meetings in which he adroitly "questions" another about his actions. Seldom making direct accusations, he implies nonetheless that the other's job performance is slipping by raising questions that seem legitimate to the unwary. He is not the friend and confidant he represents himself to be. Unable to handle his own aggression straightforwardly, he uses his dagger, sticking it in our backs and twisting it.

Of course the dagger personality practices the same techniques at home. His children may come to him seeking support and affirmation, seeking insight into some particular difficulty or other. Under the guise of helping them think things through, he manages to throw them into a grave sense of inadequacy. His wife may ask for help completing a household chore, but while he helps, the dagger husband also mocks her method for handling the chore so that the next time she needs his help she will prefer to do without it.

Several interesting things occur as the masochist approaches his repression barrier. He drops the "nice guy" pretense with increasing frequency. He becomes negative and cynical. His cynicism hurts himself (which is in keeping with his masochism) and those around him (which is the first obvious expression of his sadism). We have all been around such people. If we find nobility and beauty in someone's actions, the masochist-turned-cynic looks for the worst possible motives. If we express hope for the world, such men give us a long list of reasons why only despair is justified. For the cynic, every cloud has a dark center rather than a silver lining.

One man had his self-image so damaged by the moralistic Church in which he had been raised, he came cynically to ascribe all human evils to "institutionalized religion." In his mind, the Church was not only one of many major sources of oppression and warfare in human history; it was the *only* one. Any list of the good things the Church had accomplished in society was countered with the argument that these good things were accomplished by virtuous individuals acting in defiance of the Church. He himself had transferred his spirituality to his devotion to classical music. From the onset of therapy it was clear that his major task would be to work his way through his early wounding, received at the hands of his religious parents, to the spiritual vision his unconscious was crying out for. His cynicism barely concealed his hurt and rage. And the harder he was pushed against his repression barrier, the more negative and cynical he became. Cynicism was for him, as it is for all of us, the final defense against rage.

As the repression barrier is approached the masochist begins to change before our very eyes into his sadistic opposite. Before he does, one final defense appears, the defense of addiction. Addiction (grounded in a flood of Lover energy) serves to soothe the masochist in the face of his own mobilizing aggression. Most addictions, to alcohol, tobacco, pot, tranquilizers, and even more seriously mind-altering drugs, have self-soothing origins. The masochist returns to the oral phase he last had in the arms of his mother. The addict seeks to stay in this passive, oral-intake mode, refusing to break the childhood bond and forsake the comfort of the breast.

A man approaching awareness of repressed unconscious materials experiences a rapid rise in his anxiety level. He desperately does not want to experience or own the frightening feelings that lie beneath the barrier. Drinking excessively serves some men to release their pent-up feelings, under cover of their fantasy that they don't have to take responsibility for those feelings. For others drink anesthetizes the awakening animal. Smoking similarly reduces anxiety, by "burning off" the rage with cigar, cigarette, or pipe; the unconscious links the controlled fires at our lips with the smoldering fires within.

Addiction to more powerful mind-altering drugs goes beyond self-soothing to a more explicit, chemical *rejection* of what lies beneath the repression barrier. Cocaine in particular, by causing a massive release of endorphins in the brain, seems to remove us from the sadomasochistic system in progressive waves of "highs." We no longer feel the masochist's worthlessness or helplessness, nor do we feel the bitter rage of the sadist.

The trouble with the "escape," apart from the fact that the drug is ferociously addictive and life-threatening, is that we haven't really left the sadomasochistic system at all! The use of a life-threatening drug, one that decreases the natural endorphins in the brain until we are unable to feel a sense of well-being *without* the drug, is in itself masochistic. And sharing the drug with others is sadistic. Besides this, the cocaine hangover drops us to new, terrifying levels of depression and masochistic self-loathing. The repression barrier has not been breached. To get out of the sadomasochistic system we may not go around it. We must go *through* it. The psyche of the masochist knows that the repression barrier must be broken, and that the Sadist must be experienced directly and internally. But without adequate Ego structures the Sadist comes in exactly the destructive forms the masochist fears: as an outer assailant, or as a violent, uncontrolled inner eruption. It is to this violent eruption that we now turn.

THE SADIST:
POSSESSION BY THE
WARRIOR WITHIN

C ROSSING THE SOUND BARRIER FOR THE FIRST time provided a very difficult set of problems for test pilot Chuck Yeager, and the Bell Labs staff who built his jets. Before it happened, some of the Bell engineers believed that if he ever reached the speed of sound he would be incinerated after slamming into an invisible "barrier" in the sky. Yeager himself may have had his doubts when subjected to the enormous stresses that shook his plane as he approached Mach 1. The plane threatened to break apart as air turbulence and an incredible vibration rocketed his machine. It was hard for him to focus, even to stay conscious. Then suddenly, with a tre-

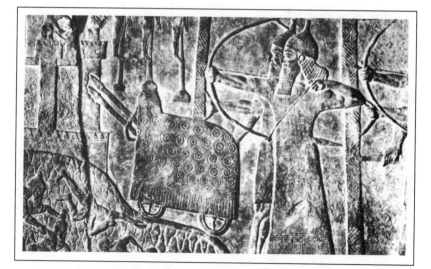

The Sadistic Warrior: Cruelty for Cruelty's Sake
(King Tiglath-pileser leading the storming of a city, probably
in Babylonia, prisoners beheaded and impaled, Nimrud,
Central Palace)

mendous sonic boom, the barrier was crossed, and the future
stretched out ahead of the jet as wide as the blue sky.

A similar thing happens to the psyche when the repression barrier is approached. The structures the psychologist
Winnicott calls the "false self organization" begin to shudder
and shake.[1] Stresses mount, and under pressure of a greatly
increased anxiety, the Ego and its defenses begin to fragment.
Paranoia sets in, bringing its attendant feelings of dread. And
then, suddenly, the barrier is crossed!

Unlike the careful test pilot, the Ego really *does* lose
consciousness. And the skies beyond the barrier are not blue,
but uncertain and dark. A blackout of the human identity
occurs, and the psyche hurtles into a state of possession by the
inhuman sadistic Shadow Warrior.

This is the aspect of the Warrior we fear so much within
ourselves and others. Whether or not we act out the soci-

opathic rage that takes us over as the barrier is crossed, we are left afterward with the feeling that we were not "ourselves." Indeed, we were not. This is the "battle frenzy" and "blood lust" celebrated by the epics of patriarchal societies and guarded against by its laws. This is the madness that overtook the Germans, after they had been emasculated by the Allies following World War I. This is the dark rage that swept through the ranks of Pol Pot's Khmer Rouge, and the barbarity that possesses the "death squads" of Latin America. This is the demon that took over Idi Amin. And this is what takes over the man who goes into a murderous frenzy, who beats his wife and hurls his children against the walls.

Out of a man's sense of intolerable vulnerability and violation, the rageful inner Sadist is constellated,[2] and his "temporary insanity" is released into the world. But these violent eruptions are not the only means of expression available to this pole of the Shadow Warrior. Dark rage *seeps* through an insufficiently hardened repression barrier and inflects the simplest of actions. This rage is the source of the nice guy's passive/aggressive behaviors, as well as his cynicism and negativity. His inability to deal with his rage fuels his pretense of innocence and purity, which gives him the illegitimate power of self-righteousness.

The repression barrier works both ways. Not only does it help keep the Masochist-identified Ego unaware of his rage, it "protects" the man whose Ego is closely identified with the Sadist from incursions of sensitivity and human feeling. Men who are clearly sadistic are terrified by the humanity inside of them, and so they shut it out of their awareness.[3]

What are some of the characteristics of the sadist? Principally, and most obviously, there is the rage. If the rage runs hot, it will be expressed in passionately cruel words and actions. A cold rage will feel subhuman, profoundly alien, and completely divorced from reality. Cold rage fuels the psychopath who has no sense of right and wrong. Either form of rage is organized into a hatred toward the "weak" and an envy of the "strong," whatever those two words mean to the individual sadist.

In *For Your Own Good*, Alice Miller shows how both of these elements were present in Adolf Hitler. He was physically and emotionally brutalized by his father. His father never called him by name, used a dog whistle to summon him, locked him in closets for days for the merest infractions, and taught him that tender emotions were unacceptable to "real men." Young Adolf admired his father's "strength"; at the same time, unconsciously, he hated him with an animal fury. From his father he learned too to hate and despise his "weak" mother, who was never able to stand up to her husband's brutality.

Adolf learned that gentleness, tenderness, and love had no power to help him. He learned to despise the human qualities that never came to his aid. Consequently, he repressed them whenever they appeared within himself. Because brutal power became his driving force, he came to admire his father, even though he hated him.

Sadists are envious of those who can feel love. Envy is a destructive emotion, uncomfortable for both the envying and the envied.[4] Envy does not inhibit underlying feelings of hurt and rage but rather exacerbates those feelings. Envious men gleefully watch or actively participate in the fall of the powerful. This is the "blood in the water" that attracts so many men, like sharks to a wounded brother. There is frequently an almost holiday atmosphere surrounding a rumored office "beheading," whether the person branded for execution is generally admired or despised.

Part of the excitement of watching another's fall in status is in feeling one's own status rise. Everybody wants a piece of

Headhunters: A Cult of Death

the kill because with each piece comes a little of the energy. This is the dynamic behind a Native American brave counting coup. The Native Americans didn't just kill a man to see him dead, they killed to get a man's power. The greater the brave, the greater his power, accumulated from all the coup he had counted. Some tribes accepted coup counted without killing an enemy—provided the enemy had been humiliated, or otherwise *disempowered*. A similar practice could, until very

136

recent times, still be seen among headhunter societies around the world.

Some classic personality disorders are located at the Sadistic pole of the Shadow Warrior.[5] The "active/independent," the "antisocial/aggressive," and the "compulsive" all are properly read as facets of the Sadist. While each disorder shows more or less unique symptoms, there are characteristics common to all three. All of these personality types involve a man's unrealistic sense of power, his self-deception concerning his imagined invulnerability, and a dangerously defiant fearlessness. These delusions mask a terror of underlying passivity, dependency, vulnerability, and weakness. Sadistic, often sociopathic behaviors are defensive maneuvers designed to ward off feelings of helplessness and worthlessness. Because of this fear of personal weakness the sadist feels the need to control others.

The paranoia always encountered at the threshold of the repression barrier is active where the sadist's fears are awakened. Vigilance becomes hypervigilance. Danger is imagined behind every bush. An innocent remark or event, or even a genuine but minor slight, is experienced as a life-threatening display of hostility. A man caught in this hypervigilant pattern is suspicious of every phone call his wife receives, imagines his colleagues to be plotting behind his back, and views a friend's compliments as an underhanded attempt to put him down.

The man who does not trust others tries to control them. He may try to confine his wife to the house, perhaps even answering all her phone calls himself. He may discourage her friendships and try to keep her from doing things she enjoys. After all, her friendships are opportunities for her to talk about him, and so undermine his control of her life. Her enjoyment of anything indicates to him an inappropriate independence. Since he is working to make her life miserable, she should have no *reason* to be happy—so if she *has* found happiness he suspects her of going outside the relationship to find it.

What this man doesn't realize is that he is really trying to control his own impulses to be free and happy. The sadistic complex is hostile toward any signs of healthy feeling because that very health threatens the complex's autonomy. Archetypal Shadow elements are self-sustaining systems that fight for their own survival, screening out any information that might contradict the assumptions from which they draw their energy.[6] If a man tries to reject his inner Sadist his Shadow will hand him a knife and encourage him to turn it against himself.

Even where there were no outer enemies the sadist's need for them creates them.[7] Unable to integrate the warring inner opposites, he fights his personal battles in the context of his interpersonal relationships. His misdirected paranoia, his rage, and his need for control will finally result in exposing his true weaknesses. He will end by driving everyone away from him. They will be forced away by the savagery of the inner dynamics he projects onto them.

He may temporarily save his relationships if he is sufficiently frightened by the course they are taking. His Masochist, with all its pretended helplessness and remorse, will break through the repression barrier. The man caught between these two poles of the Shadow Warrior will sue for peace and forgiveness—*until* his anxiety about the vulnerability he is showing starts to rise again, along with his rage at allowing others temporarily to "control" him. Through such an oscillation the sadomasochistic system is maintained.

This maintenance is enabled by the relative weakness of a man's Ego structures. These structures are formed in concert with the Ego-archetypal axis; to the extent the axis is realized, the Ego can adequately access the four archetypes of mature masculinity and the masculine Self as a whole. If the Ego cannot maintain a strong axis, then the Ego cannot manage the archetypal energies that it draws. The Ego cannot discriminate between the dysfunctional, largely unconscious Shadow processes, and the healthy energies of the archetypes in their full expression. The inner Sadist takes advantage of such a weak Ego, pushing the personality past a human sense of guilt, remorse, and responsibility. For the man possessed by the Sadist, emotional and physical brutality seem justified. In his own nightmarish world he believes himself to be battling the forces of evil that have allied themselves against him.

Accompanying this rejection of human values is another characteristic of the sadistic man: He feels strangely anesthetized. This is the dark obverse of the same anesthetic that enables healthy men, appropriately accessing the Warrior, to persevere in their worthwhile endeavors despite pain and exhaustion. But when it is not mediated by a moral outlook, this anesthetic serves to hold human feelings at bay. The anesthetized sadist has no realization of the impact of his barbarism on others. He is a man such as the Israeli soldier who does not hear the anguished protests of the men he has ordered to fire on Palestinian women and children. He is the Iraqi general who cannot recognize his crimes against the Kuwaiti freedom fighters. He is the ugly American who institutes covert operations to destabilize even those Latin American governments that are trying to better the lives of their people. He is the Nazi concentration camp commandant who can speak calmly, without human emotion, about the efficiency of his extermination project.

The man possessed by the sadistic Shadow Warrior is compulsively driven: He doesn't know when to stop because he feels no pain. And he is driven toward goals that are often meaningless or even viciously destructive. This man is constantly in motion because he can never appreciate what he has or what he has done. He often tries to do in a day what it would take others a week to accomplish. He lives to work instead of working to live. He ends up having a heart attack or a stroke.

We can see this compulsive, driven quality, and the effects it has on the lives of average men, in the Japanese business community. There the men are still in the grip of the best and the worst of the samurai tradition. At its best it urges them to be loyal to their companies, to value their work and the quality of their end product. It pushes them to strive for excellence in everything they do. But at its worst it drives them with obsessive fury. It commits them to excessively idealistic codes of honor, encourages workaholism, and often results in an early grave (as demonstrated by a recent study of mortality rates among Japanese executives). We can only wonder what effects possession by the Shadow Warrior has on their personal lives.

The Shadow Warrior anesthetic also has a deleterious effect on a man's relationship with his Anima, and consequently also on his real-world relationships with women. While the fully expressed Warrior helps a man relate his personal feelings to a transpersonal devotion, the Shadow anesthetic takes all knowledge of personal feeling away. It teaches a man that it doesn't hurt not to feel—and numbs him until he can believe it. A lie such as this has disastrous consequences upon inner health, which depends upon feeling-toned relationships with others. A man can reach a significant degree of maturity, grasping the fullness of his phallic power, only if he is intimately involved with his Anima.[8] And this normally depends upon a relationship with a significant other, where both partners affirm and enrich each other's identities.

Women, for the sadist, are not for intimate relationship.[9] The tenderness, caring, love, and respect they demand and deserve are too much for him. These nurturing feelings are unacceptable to him; he keeps them beneath his repression barrier. Women, for the sadist, are only for sex. They exist to bring him momentary genital pleasure. They provide, even more importantly, a psychological thrill when they can be overpowered. Overpowering women is a pleasure to the sadist because it is a way for him to express his hatred of the weak and defenseless. Rapists often report that they have committed their crimes *not* primarily for sexual reasons but for the feeling of power their actions bring.

This desperate and violent attempt at power is further testimony to the sadist's experience of his own inner powerlessness. Rape in any of its guises shows the bankruptcy of the sadomasochistic system in horrifying terms.

The pervasiveness of the Shadow Warrior in his sadistic form leads us to wonder why, if we can't get rid of him, we don't do something to redirect him. Freud wrote a lot about "sublimation," the redirection of the Id's uncivilized impulses into less harmful and more creative behaviors.[10] Some argue that sports aid this sublimation by raising these destructive energies and then releasing them through a cathartic process.

Several objections to this kind of thinking occur. For one thing, most professional athletes have ceded responsibility, in recent years, for the fact that they serve as role models for male children and adult men. Their behavior on the playing field has increasingly been unabashedly sadistic and antisocial. Obviously there is no catharsis working for them. Another problem is that fans have grown increasingly violent. Apparently instead of *redirecting* aggressive impulses, athletic events are more and more *evoking* latent aggression, and leaving it to the individual to deal with. Since so many men are ill-equipped to deal with their hostility, violence often results. Indeed, sports may provide some acting out of aggression, but there is no *moral* dimension to this action. When the most important struggle becomes one between the Bears and the Patriots, a lot of the positive aspects of the archetype are lost.

And when a man meets the Warrior only in his projection of this archetype onto a favorite linebacker, he misses a whole fund of energy that would otherwise be his.

But if the object is to expunge, by sublimation, the fully expressed Warrior, sports are not a helpful pursuit. We do not need to *dispose* of the archetype's aggressiveness and turn warriors into spectators. We need to bring the archetypal energy *into our own lives,* and not watch it play itself out in a Super Bowl. We need to turn the Warrior's legitimate energy against the Real Enemy in the Real War, and be prepared to fight whatever battles our lives and world demand of us.

A Bear Hunters' Ritual in the Magdalenian Culture
(10000 B.C.E.)

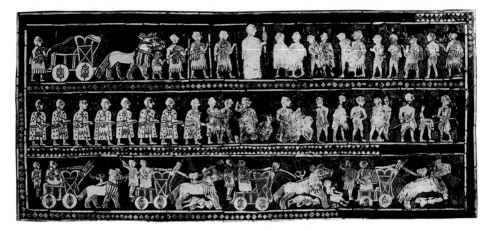

The Armies of Ur
(a military standard of the powerful city-state
of Ur, around 2500 B.C.E.)

Nubian Troops: The African Warrior on the Move
(model warriors from the tomb of the nomarch Mesehti
at Asyut, Eleventh Dynasty, 2000 B.C.E., Egypt)

The Last Battle Between Prince Rama and the Demon Ravana
(a Hindu account of the Eschaton)

The Etruscan Warrior: Calm Assurance
(terra-cotta head from the fifth century B.C.E.)

Protecting the Boundaries of Cosmos:
Samurai on Horseback

Repelling Evil:
Chinese Temple Guardian

The Warrior as Liberator *(Simon Bolívar the Liberator)*

Destroyed from Within: The Shadow Warrior

The Brotherhood of the Sword:
A Samurai Giving a Cup of Water
to a Wounded Comrade

Mixtec Warriors Expanding the Sphere of the Created World
(from a symbol-picture manuscript, three canoe-borne warriors
crossing a lake to attack an island)

PART 4

BECOMING A KNIGHT: THE CHALLENGE OF MASCULINE WARRIOR INITIATION

A Masai Warrior

9

DRAWING THE SWORD:
THE CHALLENGE OF
INITIATION

INCREDIBLE AS IT MAY SEEM, MOST MEN HAVE great difficulty integrating their power.[1] They have been taught by abusive fathers and controlling mothers that it is not good for them to feel powerful. Their real wants and needs, they have also been taught, are not meant to be expressed. Invasive parents discourage the construction and maintenance of a viable boundary for the Self. The child's Self is attacked as being shameful whenever its desires and actions do not meet a parent's own demands for mirroring.

In her series on childhood development, the psychoanalyst Alice Miller has discussed the underlying dynamics of the pervasive practice of psychological child abuse. She believes that mothers, then later fathers too, typically use their children to plug up the holes in their own self-esteem. Parents often try to fulfill their own unconscious needs and live their unlived lives through their children. As she makes plain, this is exactly the opposite of what children need to achieve—realistically self-confident, healthy, and empowered Ego structures. Both boys and girls face this invasion of the Self by inadequate or hostile parents.

For Jung the deepest Self was androgynous.[2] To the extent that this Self is attacked or neglected the wounds are, for boys and girls, similar. But often the gender-specific Self comes under fire from destructive parenting as well. This means a boy's specifically masculine identity may be jeopardized by either his mother or father or both. A mother may act out her unconscious fear of and rage against what she perceives as abusive male behaviors by habitually undercutting her son's male pride or exuberance. She may be critical of his aggressiveness, his interest in male pastimes, even of his body hair! In an extreme case, she may even engage in an angry display of jealousy when he begins to date. A father may attack his son in order to ward off what he perceives as the boy's growing challenge to his position of dominance in the home. Rather than recognizing his son as an *heir* to his masculine power, he may see the boy as a *rival* for what little masculinity he has.

Both mothers and fathers often attack the joy their sons take in life out of fear and envy. They are afraid to face the ways they have been deprived of joy in their own lives. A father may attack his son's weaknesses when these remind him of his own repressed vulnerability. A mother may attack her son out of hatred for the abuses of power she may have experienced at the hands of adult males. In addition, fathers and mothers who have little conscious contact with the archetypal

Slaying the "Bad Mother": The Witch Louhi Attacking
Vainamoinen and His Faithful Followers (scene from a
myth of Finland)

Warrior unconsciously pressure their children to live out this split-off aspect of their own psyches.[3] Violent teenagers are often only acting out what a parent isn't actualizing.

Our societies also damage our capacity to experience our legitimate masculine greatness. Societal reaction against individual empowerment is a major factor in the formation of what Freud called the superego, with an oppressive list of taboos that inhibit the true Self.[4] Christian societies are especially adept at separating men from their power. In most Christian thinking, goodness and power cannot ever be united.[5] *But just such a union is desperately needed by men in order to be generative within the larger world.* To a large extent, Christian culture aggravates our wounds and encourages our alienation from our own resources. This cultural disempowerment destroys our vital Ego structures, militates against life-enhancing Ego-archetypal axes, and drives us into the sadomasochistic dialectic of the Warrior's Shadow.

We need to become legitimately and fully empowered, in part, by reconnecting with the archetypal resources of the unconscious. But in any confrontation with the unconscious, the aim is never to *become* an archetype. The archetypes are energic structures, not personalities to adopt for daily living. As with any energy source, there is a danger threatening the person who draws too near. An archetype is *numinous*. This means that it has a certain magic; because it is a source of energy, it organizes a field around itself, just as a magnet does. When an Ego approaches this field, it becomes aware of all the powerful attractiveness and seductiveness the field holds and promises. And to the extent that the Ego is not very strong, this energy will take it over: While men can be deprived of access to the archetypal Warrior, they can also become *possessed* by it.

The process Jungians call individuation involves an active struggle *against* the archetypes. The archetypes are necessary sources of energy, but the properly individuating Ego develops its own Ego-archetypal axes in such a way that the energy can be drawn only as needed. The more *unmediated* the energy is, the crazier the man becomes. This is why an archetype is not something a man wants to *be*. The man who is infantile is very archetypal. Nobody is more archetypal than a schizophrenic, and borderline personalities are much more in contact with the archetypes than most of the rest of us. Borderlines have an impaired repression barrier, which is one of the reasons they can sometimes be so magical and creative.

Most of us have *some* protection against the power of the archetypes, including the archetypal Warrior. For example, a useful depression can result when a personality that is *not* borderline gets too close to an archetype. A person's defenses operate then like an automatic fail-safe system on a nuclear reactor. The depression helps to keep the archetype from overloading the psyche with energy. Of course a depression can also mean that a person lacks enough positive contact with the Self. Ideally what we want is to develop a workable Ego-archetypal axis and access the energy as we need it. Perhaps the best image of this is of a jet's in-flight refueling—we want to learn how to come up behind the tanker just right; we do not want the nozzle coming through the windshield. We want to refuel, then peel off and go on with our mission.

The man who learns to do this has access to the full energies of life. Jung called this fullness the *pleroma*, and getting a taste of this is really what inner work is all about. The work is challenging and can take time. We can access our inner resources without a therapeutic process, but some kind of guiding supervision is essential. The products of the unconscious can be so seductively enchanting that we need to have some other person available to keep us in touch with reality. *We* want to be able to use our inner resources, and not have them use us!

Certainly a power source should always be approached with caution, whether it be electrical, gravitational, nuclear, or psychological. Unfortunately, given the mentality of scarcity, many of us feel it is dangerous to let our own children feel powerful. The fear is that whatever power *they* have is taken away from *us*. Ironically, when legitimate power is denied a child, or stifled in him, he will embody the very sadistic powers we were so afraid of unleashing in the first place.

THE MYSTERIES OF THE SWORD

Men should be empowered.[6] They need encouragement to accept, experience, and exercise their power. The initiatory processes of premodern societies helped to teach men how to become responsible, nurturing, and *powerful*. These initiations taught men the "mysteries of the sword."[7]

Many are familiar with this idea of the mysteries of the sword through the *Star Wars* movies. A cult of the sword appears in the series alongside the sacred warrior tradition of the Jedi Knights. Their sword is a fabulous light saber. This wonderfully invokes the archetypal image of the soldier of light, who is in cosmic combat with the "dark side of the Force." His light is the light of consciousness, awareness, and will.

We learn as Luke Skywalker receives his training that the best way to use the light saber is with eyes closed. The opponent's movements must be intuited; parries and thrusts must be guided by instinct and insight. Such an energetic relationship demands that a man be comfortable with his animal nature. The aspiring Jedi warrior learns to develop a cooperative relationship between the evaluating conscious mind and the archetypal unconscious as he draws upon his own Warrior energy. When he is finally initiated, he has learned the mysteries of the sword.

How can we understand the mythic and symbolic meaning of the sword? One answer is provided by the awe-inspiring temples of the god Shiva, found throughout India. Often the most prominent feature of a Shiva temple is the lingam, usually of enormous size, sometimes unadorned, sometimes elaborately carved and decorated. The lingam is Shiva's phallus. His is a cosmic, life-engendering phallus, a fount from which flows all of life and the world of forms. In modern Japan, as in ancient Egypt and Greece, there are fertility festivals featuring huge, artificial phalluses carried in procession. The "Herms," road markers of the ancient Mediterranean, depicted the god Hermes with a huge, extended phallus. Hermes was guardian of the highways, indeed of every "way" in life, both in this world and the next. An explicit connection exists between the phallus and the sword in the Cro-Magnon caves of France. One scene shows a shaman hunter with a fully erect penis as he attacks the animals. Some of the warriors from the barbarian tribes that menaced the Roman Empire charged into battle in the same condition!

There are those who argue, in company with the ethicist James Nelson, that men need to learn what they have is not a phallus but a penis.[8] Their arguments suggest that the significant thing about the penis is that it is soft. This is true, as far as the *penis* goes. But this completely ignores archetypal psychology, because the *flaccid* penis is *not* what is celebrated as the symbol of masculine empowerment. The swollen *phallus* is.[9]

Men have trouble with potency not because they symbolically associate their penis with a sword—but because they do not understand that the phallus is both a physical *and* an imaginal representation of a fourfold psychological and spiritual reality. The phallus exists foundationally in a psychic and spiritual realm. Potency is not a question of mechanics. Sex therapists who approach masculine sexual dysfunction as a mechanical problem are misguided, except in those rare cases where a man's physical condition renders him impotent. Otherwise a man gains potency through initiatory processes, by getting a sense of what it is to be drawing on his archetypal energies.

The sword is not the only manifestation of the phallus. And both sword and phallus are incarnate symbolic expressions of something more primal, namely Libido, in its masculine form. This Libido brings to the mysteries of the sword an enormous energic potential. The other masculine archetypes are likewise infused with Libido in phallic form—the King with his scepter, the Magician with his wand, and the Lover—with his phallus. All of these are symbols of mature masculine life-force. Scepter, sword, wand, and phallus therefore are parallel images of the fourfold fullness of masculine empowerment which has to be achieved through masculine initiation.

Why do so many men fear or demonize masculine Warrior initiation? It can be frightening to draw the sword of our masculine power, because to be empowered is to risk the same attacks we sustained as boys. The sword is also frightening because of the potential it carries, of sparing life or causing death. When a man draws the sword from the stone he accepts the responsibility of holding in his hand the power of creation and destruction. Few of us really want to take this much responsibility for our lives or for our worlds. Few of us want the power to destroy what needs to be destroyed in our lives, families, companies, voluntary organizations, nation, or planet. Nor do we want the power to create what is needed to replace outdated configurations. The responsibility for deciding what needs to be destroyed, and what needs to be created, seems godlike. Yet for a man to gain maturity and generativ-

A Warrior of New Guinea with His Ritual Ax

ity, he *must* accept his sword, make decisions, and take responsibility for planning and implementing effective action.

There is another painful aspect to the mysteries of the sword. As he draws the sword, an immature hero is forced to recognize his limitations. He will have to come finally to a psychological condition of true humility. Under the power of the sword the masculine Ego submits to its own inevitable mortality. The Ego comes into full knowledge of the numinous mysteries of death, that life must die to itself in order to live, that out of destruction a new life is born, that death is the

very *generator* of life, and that all living beings are destined
to die in order that others may flourish in their place.[10] Here
is the drama of self-sacrifice, that terrifying call to surrender
individual identity to a greater cause. Here is Christ's dilemma
in the Garden of Gethsemane, as he first struggles against,
then finally accepts his fate, submitting to the will of the
archetypal King.[11] His ultimate loving sacrifice provisions the
world. The Ego dies to its old grandiose opinion of itself, and
is reborn, and reinvested with the power of a higher good.
Through masculine initiation the *hero* becomes a *warrior* in
the service of the King. This was the aim of a medieval
knight's all-night chapel vigil; with sword laid upon the altar
of Christ, his meditative ordeal initiated a knight into serving
the Lord. Samurai codes of conduct and their rituals of sword
etiquette served a similar function. Robert Bly tells a wonderful Japanese parable of the samurai period—after their king
dies, the residents of a certain pond are at a loss for what to
do, and whom to follow. So they elect the Heron king because
he is the fiercest warrior among them. And the first thing the
Heron does is eat everybody in the pond![12] This is what happens when the Warrior energy is not moderated by a higher
authority. The Warrior's aggressive potentials must be dedicated to some power beyond his own, or he becomes purely
destructive, creating unnecessary conflict instead of serving
and protecting the human community.

Jung said what he encountered most in his practice was
his patients' failure to integrate their instinctual impulses,
especially their rage and sexuality, with the "spiritual complexes" that gave them exalted visions of themselves as superhuman beings.[13] This is apparently a long-standing historical
problem, not only a modern one, because the ancient Warrior
initiations were designed to wed the same human passions to
some spiritual mission. They achieved this within the context
of highly structured processes, designed to bring the Ego into

relationship with a Center of a higher order.

In the movie *The Magnificent Seven,* we see a young would-be gunslinger so eager to prove himself that he challenges a seasoned veteran, played by Yul Brynner, to a gunfight. The young man wants to win a place among the select group of gunfighters on their way to liberate a Mexican town from bandits. With the firmness and benevolence of a mature Warrior, Brynner declines the fight. He allows the young man to expend his self-humiliating rage and then accepts him for the mission. He knows what this immature hero needs in order to become a man. He needs the chance to "draw his sword" under the supervision of a wise elder. The Brynner character accepts the role of mentor to the young man and helps initiate him into manhood. In the end the young man moves out from under the sole influence of the Warrior. Having integrated the Warrior energy into his Self structures, he marries a woman from the liberated village, settles down, and becomes a farmer and a *builder* of community.

DRAWING THE SWORD:
ACCESSING WARRIOR ENERGY

The Arthurian legends of England and France turn upon the idea of a man drawing his sword. When Arthur takes Excalibur, in different versions either from the Lady of the Lake or from out of the stone, he becomes a man and the rightful heir to the throne.

A lake, or any body of water, is a common psychic symbol for the unconscious mind;[14] also, it is a "pool" of energy. When the Lady of the Lake raises a phallus-sword for Arthur up out of the unconscious, we see how a man receives his mature masculine might from the hands of his Anima, his own

The Mysteries of the Sword: The Lady of the Lake Offering
the Power of Life and Death

inner feminine aspect. Unless he can accept his own tenderness, vulnerability, and sensitivity, he cannot be trusted with
empowerment, and he cannot really receive his sword. In
medieval lore no man can be called a knight unless he serves
a lady. The inner feminine works with the male structures to
actually support and *enhance* a man's masculinity, enriching
what would otherwise be an empty macho caricature of a male
personality.

There are several interesting aspects to the related story
of Arthur's drawing the sword from out of the stone. The
stone is a collective symbol of the masculine Self.[15] The

Ka'aba in Mecca, the Pegasus Stone in Jerusalem, the royal Stone of Scone of Scotland and England, Ireland's Blarney Stone, the menhirs and standing stones of the megalithic cultures, even the stones we place over our graves, all are symbols of the enduring center of the human psyche. Counselees often find it helpful to imagine a jewel or crystal pyramid at their inner centers.[16] The image seems to help restore order and calm to a fragmenting psyche.

So Arthur's image of masculine might is embedded in the mysteries of the Self. No one can dislodge the sword by main or might, which is to say by an effort of egoistic will. Many knights of the realm strain their muscles trying to pull the sword out, since an oracle promises that the man who can do so will become the King of England. All who try fail. When a young squire, Arthur, happens along, looking for his brother Kay's sword, he sees the sword resting in the stone and casually pulls it out. The humble Ego (serving as a squire), acting out of goodwill rather than self-aggrandizement, succeeds where heroic Egos failed. The story notes that only the "right man" can draw the sword. That right man is *any* man if he accepts his Anima, his tenderness, and true humility as prerequisites for his empowerment.

Another instructive message of the Arthurian legends is that once a man has drawn his sword it can be difficult for him to keep it. If he misuses it, it may break, or he may have to cast it back into the lake from whence it came. Misused power leads to psychological impotence.

We misuse our power whenever we are abusive, both in our minds and hearts and in our words and actions. We are abusive to our own personalities when we split off or repress pieces of ourselves. When we treat employees in a manner intended to humiliate them and render them powerless, we are abusive. When we look for ways to fire long-term employees just before they reach retirement age, we are abusive. We may

Arthur's Knights Accoutred by Their Ladies Before Going
into Battle (detail of a tapestry by Edward Burne-Jones and
William Morris)

be abusive toward customers by advertising false sales. Of course, there are an endless variety of abuses at our disposal. Obviously we are abusing others if we are involved in criminal behaviors, whether white- or blue-collar, or in theft, drug sales, violence, rape, or murder. When we use power in an abusive way we may feel a temporary rush. But the rush stems from infantile rage, and the fires of rage quickly turn and burn back inward!

If a man humiliates his children through ridicule or criticism, if he becomes bored with them and fails to support them in their interests, he is using his power as a father to harm them. If he verbally or physically assaults his wife, he is misusing the psychological force and physical stature nature has given him. The result of these rageful abuses is always the same: a terrible sense of guilt, a crippling sense of self-humiliation and degradation, and ultimately, impotence. When we abuse the sword, we end by losing it.

There seems to be an inner critic in place to keep a check on a man's immature and illegitimate grandiosity. The Greeks referred to this system of psychological restraint as the interacting dynamics of *hubris* and *nemesis*. Hubris is a man's overweening, abusive pride, which leads inexorably to nemesis, or his destruction. The misused sword is snatched from his hand, and he is deprived of self-worth and station. Probably we have all seen an arrogant person take such a fall. With a moment's reflection, we can probably think of instances of it within our own lives. Thus it is vital that we learn how to draw the sword and use it in such a way that we do not hurt ourselves or those that we seek to serve and protect.

The problem for most men is that no one has ever shown them how to do this! One reason so many men find mentor characters like Yoda and Yul Brynner's gunslinger so appealing is that there is such a lack of real mentoring in American life. Most men have never been given the permission they need to be legitimately powerful. Consequently they do not know how to use their power without being abusive. Older men spend their time and energy, more often than not, ignoring or humiliating younger men when they should be mentoring them. In our age of absent fathers and discredited ritual and spiritual experience, younger men are left completely alone in this business of drawing the sword. Mature men in our society neglect their responsibility to these younger men. They have often abandoned the spiritual realm to women; the masculinity they pass on is a "practical," hard-boiled version that completely rejects a young man's emotional and spiritual needs.

One thirty-year-old counselee, after some defensive maneuvers designed to deny his rage toward his father, describes the following core childhood scene. As a young boy, and even as a teenager, he would come into the room where his father sat drinking a beer and reading a paper. He would try to describe some recent event with great feeling, his enthusiasm over making the farm league baseball team, for example, or his fear of the neighborhood boys who had stolen his lunch box. Sometimes he would show his father a drawing he had just completed. His father's response was always essentially, "Get away from me, you little faggot!" The boy needed encouragement and his father's blessing. He received only abuse from the Shadow King and Shadow Warrior in the father.

Another counselee reported as a very small child wanting to be physically close to his dad. He wanted to cuddle up next to him. He was fascinated by his father's chest hair and wanted to touch it, to make contact with the primitive masculine energy he shared with his father. This father brushed the boy away saying, "Don't touch me! What's wrong with you? Sometimes I think you're a sissy. Men don't touch each other like that!" And this was how the boy learned to be a man.

Still another father answered his son's "cosmic" questions—about the stars, about dinosaurs, about God—with the admonition that these were not the things "real men" cared about. He told his son "stuff like that" was for women. It was fine for his mother to go to church, but if he was a real man he would start enjoying with his father the obligatory Sunday fishing trips. The damage to this man's eventual sense of masculine empowerment was enormous. Through his abuse of his son's tenderness, sensitivity, and natural spirituality the father made a *Warrior* initiation much more difficult for his son.

WHITE KNIGHT, RED KNIGHT, BLACK KNIGHT: THE PATH OF WARRIOR INITIATION

Other imagery from the knightly tradition gives further clues about the initiatory process a man must follow in the context of the mysteries of the sword. This is the imagery of the White, Red, and Black Knights.[17] While not directly related to the Arthurian legends, the implications of this psychological imagery certainly apply to the Camelot myth.

The White Knight is like Lancelot when he first rides into King Arthur's court. He is innocent, adazzle with the light reflected from his polished silver armor, astride a white horse, whose mane tosses triumphantly in the breeze. He believes that he can do anything, as all heroes do, through the force of his goodwill and the purity of his heart. Where others are frail and fallen, he is pure, invulnerable to all temptations. His purposes are "spiritual," not "carnal."

Lancelot's exaggerated purity does give him extraordinary power initially. His single-mindedness allows him to accomplish great things for himself and for Camelot. The White

Knight is at the adolescent stage of masculine development. He is possessed by what Jung called a "spiritual complex," unable to incarnate, to come into his earthly body and accept his animal nature. For Lancelot the body is only a tool for the exercise of his spiritual purposes.

Of course this despised animal body is what brings Lancelot down. He falls irrevocably and disastrously in love with Guinevere. He has neglected his animal passion at his own peril, and the animal now comes forward and muscles the spiritual aside. He becomes the Red Knight, whose repressed and denied instincts possess him with overblown passion and fiery rage. Lancelot is still clinging to the illusion of his innocence, however, so that his self-righteousness takes on a more sinister guise.

The Red Knight is unable to abandon his inflated view of himself. But all his actions are now tinged with doubt. He is a tortured soul, caught between his innocence and his rage and sexuality. He turns on himself, punishing himself for his inner conflict. And he turns on the others who dare to point out the discrepancies between his values and his conduct. Unable to accept his passion and his rage, the Red Knight becomes anxious, defensive, and paranoid. He rightfully fears that others know the truth about him. His purity and innocence have become lies, but they are lies he is not ready to face. His paranoia and anxiety push him to a frenzy of sadistic destructiveness.

This passionate, embattled animal within is what Jung called the "instinctual complex." As the tension of his inner battle mounts, a man caught between the "spiritual" and the instinctual complexes is tempted to act out his angry bewilderment. He is in the Red Knight stage of initiation and is dangerous to himself and others. He is a "loose cannon," rageful and violent.

One twenty-five-year-old counselee experienced this

inner conflict as a struggle to the death between the "Asshole" and the "Nice Guy." We will examine his case in more detail in Chapter 10. For now, the following dream is of interest:

> I am in a convenience store late at night with a buddy, the Nice Guy. Suddenly, a young man, a friend who has accompanied us to the store, after shoplifting some things and stuffing them into his pockets where they were still clearly visible, grabs a red flag and begins waving it wildly. The Nice Guy and I are horrified by our friend whom we now see is an Asshole. We say to him, "Cut it out! You're going to get us all in trouble!" And the Asshole replies with a sadistic laugh, "What's wrong with you guys? Don't you want to have a little fun?"

The counselee was struggling to integrate his White Knight (the Nice Guy) with his Red Knight (the Asshole). The Red Knight had a hold on his passion and rage and was using it against him. The denied life-force was waving the red flag of revolution in the dream, demanding to be noticed. The counselee was overidentified with the Nice Guy and needed to hear from the Asshole in order to move toward a condition of greater psychological integration and wholeness.

The unintegrated Red Knight launches crusades, commits atrocities, and tramples the weak and helpless under his iron-shod feet. Possessed by the Red Knight, Lancelot defends his own and Guinevere's honor with misplaced outrage. He is unfaithful to his King (the archetypal King beyond Arthur), unable to take responsibility for his own Shadow, and ultimately much to blame for the destruction of Camelot.

Eventually Lancelot was forced to face the fact that he destroyed the very thing he started out to build. How often do we see this in our lives? The real world does not sustain the man who cuts himself off from instinct and animal pleasure. When a man comes to integrate spirit and animal within

SADOMASOCHISM: THE SHADOW WARRIOR

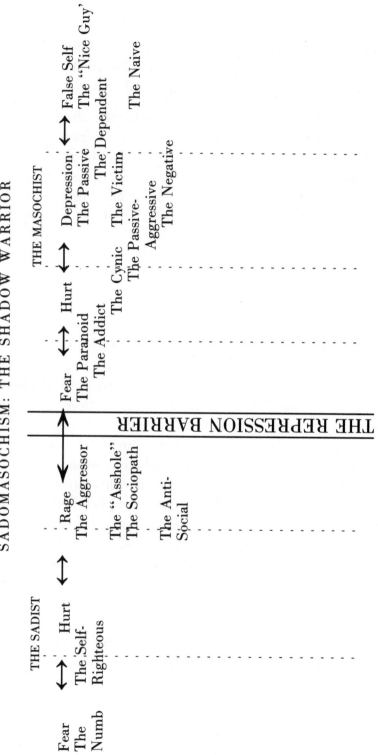

THE SADIST

Fear ↔ Hurt
The Numb   The Self-
           Righteous

Rage
The Aggressor

The "Asshole"
The Sociopath

The Anti-
Social

THE REPRESSION BARRIER

THE MASOCHIST

Fear ↔ Hurt
The Paranoid
The Addict

The Cynic   The Victim
The Passive-
Aggressive
The Negative

Depression ↔ False Self
The Passive   The "Nice Guy'
        The Dependent

The Naive

164

himself he moves to the Black Knight stage of initiation. He looks with a critical eye at the damage he has caused himself and those around him. He wears somber black armor and carries a black pennant adrift in a sadder but wiser breeze. He comes to accept that he is a *part* of the tragedy of life, and neither its victim nor master. His soul is inextricably bound up in the forces of both creation and destruction.

The White Knight uses his sword in innocence, unaware of the harm he causes. The Red Knight lifts his sword in outraged self-righteousness, uncaring about the damage he leaves in the trail behind him. The Black Knight wields his sword reluctantly and only when he has reached the sober realization that it is necessary. The man who has integrated the White with Red Knights and accepted Black Knighthood has confronted his own Warrior Shadow and moved toward taking moral and spiritual responsibility for his own aggression.

Once we take responsibility for our own destructive potentials, we have our first real chance at masculine maturity. With this maturity we can take up our swords and use them in generative ways. We will be able to assert our realistic greatness, and defend and promote our interests and needs. As we gather strength to live true lives we will find ourselves pledging fealty to something that is greater than ourselves. We will wear our swords with confidence and integrity, and for everyone to see!

THE APPRENTICE KNIGHT: ACCESSING AND MASTERING WARRIOR ENERGY

T HERE IS A TERRIFYING SCENE IN THE MOVIE
Dragonslayer after the young hero descends into the
dragon's cave. The hero is standing on a rock in the middle of
a fiery lake that covers the floor of the huge cavern. With his
sword and shield in hand he is scanning for the monster.
Behind his back a dark form rises from the water. The form
is so huge it blocks our view of the cave beyond. For the first
time in the movie we get a look at the size of the hero's foe.
Our instinct is to shout a warning to him to turn around, see
the danger, and considering the size of it, to get the hell out
of there! Just in time, he hears the terrible sound of the dragon

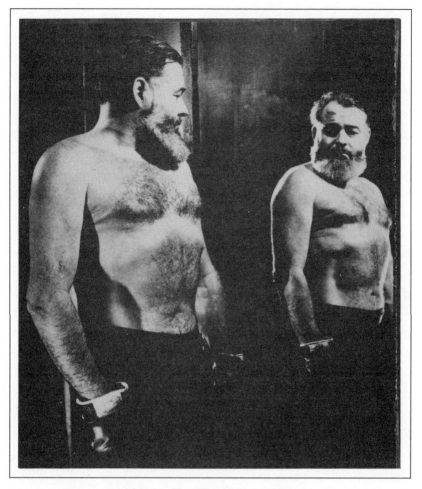

Admiring Men: Ernest Hemingway

inhaling as it prepares to blast him with its fiery breath.

This scene has such frightening power because it is a true representation of several aspects of the psyche. First, the danger of proximity to archetypal energy is far greater than we usually realize. Our immature Ego is woefully unprepared to deal with an archetypal presence rising from the fiery depths of the unconscious. Second, the Shadow aspects of the archetypes are always positioned in our blind spots, just as the dragon is in the scene. They strike at us from exactly the direction we least expect. Third, archetypal danger is, in its most primitive form, reptilian.

The primordial notion of the danger of the reptilian dragon reflects the reality of actual structures within our brains.[1] The locations in the brain that give mammalian expression to the raw emotions of fear and rage are within our paleomammalian brain. This brain includes the most primitive level of the cerebral cortex and the limbic system. But beneath this level lies the *reptilian brain*, the locus of overwhelmingly powerful appetitive impulses. Since the feelings arising from these primitive structures tend to be extremely powerful and straightforward, they appear to the rest of the brain to be alien and dangerous. They threaten to overwhelm the tiny Ego just as the dragon threatens the hero of the movie.

As it happens, the movie's hero is unable to do anything more than run for his life. He doesn't try to face the dragon as an equal combatant. Such a decision shows a certain psychological wisdom. Important as the hero's courage and will are, they are not enough to slay the dragon. Nor does the phallic might of his magical sword strike the final blow. In the end, a wizard fells the dragon, a man whose life is inextricably bound with the dragon's own. This character, an expression of the Magician archetype (which, along with the Lover, is an absolutely *vital* ally of the Warrior), understands the uses of dragon power within the psyche and knows how it can be contained and channeled.

The task before the Ego is the realization of true humility. In order to recognize its true stature it must confront the size and power of the archetypal energies. Once the Ego has done this, it can draw from the inner Magician the technology and wisdom necessary to tame the scaly beast within. A large part of the Ego's task is building an identity sufficient to maintain a distance between the human personality and the

Admiring Men: Winston Churchill, the Decorated Warrior

archetypes, without blocking any of their sustaining energy.

There are a number of techniques we can use to gain this kind of access to our inner resources. Jungian active imagination techniques, including such traditional spiritual processes as prayer and meditation, are among the most effective.[2] Since everything we experience is mediated by the imagination, it is the imagination we must activate in order for us to achieve more generative lives for ourselves and for our world. Besides exercises in active imagination, and the internalization of positive images of the archetypes through art, music, literature, and the movies, there is a real importance in bonding with men further along the road to masculine maturity than ourselves. A psychotherapeutic process can also be extremely helpful in bringing the Shadow to the light of day. "Demons" cannot withstand the light of consciousness. And as the ancient exorcists remind us, "To know the name of a demon is to have power over it."

Biographies can be a good means of bonding with men by admiring them. Useful Warrior material can be found in the

A Martial Artist (portrait of the Imperial Bodyguard
Huerh-chia, Ch'ing Dynasty, dated 1769)

biographies of men like Douglas MacArthur, Winston
Churchill, George Patton, and George Marshall. Of course
these men were not perfect. They were merely human beings
doing their best in a difficult and dangerous time. But their
strengths can be inspirational. And their weaknesses can illu-
minate our own inner landscapes, showing us more clearly
what we ourselves are up against in our battle for an integrated
Self. Their shortcomings will help to give us an idea of our
own. Through a humble appreciation of other men, we can see

what we need to do for ourselves in order to become mature warriors in a world that is crying out for world-making efforts.

Some form of martial art or athletic discipline is also a useful way of channeling the archetypal Warrior. Any athletic pursuit that requires a disciplined mind and body, develops a capacity to withstand pain, and releases aggressive instincts, is a close modern equivalent to the ancient warrior activities. If the essential task of the inner King is to constellate the *axis mundi,* the inner Warrior's essential task is to constellate the structure and dynamics of the cosmic combat. One-on-one sports simulate combat and draw on the resources of the Warrior. Please bear in mind that combat sports should not serve as a substitute for engaging the Real Enemy—they are better used as a stimulus to a fuller investment in the Real War.

In the remainder of this chapter we will follow the dream material and active imagination dialogues of a young man attempting to overcome an inner sadomasochistic split. We can see in this way a split we all face to some extent, and find a means for overcoming it. Following his difficult and vital work in self-integration may help us in our own Warrior initiations.

THE MASOCHIST AND SADIST
AT WAR IN MARK

Mark first became involved in a psychotherapeutic process because of a malaise he experienced in his professional and personal life. He wanted to bring his cocaine binging to a close. He felt his behavior was, as he put it, "awkward." He felt chronically "inept" around co-workers and dates. Constantly afraid of doing or saying the wrong thing, he would wonder day and night, "Why am I such a wimp?" At the same time he experienced violent fantasies about attacking anyone who got in his way, especially his boss and other men he would run into at bars or parties. He had been divorced for about a year from an abusive and materialistic woman. She had run his credit cards up to their limits, and once she had pulled a gun on him! Finally she left him for a professional football player!

According to his account Mark had been abnormally passive throughout his marriage. He assumed the "nice guy" role in the marriage. When asked why he had ever put up with such a volatile, hostile woman, he attempted to answer in a caricatured gruff voice. His exaggeratedly macho bearing dramatically revealed his fear that he was not presenting a manly enough front.

Immediately following the first few sessions Mark had a series of prognostic dreams. Such dreams often appear at the onset of therapy. The unconscious is apparently eager to suggest ways to work on a problem, whenever invited to do so. It provides the Ego with an overview of the therapeutic process from a perspective beyond chronological time. There is a great deal of evidence to suggest that the masculine Self experiences time and space in a way that closely resembles what mythologists call *mythic* or *sacred* time and space. The total life of the psyche is viewed as if it were a painting or tapestry, a whole work already completed with every event of note simultaneously visible. A prognostic dream offers a glimpse of this tapestry.

A SERIES OF DREAMS

I'm at work with all the other company sales reps. It's 5:00 P.M., dark outside, snow has fallen, making the street slippery. I leave work, get into the car, and soon must make a U-turn; I step on the gas to purposefully fishtail for a little fun. The car starts spinning down the street uncontrollably. I think I'll hit something; I make a minor adjustment on the steering wheel—I find I have a little control—and luckily I don't hit anything. After traveling one block, spinning down the street, while making two minor steering adjustments, my car comes out of the spin and I go down the street in control.

In this first dream we see an aggressive element in Mark's personality. For "a little fun" (read *rage* and *passion*), he deliberately accelerates the car (the course of his life) to dangerous levels considering his environment (his present life situation). Frighteningly the car does spin out of control, threatening an accident. The implication is that the inner aggressor wants to scare, maybe even hurt Mark. The Ego still retains enough control to pull the car out of the dangerous spin, and proceed on its life's course with more control. This first dream offers an optimistic prognosis. Despite a sadistic aggressor within Mark, which is putting his life in a tailspin, he has enough psychological structure to eventually restore control.

I'm with a group of friends. They are going golfing; I ask if I can go too. They say, "Sure, no problem." They all hit balls first. I hit last; the ball dribbles about a hundred feet. They are not waiting for me. I must hit the ball several times to reach the green. I am trying to catch up to the group.

This second prognostic dream provides several indications of Mark's view of himself. He sees himself as isolated and left behind by other men. This reveals his underlying failure to bond adequately with other men. As we've suggested, this can be a vital resource to a man. Mark also has no legitimate sense of his own empowerment. Notice the dream Ego's weak, petitioning stance: "I ask if I can go too." This indicates that his Ego structure may be identified with the passivity of the Masochist. Notice too that Mark's drive is a pitiful dribble. The dream makes use of a pun on the word *drive*, which makes sense in the golfing context, but also hints that Mark has lost his drive for day-to-day living. Again this confirms Mark's self-assessment that he is alienated from his inner energy resources. The men in the dream do not wait for him. He is left behind with a sense of inferiority and ineptitude.

> I'm sitting in the stands at the Bears-Packers game in Chicago. I'm rooting loudly for the Packers. A person sitting in front of me with his arm in a sling tells me to shut up or he'll beat the shit out of me. I won't listen to him; I keep rooting for the Packers. The person gets up, and I think he's going to attack me. But he extends his good arm to shake hands with me and make peace.

Here the Ego demonstrates aggressive self-affirmation by rooting for its team. But the inner aggressor appears again, rooting for a team exactly opposite to the Ego's. The aggressor sadistically threatens the Ego. But the Ego "won't listen to him." This is a healthy sign that the Ego may not be as weak as it has seemed. At the same time, there is dangerous evidence that Mark's psyche is divided against itself. Hostile dream figures will, as a rule, only modulate their hostility and offer themselves as valuable allies to the Ego if they are approached as friends.

As we'll see, when the Ego shows enough strength to stand up to the inner Sadist, the Sadist will begin to change his threatening aspect. Two other points are of interest here. The first is that the aggressor's arm has been injured: His arm is in a sling. The aggressor shows the Ego his actual wounded condition. All sadists are wounded, but this one still has a good arm, which he extends to the Ego in an effort to make peace. This is the second interesting point: The movement toward reconciliation comes from the *aggressor*! This shows the aggressor's humanity and goodwill and also shows that he is not *completely* possessed by the Sadist. Again the prognosis for an eventual integration of Mark's fragmented Warrior is positive.

After these three prognostic dreams Mark began to couch his descriptions of his inner conflict in terms of the Health Nut and the Drug Abuser. His terms show his unconscious awareness that the clean, sparkly eyed athlete within him was a little "nuts," and that the drug user was actually an abuser. Using active imagination technique, the following dialogue ensued between the Health Nut and the Drug Abuser. Significantly the dialogue was moderated by the Ego. Since moderating between various aspects of psychic material is one of the Ego's proper functions, Mark's Ego shows greater cohesivesness and structure than had hitherto been present. The dialogue also shows that his Ego has already achieved some measure of distance from the Health Nut with whom it had earlier been overidentified.

EGO

We both need excitement in our lives.
(Who is the "both"? With which complex is the Ego identifying most?)

HEALTH NUT

I just like doing different things. It doesn't have to be strenuous to be appreciated by me. Just something novel or active. Like a walk or a drive. I want to do it with somebody I like, though. Sharing makes it more exciting or enjoyable.
(Here the issue of relatedness comes up, and the excite-

*ment that it brings. Mark's need for bonding and being
with people is a powerful one for him.)*

DRUG ABUSER

Drugs are an easy way to reach the zenith of excitement.
But, as I know too well, they also cause me to fall. I
usually do drugs with someone—Frank, Joe, or Josh.
Sharing the entire drug experience with them is very
bonding. I have a special relationship with them.

EGO

Sharing seems to be a common desire.

HEALTH NUT

Yes and no. Sometimes I want to be alone when doing
things. Like driving to Wisconsin after a long week. The
feeling of freedom in the open spaces of the farmland I
savor alone. Or watching passenger jets from O'Hare. I'm
fascinated with them, wondering where they've been,
how many total miles each jet has on it. The older planes
excite me more, DC8s, 747s, the older 727s. If an older
707 happens by I'm in heaven . . . Otherwise, I love doing
things with people I feel comfortable with, like Jane, or
even my drug friends. Being on the move, enjoying what
I'm doing, sharing certain experiences, gives me a swim-
mer's-type high.

DRUG ABUSER

I can't do drugs alone. I should say, I can't start off doing
drugs alone; but when everyone goes to bed and the
party's over, I don't want to crash. If any drugs are left
I'll do them until they're gone. Sometimes it takes
twenty-four hours, with cocaine. Pot I can leave. The
most depressing part of my drug experience is after the
party and before falling asleep. I've lain awake in bed for
hours, not being able to sleep, with negative thoughts on

my mind. I think the best thing about the drug experience is the close personal bonding I get with whomever
I'm sharing the drugs. The bond continues after the high
because most of my drug buddies experience some sort of
downfall afterward. Mine seems most severe, however.

EGO

I really believe that Drug Abuser is sick and tired of
drugs, but he wants that closeness or bonding with
friends that is built during drug experiences together.
Health Nut doesn't quite have those intense feelings.
But, I believe the potential is there to form tight bonds
through shared experiences. I believe Health Nut has to
concentrate more on his partner's feelings *(a woman is
implied here)* about an experience just as Drug Abuser
concentrates on the state of his friend's highs or lows.
Where does novelty fit in?

DRUG ABUSER

Nowhere. It's not novel anymore. Unless I do LSD again.
That may cause a few novel things to happen!

HEALTH NUT

Novelty is more important here. It serves to enrich experiences. But, I could go to the same park, or hill, or to my
apartment view, and still have different thoughts. Cocaine seems so confusing.

DRUG ABUSER

The thought of doing LSD again is tempting. The drug
version of novelty is to vary the type of drug ingested.
Peyote one day, LSD the next, MDA the next, etc.

HEALTH NUT

Yes, but you must supplement these drug experiences
with real-life experiences and sharing with others. Drugs

are individualized. I think if I reverted to a drug abuser, drugs would dominate my life, like cocaine, and I wouldn't experience those rich feelings I get from others.

The dialogue ends here, for the time being. There are many important features to this dialogue. For one thing both the Health Nut and the Drug Abuser show a great capacity to reflect upon their feelings and their motives. To that extent, they are both invested with a great deal of consciousness, though it is split between them. For another thing they both have the same goals—bonding, sharing, novelty, and excitement—though their methods for achieving these ends differ profoundly.

There seems to be a little of the "good boy" in the Health Nut, the naïve male who assumes a holier-than-thou attitude and likes to demonstrate laudable attitudes (the White Knight). This was confirmed later in an in-depth reflection on the dialogue in which the "pure" Health Nut became arrogantly self-righteous during an angry denunciation of the Drug Abuser. Likewise the Drug Abuser's (the Red Knight's) apparently sweet and reasonable demeanor disguises a sadistic attack on the Health Nut. This also became clearer during later reflection. The Drug Abuser was pressed to account for the negative effects drug use was having on Mark's total personality. These effects included physical exhaustion, pain, hangover depression, guilt, and self-recrimination. In the dialogue itself neither the Health Nut nor the Drug Abuser is willing to admit the intensity of their mutual hostility.

A few sessions later Mark gave some childhood background information that showed the genesis of his split. Here are his notes:

Throwing rocks at cars, six years old, spotted by police. I run home, and a police car follows. Run in house and hide under bed. Police officer comes into the house to talk to me. I refuse to come out from under the bed.

Kindergarten, five years old. Fellow student steals my beanbag. I tell the teacher, and she yells at me for being a tattletale. I feel terribly confused.

First grade, I have to use the bathroom. Nun says no. I start to cry, feel humiliated.

Move to a new school, second grade. Neither the kids nor the teachers are welcoming. Humiliated a lot in class. Hate talking in class, afraid of looking stupid or making a fool of myself.

Remember Father ridiculing me when I tried to help him build a bird house or repair things. He would say, "You can't do anything right!"

Mother made me go down a slide when I was afraid. I cried and begged. But she made me do it, saying "Boys don't cry."

Got beaten up by boys in fifth grade. Came home crying. Father made fun of me.

Was afraid to approach kids I wanted to be accepted by for fear of rejection. Would sit and watch a group play, wishing I had the guts to join them.

Paula liked me, seventh grade, was very forward and aggressive with me. Made it very obvious she wanted me. I was afraid of her. But did a lot together, hayrides, bowling, dances, etc. Could never get very far with the girls I liked. Too nervous to put my arm around them, even if I could tell they wanted me to.

Ninth grade, sports dominate my life. I was a track star and wanted a girlfriend, but I was always too shy and nervous. Didn't want girls to know my lecherous thoughts. Therefore, afraid to do anything.

At six years of age, Mark's inner aggressor has already put in an appearance, throwing rocks at cars. We also see Mark was subject to an unfortunate pattern of humiliation by both parents and teachers. Even though Mark could remember little before his sixth birthday, we can surmise that such scenes of humiliation were a regular feature of his earliest boyhood and infancy.

Regular humiliation, shaming, and ridicule can easily give rise to a six-year-old rock thrower. No sooner had he begun to act out his growing rage than it was squashed by his run-in with the police. This incident deepened his sense of humiliation and fear. Throughout his account of his grade school years, we see Mark experiencing himself as a target for the rejection and attacks of others. In each event he makes note of the fact that his Ego-structure is coming under fire. He becomes immobilized by his fears—of rejection, and when with girls, of their discovery of what he regards as illicit sexual desires. He has been taught to fear the legitimate power of his masculine might. Paula is the only girl he connects with, but it is *she* who pursues *him*. In later counseling sessions it came out that even with her he had felt invaded, harassed, and overwhelmed. But his weakened Ego had been unable to say no. It is not hard to see how a masochistic Ego had taken form in young Mark.

Shortly after starting work on his childhood, Mark had the following dream. We can see his rage is still beneath his repression barrier.

I'm cleaning my old car, an '82 Grand Prix. Cleaning every inch with soapy water, the black exterior, the red

180

interior. I'm trying to fix some electrical wiring. Some of the parts come off in my hands and fall on the floor, making a hopeless mess. Dad hears the noise and comes into the garage. He laughs at me and says something like, "You just can't seem to do anything right, can you?" I cringe, my whole effort and happiness is ruined.

Asked if he felt anything other than ruined happiness, he answered no. In further active imagination work, Mark's Drug Abuser gave a glimpse of his rage and what it was all about. He said sneeringly to the Health Nut, "You were a star on the track team when my drug abuse started. Nobody suspected I smoked pot, me, Mr. Clean. I'll never forget how exciting it was to experiment with drugs in high school. It was exciting because I was taking a chance. It was against the law and forbidden by most parents."

About six months into counseling, Mark began to call the consciously dominant part of his personality the Nice Guy. The Nice Guy included all but the aggressive traits of the Health Nut. But both viewed themselves as "pure" and "innocent," and both used the word *should* a lot. Mark's Ego was also more or less aligned with the Nice Guy. Still there was some distance between the two, as is made clear in the following dialogue.

EGO

What do you feel inferior to?

NICE GUY

I don't feel inferior to any one thing. Well, I guess I feel inferior to my father's image of me, or what he wanted me to be. I couldn't find a comfortable niche in school that I could settle in to and become an expert. I can do everything so-so.

EGO

Why would you have to become an expert at something?

NICE GUY

I feel like I have an inferior intelligence.

EGO

When did you start to feel you have inferior intelligence?

NICE GUY

I remember distinctly once when our mothers were invited to class. Somehow, I did not get the assignment for
that class. Mothers were given a list of questions to ask
the kids about the assignment. Of course, mothers asked
their own kids the questions. My mother asked me a
question. I had no idea what the answer was. I was totally
humiliated. Things like this happened enough times that
now I don't trust myself, or my basic intelligence. My
confidence is fragile. I'm afraid if I change my familiar
environment (new job assignment, boss, etc.) this will
expose my weaknesses.

Again the wounding of the Self structure is clear. It is also
interesting to notice that "somehow" the Nice Guy did not get
the assignment necessary for the class. This almost certainly
indicates that the inner Sadist set Mark up for a fall.

Shortly after Mark began to get cognitive and emotional distance from this material he began to internalize the idea that
the Nice Guy was a false self organization, and by no means all
there was to his personality. In the sessions the masochistic
Nice Guy began to talk about his need to please others at all
costs, something Mark himself did not go along with. Once in
the middle of a dialogue between the Nice Guy and the Ego,
the Sadist interrupted and with barely concealed rage described the origin of his extreme hostility.

Dad was the enforcer. If I was bad, he'd use the belt. I'd talk back to him. He'd keep whipping me with the belt until I would shut up. I'd scream with rage until I couldn't take it anymore. But I'd always try to get the last word in. The whippings always were too severe for the "crime." This happened frequently. I got so much shit from my old man that I hated him.

Then came a revelation about the origin of the Drug Abuser as an expression of the Sadist. "When I started smoking cigarettes in grade school and doing drugs in high school, I remember doing it to spite my dad."

About eight months into counseling Mark was introduced to the Jungian concept of the Shadow, as it related to his inner aggressor. In Mark's case the Shadow was the totality of forces working to undermine the Nice Guy's dominant position in his personality. Fresh revelations were forthcoming. Here is one of several dialogues between Mark's Ego and his Shadow.

SADIST/SHADOW

I am lazy and depressed. I have a lot of hatred. When I'm in control, the body grinds to a halt.
(This is a strategy the Shadow uses to unseat the Nice Guy.)
It's easy for me to be in control.

EGO

I hate it when you're in control. It's difficult to fight you. If I let you dominate I couldn't survive.

SADIST/SHADOW

Yeah, we could watch TV all day. Watching TV is safe. You don't have to expend all that energy it takes to do things. You know, when you try to relate to people, you have to spend a lot of energy being scared.

EGO

But I love relating to people.

SADIST/SHADOW

I get so sick of it after a while. Usually they offend me, and then I want to kill them. Or I get bored. I think it's safer just to stay at home.

EGO

But the more I stay locked up the more power you drain from me. Sitting at home with you in control is depressing.

Here we see, as is true for many men, *the Sadist manifesting in order to protect the Ego from pain!* When Mark is relating to people, trying to be active and vital, the Sadist senses his growing anxiety and shuts him down, confining him to the house. The Sadist claims to protect Mark. The claim is somewhat reasonable, since Mark learned through whippings and verbal abuse that it was unsafe to express his legitimate power as a person.

Mark had the following dream nine months into his counseling work. Notice that the Sadist appears to the Ego more directly and confrontationally. The unconscious refers directly to Mark's "assignment."

I'm on a city bus, sitting in back, with several work friends on a job assignment to uptown. Our assignment is to confront some "bad" individuals.

The mode of transportation switches from bus to cop car. My friends are in one cop car, and I'm alone in another. We get to the bad-people area. I lose my friends at a busy intersection. I run a red light to follow them but can't find them.
(Here's the theme of being left behind again. Mark is

alone and will have to face the danger alone. This is a
healthy sign, as we'll see.)

I find myself walking down a ramp leading to a dark and
dangerous subway entrance. To my left I see a passage
leading back to the street. I turn to enter the passage-
way—
(The Ego is trying to escape the confrontation.)

A dangerous street man blocks my way. I try to walk
around him, but he won't let me. He's right in front of
me, and I *hear* his switchblade open. I see his knife, he
tries to stab me, but I catch his hand with mine. I realize
my strength is much greater than his. I simply push him
out of my way.

Obviously his "assignment" is to deal with his own repressed aggression. The important message in the dream is
that he can do this only by himself. The Ego tries to escape
dealing with the Shadow. But then the Ego realizes it is much
stronger and more aggressive than Mark had thought it was.
This is an encouraging sign. Among other things, this signals
that Mark's Ego is no longer so identified (at least in the dream
state) with the masochistic subpersonality of the Nice Guy. A
possible negative note is that by simply pushing the aggressor
out of the way, the Ego is still rejecting the inner Sadist, and
probably underestimating the Sadist's true force.

This suspicion was confirmed by two dreams Mark had in
the days following the switchblade dream. In them his Ego
again identified with weak, depressed, hysterical, and intimidated subpersonalities. In one the Ego was identified with a
masochistic "woman from work" with whom he shared a pink
parka. Mark feared allowing himself to really feel his vulnerability because he would have to accept that this weak part was
partially identified with his inner feminine. The thought that

a part of him might be "womanish" was unbearable to Mark at this stage. In the second dream he was terrorized by his ex-wife in his new apartment. He found traces of her everywhere, including most strikingly "a pile of sheets and blankets on the bed which were moist" from her perspiration. He reported waking up feeling very anxious and weak.

After ten months of counseling Mark accepted a new position with his company in the rough South Side of Chicago. He loved rough neighborhoods. They were symbols for him of masculine adventurousness. The job was a major step up in the company. But despite the rush of masculine pride he felt from receiving his promotion, he also felt anxious. When pressed about this anxiety, he appeared to feel incompetent. He began expressing the idea that he had only fooled himself into believing that he was competent, even in the one area of his life where he felt most comfortable. He began making serious mistakes in his paperwork at his new office, and he lost a file of important documents. He felt intimidated by his new boss. Then he had a car accident.

At this point we began to investigate the Trickster element of his inner persecutor, which it seemed was undermining what should have been an exciting, Ego-bolstering experience. The Sadist appeared as Trickster in the following dialogue, in a more virulent form than he had before. Evidently Mark was not going to be able to just push his inner attacker aside.

EGO

What are you trying to do to me?

TRICKSTER

Keep you off balance.

EGO

Why make me feel like shit?
(Notice the Ego's increased aggressiveness.)

TRICKSTER

It's the most effective way to keep you down.

EGO

But I don't want to be down.

TRICKSTER

When you reach a certain point of success I'm automatically going to get you!

EGO

Even though I'm afraid of certain things, I want to overcome them.

TRICKSTER

I just won't let you!

EGO

Why?

TRICKSTER

Because you can't handle them. You're better off being stupid and slow!

EGO

How do you know?
(The Ego said this sarcastically, showing increasing aggression.)

TRICKSTER

Because you've always made an ass of yourself, your whole life.

EGO

You do that to me. If I can shake you, I'll be happy.

TRICKSTER

(Tries a seductive tactic in the face of the Ego's increased aggressiveness.)

I show you where your limitations are. You can't talk in front of people. You can't sustain conversations with girls. You fuck things up eventually at work. You can't do manipulative things with your hands, etc.

EGO
You make me feel like shit! It's almost better to be humiliated by a woman or to make an ass of myself than to listen to you!

TRICKSTER
It's going to be real tough to get me out of your life!

Mark has come to a point where his Ego is much more assertive, the Sadist is much more direct in his attacks and is also feeling exposed and anxious that the Ego is discovering his true intentions. Mark is poised to really begin taking control of his life now.

In the next couple of dialogues Mark's Ego attempted to negotiate a truce, and then a working relationship with the Sadist. The Ego tried explaining that they were both "in this thing together" and that if the Sadist succeeded in destroying Mark's life, the Sadist would be destroyed too. The Sadist seemed to agree with the Ego. But it turns out this was only a subterfuge, born of the Sadist's increasing frustration at being unmasked and confronted.

After having been in counseling for a year, Mark met a woman and they fell in love. Once again this positive development was threatened by the struggle between his Ego and the Sadist. There were battles between them over how to go beyond the first kiss to further physical intimacies. Through the course of several dialogues, Mark challenged the Sadist about his attempts to sabotage any further expression of physical interest. During these confrontations the Ego was able to draw strength from the Sadist. He converted the Sadist's rage and passion into the energy he needed to mirror and affirm the woman and himself. This was an amazing breakthrough. In subsequent dreams the Sadist attempted to scare Mark away from further progress by showing him how threatening women can be. Here is one of those dreams.

I'm in a classroom in a hospital with a bunch of Filipino nurses. There are white pans with body parts soaking in blood in them. The women are examining the body parts, arms, legs, heads, coldly and casually. I am repulsed, and try not to look at them. (Mark's ex-wife was Filipino.)

The hospital and the nurses signify his attempts to get the healing he needs. But the nurses have a sadistic, detached attitude toward his inner fragmentation. When the sadistic intent of the dream was confronted, the following active imagination dialogue emerged.

EGO

Who are you?

SADIST

Some asshole!

EGO

What the hell are you doing?

SADIST

Making myself known. I want everyone to notice. I want to bug everyone!

EGO

Why do you want to bug everyone?

SADIST

Because you're such a pansy!

EGO

Why do you think that?

SADIST

All you care about is other people, other people! I get sick
and tired of your thinking about other people, and caring
about what they think, wondering if they like you, wondering if you're "bothering" them! Fuck them!

EGO

So, you want to bother other people.

SADIST

Yeah. It's better than worrying about them. I'd rather
bother *them* than have them bother *me!* I feel more
powerful when I bother other people.

EGO

I felt bothered when you put those body parts in the
pans, in the dream you sent me! I'm not going to put up
with sadistic dreams like that!

SADIST

I don't give a damn what you do!

EGO

What if I take those body parts and shove them down
your throat?

SADIST

You wouldn't do that here, in public, where you would
create a scene. You know, you really have to be pushed,
you really have to be bothered to react!

EGO

What if I challenged you anyway?

SADIST

I wouldn't back down. Not even against you. You think you're so powerful now, after a little therapy! You're still a weak, masochistic little shit!

EGO

You are out of place here. There are times to be rough and times not to be.

SADIST

Yeah, but I really don't know when it is appropriate, and neither do you! So, I'm this way all the time. I don't want to get fucked, so I do the fucking! Like I said, it's a power/control thing. Ain't nobody gonna push me around. I will look at them, right in their eyes, and tell them to fuck off!

This is a very interesting dialogue. For one thing, we see how much more aggressive Mark's Ego has become by now. He is no longer trying to sidestep his inner Sadist. He is challenging him head-on and not allowing himself to be intimidated. The Sadist grows increasingly desperate about his waning power and control over Mark, and resorts to name-calling, and even to direct statements about his intentions. He reveals his mind-set—"bother them before they bother you." The Sadist's game is power.

This is a plain example of Schmookler's "mentality of scarcity." Mark no longer believes with the Sadist that there isn't enough good to go around so that the best strategy is to grab everything before anybody else has a chance. When the Sadist was pressed in the counseling session that followed to define what he meant by "bother," he snarled, "Fuck! fucked!" Thus his intention was not merely to avoid being irritated. He wanted to fuck Mark over before Mark fucked him.

Further work also demonstrated that there was some truth to the Sadist's original claim to be protecting Mark. Considering the level and severity of the attacks against Mark during his childhood, the sadistic rage had formed within him to protect him from feeling completely overwhelmed and hopeless about himself. The sadistic Warrior helped form protective boundaries for Mark's besieged Ego and Self-structures.

It may seem to a child, and it may literally be true, that challenging an adult persecutor puts life and limb at risk. Mark's Ego had to identify with the part of him that always endures the attacks of others, the archetypal Masochist. Once this had happened, the Sadist rightly felt that Mark was allied with his attackers. The Sadist felt there was no choice but to express the anguish of his lonely and impotent rage against Mark as well as against others.

For the first time in his life Mark could prove to the Sadist that he and the Masochist were not one and the same, now that he was beginning the work of disidentifying his Ego from the Masochist. His Ego became still stronger. And as it did, the Sadist began to express doubts about his own capacity to know when to bring the "fuck or be fucked" mentality into play. This was the first admission by the Sadist that he could be wrong.

After this dialogue Mark's job performance improved rapidly. He felt much more confident in his new assignment. And even though he felt some intimidation when his boss still yelled at him, he didn't allow his boss to see his fear. He was much better able to maintain his legitimate boundaries, and even face his boss down when the occasion arose. His relationship with his girlfriend moved forward steadily. He experienced growing confidence in his right to be happy with her. And she responded eagerly to his growing self-confidence.

After another month Mark had a dream in which he saw

a large dark godlike figure silhouetted against a bright light. Mark reported that this God had long hair and a beard, and a huge, erect phallus. It was clear that Mark was now drawing the sword of his phallic power!

Several weeks later Mark recorded the following dialogue. In this dialogue he calls the Masochist the Nice Guy, and the Sadist the Asshole, and his Ego is fully disidentified from them both.

EGO

I need both of you. But I can't use either one of you alone.

NICE GUY

The Asshole *is* an Asshole. How can I deal with him?

EGO

The Asshole needs some Nice Guy traits. I'm more like you; but, I'm tired of being pushed around, whether in reality or in my mind.

NICE GUY

I feel safer being the Nice Guy. The Asshole takes chances.

EGO

The Asshole just blows up easier. Nice Guy waits for something bad to happen to him. Expects something bad. That's no way to live.

ASSHOLE

I'm an asshole and I know I'm an asshole. And I enjoy it. I'd rather be the pusher than the pushee!

EGO

We have to tone you down a little.

NICE GUY

The Asshole is going to push the wrong person.

EGO

You must talk to the Asshole. He'll keep you from submitting so easily. There are values I need from you, like sensitivity and observations, your coolheadedness. The Asshole gets himself in trouble because he's too quick to pull the trigger. He's full of rage. But, also, he's full of life and energy. You are kind of dead.

ASSHOLE

Yeah, you never do anything to stand up for yourself. You say yes when you mean no. You just sit there and take your lumps.

NICE GUY

If you keep pushing, you'll get your lumps too!

EGO

So both of you guys, if you keep acting inappropriately, will get your lumps. I think the best way to handle this is to have a conference when one of us feels like he's about to get lumped.

ASSHOLE

Like when I want to be an asshole, I should ask the Nice Guy if it's okay?

EGO

Yes, something like that, until it becomes natural. At least the Nice Guy won't lie down and get beaten up if he talks to you. Both of you guys just think one way. You have to get together. You each have something to learn from the other. I want the energy, confidence, and life of the Asshole! And I want the Nice Guy's thoughtfulness, gentleness, and sensitivity!

The Ego demonstrates real power here. It brings the two poles of the sadomasochistic Shadow Warrior into relationship with each other. Each puts up resistance to the other. But their mutual attacks are much less virulent than in the past. And neither argues with the Ego's insistence that it needs to integrate the two. Both grant the Ego its proper hegemony in the total psychological system. The Ego has transcended the system and, by shoving neither pole aside, can begin to bring the two quarreling halves into the lost whole they were to begin with. The last few dreams indicate the depth of healing that is now under way.

> Sitting at Frank's house, my cocaine friend. He's having a coke party. Frank is getting loaded from coke. I'm not doing any. I feel free and not obsessed with the coke. I'm talking and flirting with girls at the party. I feel powerful. Frank looks distracted and bothered. I feel great compassion for him.

Mark's Ego has overcome the Masochist's desire for cocaine. The Ego identifies the Masochist as his friend Frank and with emotional and cognitive distance can see how "distracted and bothered" the Masochist is. The "great compassion" the Ego feels is possible now that the necessary boundaries and internal Ego structures are in place. Mark can feel compassion because he feels secure in his new strength, a strength drawn partly from the Sadist. He feels comfortable relating to his Anima (the "girls at the party") and feels "powerful." Because of this sense of security and power the Sadist rests undisturbed, since he was activated in the first place to protect an overly vulnerable Ego.

A final dream:

> There are wild dogs, asserting their dominance and submissiveness with one another, determining their legitimate internal hierarchy. I feel no fear. I'm just observing their feigned viciousness. Seeing exposed teeth and hear-

The Structure of the Pack, or Is It the Psyche?

ing their growling. I feel at the level of the most dominant dog, the "leader of the pack." I feel that the dogs' aggression is not fatal, just instinctual. I feel comfort and reassurance, and vigorously alive!

Here we see the Ego experiencing the natural aggression residing in the psyche without fear. Furthermore Mark is identifying with the "top dog." He has also learned that aggression is "not fatal." It is "instinctual," for sorting out an orderly and stable hierarchy of power (his self-structures). Finally, as this ordering occurs the Ego feels both the sense of "comfort and reassurance" craved by the Masochist, and "vigorously alive" as the Sadist prefers. Thus the prognosis of the dreams of a year and a half before are proving to be right. A reconciliation between the warring poles of the Shadow Warrior is occurring.

This final dream is striking too because with the dog pack imagery it seems the masculine Self is providing Mark a vivid allegory of the origins and management of masculine aggression. The dog pack is a version of the hominid "primal horde" and an image of a social structure that in no way seeks to deny either the reality of or the social implications of masculine aggression. The dream provides an image of a masculine psyche that is no longer putting its aggression in the Shadow— either by projecting it or denying it. Mark has managed, through his active imagination dialogues, to *access* the Warrior within. *This dream will, of course, horrify all of the nice people*—those who *lack a Warrior initiation and prefer to retain views of themselves as nice, harmless, untainted by aggression, and who nevertheless remain unconsciously at the mercy of their sadomasochistic Shadows.* For those who don't really get what we mean here, we can do no better than recommend the humorous but devastating critique of such nice people in George Bach's excellent *Creative Aggression.*[3]

We, however, believe that this dream represents an enormously significant initiatory step, which the great numbers of "nice" men *and women* have never achieved—*getting aggression not only inside the Self but up into consciousness where it can begin to be mastered and stewarded.*

In our previous books, *King, Warrior, Magician, and Lover,* and *The King Within,* we have suggested a number of psychotherapeutic and behavioral techniques, including active imagination; as seen here, to utilize in accessing and mastering the four powers of the masculine Self. We feel that it is especially important for us to emphasize here that *integration and mastery of masculine aggression cannot be done solely through study, psychotherapy, workshops, or even team sports.* While we believe all of these can be important components in a program of initiatory empowerment in the four powers, a Warrior initiation is far more challenging. George Bach rightfully emphasizes the importance of assertiveness training for both men and women. We support his point of view on this and believe strongly that psychotherapists, clergy, and professors especially need this kind of training to aid them in coming to a more honest, realistic, and effective stance with regard to their societal leadership roles relating to the challenge of managing human aggression for the human community. *Each of these professional groups tends to have aggression more in the Shadow and to so demonize its role in human culture that they are often worse than useless in helping us face up to our challenge in this area.* With regard to psychotherapists, those without a Warrior initiation will unduly pathologize rage and aggression in their patients, both men and women. This is seen in a particularly insidious way when male psychotherapists who lack a Warrior initiation dismiss angry or rageful women clients as "borderline," rather than helping them to mine the gold ore of their rage for the effective assertiveness and the boundaries that would issue from it if the therapist feared it less, contained it, and blessed its role in her emerging selfhood.

But for a realistic and adequate approach to mastering these energies, even assertiveness training is woefully insufficient. Training in self-defense techniques and learning the information necessary to secure the safety of one's home, family, and community in a dangerous world will begin to erase the naïve denial and sense of invulnerability that so easily blots out the actualities of our social reality. *Serious engagement in at least one major martial art is an activity with unparalleled effectiveness in mastery of one's Warrior energy.* One could effectively argue that the dojo of the martial arts traditions is one of the more important contemporary "temples" for this divine energy of the human soul. It is a space equally as "sacred" as any church sanctuary—and one perhaps far more promising as a resource for harnessing and channeling the energies of masculine aggression for the human community.

We are all aware, of course, that there are misguided

senseis (martial arts teachers) out there who are unprincipled charlatans and who are an embarrassment to the rich spiritual and knightly traditions they claim to represent. This was portrayed powerfully in the *Karate Kid* series of movies. We must find ways to help men, women, and children find those *senseis* who have become "Black Knights" and who seek to serve and protect, not only their tribal tradition—but the human community. We know that these teachers exist and we must now call upon them to take a more active role in the initiatory process of our homes, schools, and communities.

Is it unrealistic to expect that ordinary men (and women) could begin to utilize martial arts training in a way that could serve and not harm the human community? Isn't this just a naïve fantasy? Just before this book went to press we were reading a publication of the Community Renewal Society in Chicago—one of the most committed organizations contributing to positive interracial and multicultural cooperation for the welfare of our city. In this publication there was a lengthy article describing the crisis of gangs, guns, and violence in our city schools—a problem, of course, that is facing cities not only in America but increasingly around the world. There, on the pages of this progressive social justice organization was a picture that brought tears to our eyes because of the hope it represents. It seems that Field Elementary School has been adopted by an interracial group of Guardian Angels who not only protect the students from gang activities, but also provide them with a positive alternative. This one picture of Jose Cruz, Elias Alcazar, Ricardo Davila, Landis Davis, Mike Fuentes, and Aaron Gillespie—young men of different races—standing proudly and resolutely together to defend and help initiate the children of their community offers a bracing challenge to our spineless cynicism and hopelessness. We should make thousands of copies of this picture and distribute it to those who demonize masculine aggression and who disparage even the hope that a new breed of post-tribal, multicultural, and nonracist EarthKnights just might be on their way to help us fight the Real War of our planet.

Those who don't know of the work of the Guardian Angels in demonstrating Warrior energy in the service of human community should read the recent article by the Native American Ambrose Redmoon in a recent issue of *Gnosis Magazine*, "No Peaceful Warriors."[4] In this article Mr. Redmoon delivers what seems to us to be a decisive clarification of the requirements of an authentic Warrior initiation As he puts it, in his native tradition the warrior "protects the innocent, weak, and vulnerable; the home; the sovereignty of the individual; the Mother." The warrior protects "in spite of danger, fear, difficulty, pain, and personal cost." As the protector he must show "judgment, restraint, courage, and skill." In a scathing indictment of those who trivialize the word *warrior* by turning it into a form of spiritual or psychotherapeutic psychobabble, Redmoon emphasizes that the warrior's purpose is *outside the self, confronting willful evil with courage and restraint.* If you want an example of the initiated warrior today, Redmoon, suggests, the Guardian Angels are warriors "true and real." He closes his article with the following lines that capture the essence of the warrior initiation:

> Courage comes next, as it should.
> For you need not be good to be brave,
> But you have to be brave to be good.

The point that we should glean from Redmoon's powerful challenge is clear. An authentic Warrior initiation presupposes not only getting through one's denial and projection to *access* Warrior energy, but also developing the *discipline* and *courage* necessary to *master* and *channel* this golden masculine energy with *restraint* and *effectiveness.* Redmoon's final admonition—"For you need not be good to be brave,/But you have to be brave to be good"—raises the most important issue: that of the *purpose* for this disciplined, carefully honed Warrior competency. We write these words in the wake of the Rodney King verdict and the subsequent Los Angeles riots. Police, street gangs, and all the rest of us need to face our *common* challenge—to steward Warrior energy in a nonracist, inclusive way that is worthy of the human community.

In the *Star Wars* saga, we were given a powerful cinematic image of the *empowered* individual who has accessed and become a master of his Warrior aggression, but who has failed the "seventh degree" of his Warrior initiation—Darth Vader. *The final—and most important—initiation for the masculine Warrior line of development is that of honoring a pledge—a commitment to steward this power for the good of an inclusive community:* not only to serve and protect, but aggressively to seek to extend the boundaries of Shalom— peace *with justice.*

As Redmoon has noted, the Guardian Angels have modeled, admittedly on a small scale, this highest degree of Warrior initiation. *It is our challenge to widen the beachhead that they and others have established to initiate new ones.* The Real War for justice on Earth has enough "fronts" and "theaters" to occupy all of us for the foreseeable future. Effective challenges to the reign of "monster boys" on Earth will have to include actions ranging from effective countering of rape and domestic violence to ending the rape of the ecosphere! Those who cannot see the magnitude of the Real War to secure a humane future for the children of our planet are simply in massive denial. For those who do not want to give themselves over to passivity and resignation—to live their lives without fighting for the good—let us turn to some final reflections on what "seventh-degree" masculine Warrior initiations require in our time.

BECOMING AN EARTHKNIGHT: STEWARDING MASCULINE WARRIOR POTENTIALS FOR THE REAL WAR

I N THE TALES OF MASCULINE INITIATION THAT WE know as the legends of King Arthur there was, as we have seen, a simple formula by which one could recognize the "true King," the one who could be trusted to lead and steward his power in a responsible way. The true King could "draw the sword from the stone." This ancient story gives us an image with which we can summarize the central themes of this book. We have written this book to challenge us all to face the enormity of the task captured in this mythic image of masculine initiation and maturation. In the foregoing pages we have presented the biological and psychological factors that make the uninitiated, immature male of our species an extremely dangerous animal. We have argued that the male propensity for coercive force and violence that we see acted out daily around the globe is—contrary to popular views today—not just a result of a socially constructed image of masculinity that could be erased by doing away with violence in movies and GI Joe toys in the playrooms of our children. We have argued elsewhere that the biosocial developmental trajectory of the feminine brings aggression to the fore in mid-life in a context of relatedness and substantial life experience. The masculine developmental trajectory, however, floods young males with instinctual aggressive energy at a time when relatedness seems threatening to the survival of the self and before life experience can provide wisdom for the modulation of these energies. We are convinced that the preoccupation of most tribal cultures with the task of initiating young men was grounded in their understanding of the crucial task of channeling male aggression in constructive ways lest it destroy the world the tribe was attempting to build. In other words, we are certain that, in general, tribal cultures engaged in less denial about masculine aggression than is common today and that consequently they did a much more adequate job of confronting the problem of limiting its destructiveness for the intratribal human community as they knew it.

What fundamental reality do we continue to deny? *Most of us refuse to see that the loss of an understanding of the necessity of Warrior initiation for young males has left us in a situation in which immature expression of male aggression terrorizes the global community, including the world of women and children.* In this book we are challenging both men and women to face the gender asymmetry that lies behind this problem and must be addressed if the "dragon" of monster-boy behavior on the globe is to be slain. To deny that human violence and destructive aggression is predominantly a male phenomenon is simply to ignore enormous amounts of evidence available from many different disciplines—some of which we have outlined.

We have not, however, made the mistake, so common today, of demonizing aggression, either masculine or feminine. We have argued that the human potentials encoded in human Warrior circuits constitute a line of development in their own right without which the human Self, either masculine or feminine, cannot become cohesive and mature. Without a mature accessing of aggressive potential, healthy differentiation and effective action is impossible. In our discussion we have outlined what we believe to be the potentials encoded in these masculine instinctual powers. We have described what happens when these important biosocial capacities are not accessed and channeled adequately. And finally, we have offered some suggestions as to how we might begin to face the task of initiation in this sector of the masculine personality once again.

INITIATION FANTASIES AS
MAGICAL THINKING
VERSUS WARRIOR INITIATION AS
TRANSFORMATION FOR
ACTIVIST ENGAGEMENT

It is our position that men who have bypassed their Warrior initiations and women who have not yet drawn their own swords from the stone will continue to demonize aggression while engaging in life-styles and cognitive styles that are sadomasochistic in their fundamental structure, enabling destructive aggression in others while avoiding responsibility for their own victimization and the victimization of others. Academics, clergy, and psychotherapists are often among the forefront of those demonizing human aggressive instincts. These professions are more vulnerable than most to what we have elsewhere called the grandiosity of the Magician, "Magician inflation," a stance that overemphasizes the virtue and effectiveness of reflection and contemplation and tends toward the depreciation—even demonization—of legitimate aggressivity, engagement, and action. This stance limits human knowing to a kind of magical thinking and neglects the importance of the kind of knowledge mediated in tribal Warrior initiations. Those who do not consciously affirm both their own legitimate need for aggressive expression *and the public challenges that await their assertive engagement* still face the unfinished developmental task we have been discussing here.

We have been arguing that an adequate treatment of this sector of the human Self—either masculine or feminine—will emphasize that *this capacity of the Self is that which not only makes possible sacrificial action beyond private concern—it requires it as its most central embodied expression.* Masculine personality maturing in this sector of the Self will always move toward expressing itself in a spiritual, moral, and public commitment. Let us examine next some of the ongoing problems and potentials that will increasingly challenge us as we mature in this sector of masculine personality.

MERCENARY, TRIBAL WARRIOR,
OR EARTHKNIGHT:
STEWARDING MASCULINE AGGRESSION

When the energies of masculine aggression become accessible
and available for channelization, the importance of containment provided by a maturing initiatory experience becomes
all the more imperative. In our culture and even more so in
contemporary Japan, the language and ethos of the Warrior
have been appropriated to serve the interests of business organizations, without any commitment other than the profits of
the corporation. Executives will often study the work of Sun
Tzu, Genghis Khan, or George Patton and apply their insights
to business strategies and practices. Corporations often designate a conference room as the "war room" in which the top
"generals" will meet to plan their "attack."

While there is no doubt that business or professional
effectiveness in many fields will benefit from the appropriation
of principles derived from such studies, we have emphasized
here that such studies and merely operational or utilitarian
applications in the service of self-interest do not in fact express
the essential criteria for mature masculine functioning in this
quadrant of the Self. *At best, such endeavors reflect what we
would call a pseudo-Warrior or the phenomenon of the mercenary. Mature masculine functioning in the sector of Warrior
initiation requires that a man have a mission that is beyond
the merely private and self-serving agenda—one that serves
the most worthy authority and ideals that he recognizes.* Just
as in tribal cultures a Warrior initiation put masculine aggression in the service of the highest moral and spiritual vision of
the tribe, so today maturation in the utilization of aggressivity

requires that the aggression serve the widest possible public moral vision available to the individual. *Anything less is in fact a bastardization of an instinctual potential that contains the code for much of the nobility of our species.* We all know this human nobility when we see it—and we usually mistakenly call it heroism. It is, in fact, the *knightly* potential within us which is a part of our evolutionary heritage. As we have seen, the Hero journey leads beyond its own self-involvement to a self-transcending public commitment—one that may lead to self-sacrifice but is not masochistic in nature. *The masculine Self is never stronger or more cohesive than when it is clear about its mission and when its vision of world (cosmos) and related ideals that it serves are worthy of the supreme commitment.*

We want to emphasize again, however, that a highly developed capacity in this sector of the masculine Self can be recruited for the service of unworthy and outmoded tribal, racist, sexist, nationalistic, or fundamentalist religious visions. Indeed, as long as tribal cultures had only minimal encounters with other tribal worldviews and realities, the destructiveness of masculine Warrior energies in the service of those visions was limited. Even when growing populations increased intertribal conflict, tribal peoples learned how to ritualize warfare and limit the destructiveness of masculine Warrior energy in contexts where tribal visions were in conflict. This is not to engage in "new age" romanticizing of tribal cultures which is so popular today. It is simply to acknowledge the increase in the destructiveness of masculine aggression that has followed in the wake of the decline of tribal cultures and has accelerated rapidly since the American Civil War introduced the practice of modern, high-tech total war.

Malignant tribalism is, therefore, much more dangerous today than ever before. We have lost the ritual knowledge that enabled tribal cultures to limit destructiveness in tribal conflicts, yet we find ourselves in a situation in which masculine Warrior energy, equipped with the latest high-technology weaponry, is increasingly pressed into the service of tribal visions far less worthy than those of our archaic past. The Nazi Holocaust provides us with an example of what can happen when masculine aggression is evoked and then cast in the mold of a pseudo-speciating tribal vision. The instinct to serve and protect quickly becomes perverted into the cold SS willingness to commit any act—including genocide—if it can be construed to further the purposes of Führer and Reich. *Vulnerability to such malignant Warrior madness is not just a German phenomenon*—it is a human one. Today, in the Middle East, in Northern Ireland, in India, in the streets of America, in Eastern Europe, and in the former Soviet Union, to name a few, appeals are continually made to recruit masculine aggression and hate for racist, sexist, narrowly religious, and other malignant tribal visions. Today's technology makes masculine Warrior energy more dangerous than ever before when coupled with such pseudo-speciating visions.

Those who would like to demonize masculine aggression are quick to call our attention to the widespread diversion of these masculine energies into such destructive expressions. *From our point of view, however, it is not masculine aggression that is the culprit here, but the tribal vision. The problematic issue is not that of Warrior initiation—but that of inadequate development on the King and Magician lines of development or initiation.** We will address the intricacies of the development of the Magician sector of the masculine self in our volume *The Magician Within*. For our current discussion, the deeper question can be phrased as follows: Could the crusading potentials of masculine aggression be placed in the service of an inclusive, nonracist, nonsexist, post-tribal vision?

*We have discussed the challenge of King energy in *The King Within*.

208

We are convinced that not only is such an employment of masculine aggression possible—it is necessary if we are to address the critical challenges that face the human species at this point in our history. Rather than trying to eliminate masculine aggression we must harness it in order to achieve an effective engagement of the very real struggles we face— struggles against very real enemies.

THE REAL WAR AND THE NEED FOR EARTHKNIGHTS

Tribal peoples sought to accept the reality of masculine aggression and to channel it in support of the best vision of world (cosmos) that the tribe could muster. We live in a revolutionary time in terms of the potential inclusiveness of our "tribal" identification. We agree with Joseph Campbell that the capacity to view Earth from space has now made possible an unprecedented inclusive vision for humanity. It has now become possible for us to conceive of "EarthMen," "EarthWomen," and the "home planet" in a manner that would have been impossible prior to our access to the view of Earth from space. It is now possible for our experiential "cosmos" or world to expand to coincide with the planetary community. This new inclusive world—a planetary ecological vision—that is struggling now to become an alternative to the outmoded tribal visions of the past is in its earliest phases of development and consequently still quite fragile. It is probably no accident that on the threshold of the greatest move toward inclusiveness in human consciousness and empathic connection we are seeing the resurgence of archaic tribal allegiances everywhere on the globe. There is an enormous and growing need now for men and women to come forth and pledge their allegiance to the new, inclusive Earth-Community—to step forward and begin to strategize how to fight effectively for the establishment and preservation of a viable and humane planetary community. The first step is clearly for us to organize far more effectively on an international basis to defend our ecological habitat from those who are now systematically attacking its integrity on many different fronts. Without global networking and aggressive cooperative action to protect the ecosphere all of our other dreams for a humane global community will be in vain. Playing the "Ain't It Awful" game and whining a lot will not suffice. Neither will meditation, prayer, or new age awareness alone. We must be about the business of consolidating our Warrior initiations and putting these energies into serving and protecting the "home planet." The work of organizations like Greenpeace is only a very small beginning. If we are to have a chance to win the war for the environment, we must see a widespread mobilization of EarthKnights, both male and female, who are deadly serious about service in this real, perhaps final, war. Positive ecological warfare is, of course, only the beginning. Progress on the ecological front only buys us time to address the other plagues that now afflict most of the human population on earth.

Without an adequate Warrior initiation we can read the Sunday *New York Times* without any sense of crisis. We can read about the needless famine, disease, poverty, homelessness, ignorance, tyranny, and so on without much sense of outrage. We are becoming more and more aware that the only warriors with fire in their eyes and steely resolve are all too often those serving narrow nationalistic or religious "tribal" visions—not an inclusive, human one. We want to leave you with this fact: *Our species—and particularly the males of our species—can do better than this.* Males of our species have in their evolutionary heritage the capacity to mobilize, to cooperate in self-affirmative and sacrificial action to secure the safety and well-being of their communities. Males of our species have not yet been able—in a decisive way—to harness that wonderful masculine Warrior energy in the service of an inclusive humane world vision of the great Earth community. We think that now is the time to do so. The Real War for the future of the planet has already begun. With your help we can win it on behalf of generations yet to come!

AN EARTHKNIGHT
MANIFESTO

1. There is no such thing as a harmless or unarmed human being. Those who would deny that they either possess or need Warrior energy are merely in denial and expressing the Warrior in shadow forms.
2. This denial of human aggression—particularly male aggression—must be confronted and worked through until one can engage aggression in oneself and in others maturely and responsibly. This is not just a private issue—it is a matter of public responsibility.
3. Warrior responsibility cannot be delegated—if your community, your city, your world is unsafe for your brothers and sisters and their children, the buck stops with you.
4. Competence in the discipline and skills of the Warrior must be learned—and no one can do it for you.
5. Martial arts in some form should be a required part of the educational curriculum for boys and girls, and men and women of all ages.
6. All education in martial arts should be framed under

the vision of shared responsibility to promote and defend an inclusive, *post-tribal* humane human community on our home planet.

7. There are real enemies of this just and peaceful planetary community that are not a creation of paranoia and that if left unopposed will destroy our potential for a humane human future. This "monster boy" landscape is populated by well-organized, financed, and politically connected interests that are happy if you ignore them, at most just say bad things about them, or limit yourself to whining and playing "Ain't It Awful." Most of these real enemies of a humane planetary future could be helped toward more mature masculine and feminine initiations. But in the landscape of "monster" country, it is usually necessary that confrontation precede such transformations. At any rate, so far as men at least are concerned, many will never experience this transformation into responsible masculine maturity—but must be checked through active opposition. Their destructiveness must be stopped, or at least decisively limited: This will not make them happy. If you have assumed your Warrior responsibilities, it will make your life more challenging—and more dangerous.

8. Effective engagement will require effective warrior initiations leading to preparation, mobilization, strategic thinking, networking, and cooperation on international and local grass roots levels.

9. The confrontation and engagement that must be planned for, resourced, and expedited must be seen in a global, international, intersystemic context with the ecological struggle among the top priorities, and expanding as soon as possible into other fronts.

10. As Saul Alinsky noted, you don't need everyone to win: 1 percent of the male population of our species, with consolidated Warrior initiations and committed to an inclusive vision, could make a decisive difference for the world future.
11. The buck stops with you. Prepare yourself. Step forward. Accept your Warrior responsibilities. Fit your talents and resources to the arena or theater that seems to need you the most.
12. Victory is not an outmoded or demonic concept. We *shall* overcome!

Other magnificent men are already engaged in struggles against chaos and destructiveness in all its many forms. If there isn't a men's organization in your community that engages in the struggle, start one and become part of its leadership.

Become a general in the struggle for a humane planetary future. If this is asking more than you are competent to give now, find your level; get more experience and training, then assume all the responsibility that you can carry. Future generations on our planet may not know your name, but they will remember you and bless you as part of the magnificent vanguard who stepped into the breach at this very decisive time in human history and fought to secure a viable future for the children—the sons and daughters—of this beloved planet Earth.

BE GLORIOUS!

DECODING
THE DIAMOND BODY:
BEYOND JUNG

IN THE FOLLOWING BRIEF DISCUSSION WE WILL
show how we believe we have furthered Jung's work on the
deep structures of the Self. Our work builds upon his fundamental metapsychological assumptions.

Many Jungians have forgotten the nature and depth of
Jung's commitment to the *quaternio* and *double quaternio*
structures of the human Self. Jung believed that the human
preoccupation with quadration reflected a structural reality in
the collective unconscious. His best-known work on quadration is his typology—particularly in his explication of the four
functions of intuition, sensation, thinking, and feeling. Less

well known is his idea that the totality of the archetypal Self has been imaged clearly in the octahedron.

He presented his most extensive exposition of this double quaternio of the deep Self in his essay "The Structure and Dynamics of the Self" in *Aion*. Jung's intent was to articulate the various ways in which an octahedral shape of the Self may be shown to contain psychological insight (Figure 1). While he struggled mightily to make his case, many have found his exposition hopelessly opaque.

A few prominent Jungians have continued to search for the key to Jung's fascination with this particular octahedron. Others have adopted a similar octahedral shape to explain the deep Self, but have reinterpreted the meanings of the diamond's various facets and planes. Notable among these is John Layard's exegesis in *A Celtic Quest* (Figure 2). Layard suggests that an analysis of Celtic mythology leads to an octahedron that locates the archetypal Self in the lower pyramid and the human individuating Ego in the upper. The archetypal feminine joins the Self below. While somewhat more intelligible than Jung's study, Layard's ingenious interpretation of the diamond body has not become widely known for any clinical usefulness.

One more useful schema has been offered by Toni Wolff. In her essay *Structural Forms of the Feminine Psyche*, Wolff demonstrated how a feminine quadration could be seen to be expressed by more than typological distinctions (Figure 3). She delineates the four major feminine structures as the Mother, the Amazon, the Medial woman, and the Hetaira. Her work comes closest to anticipating our structural decoding, though her model has certain limitations. For a more thorough study of these, see Appendix C. Suffice it to say here that while she correctly sees these four forms as important feminine structures, she nearly misses their underlying archetypal dimension. In our terminology these dimensions are described

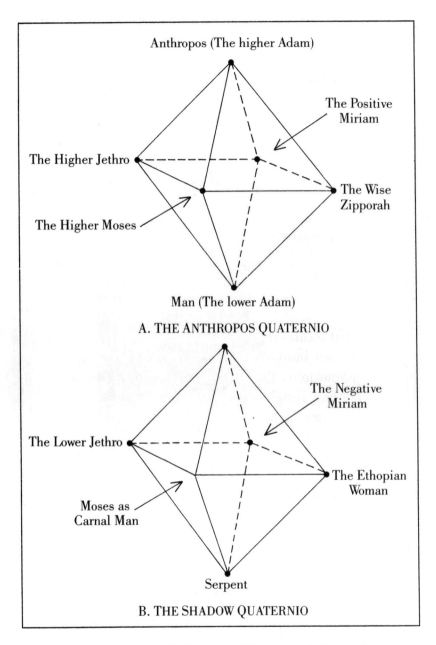

A. THE ANTHROPOS QUATERNIO

B. THE SHADOW QUATERNIO

Figure 1: From Carl Jung, "The Structure and Dynamics of the Self" in *Aion*, Volume 9, Part 2, of the *Collected Works*, p. 231.

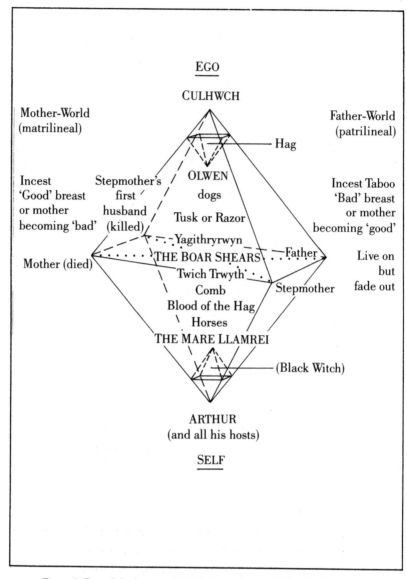

EGO

CULHWCH

Mother-World
(matrilineal)

Father-World
(patrilineal)

Hag

Incest
'Good' breast
or mother
becoming 'bad'

Stepmother's
first
husband
(killed)

OLWEN

dogs

Tusk or Razor

Yagithryrwyn

Incest Taboo
'Bad' breast
or mother
becoming 'good'

Mother (died)

THE BOAR SHEARS

Father

Live on
but
fade out

Twich Trwyth

Comb

Stepmother

Blood of the Hag

Horses

THE MARE LLAMREI

(Black Witch)

ARTHUR
(and all his hosts)

SELF

Figure 2: From John Layard, *A Celtic Quest* (Dallas: Spring, 1975), p. 202.

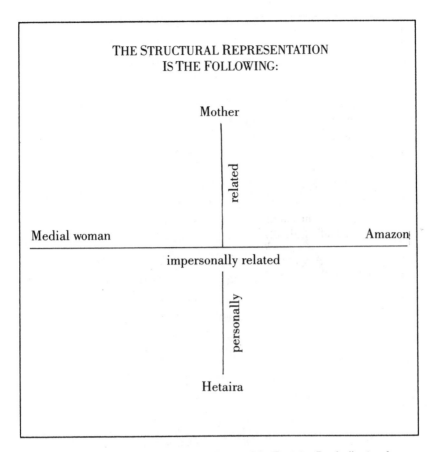

Figure 3: From Toni Wolff, "Structural Forms of the Feminine Psyche," privately printed for the Students Associations, C. G. Jung Institute, Zurich, July 1956, p. 4.

as the Queen, Warrior, Lover, and Magician. Wolff discerns aspects of the archetypes but describes for the most part traits of the feminine bipolar Shadows. Her model omits a necessary emphasis on balancing these four aspects in the movement toward individuation. Also she seems unable to interpret the dialectics that she correctly observes to exist between the Mother and the Medial woman, the Amazon and the Hetaira.

Ironically, we investigated these other models only after

constructing our own. We did not approach this topic deductively, fitting psychological data into an a priori octahedral structure. Rather, we came to the double-pyramid model inductively, seeking to understand the shape our research findings seemed to be urging. Later we were astounded and gratified to find that others had struggled to decode the same diamond body.

Our model (Figure 4) has grown out of over twenty years of anthropological field research and clinical psychoanalytic process and reflection. If you examine this model carefully, you will note the two fundamental dialectical oppositions built into the psyche's deep structure. These are between eros and aggression (the Lover and the Warrior), and ruler and sage (the King/Queen and the Magician). Freud focused of course on the eros/aggression dialectic, and Adler on the ruler/sage (compare his work on superiority and social interest). Thus Jung was not entirely correct to ascribe Freud and Adler's conflict purely to typological differences. The two were focusing on different structural dynamics inherent in the deep structures of the Self.

We believe the human predilection for fourfold structures is grounded in an intuition of an inner quaternio. Each quadrant represents in a way a distinct "program" or biogram encoded with psychological potentials necessary to a cohesive and fully functioning human self. The King program contains the ordering and nurturing potentials. The Warrior program holds potentials for boundary foundation and maintenance, effective organization, action, vocation, and fidelity. Within the Magician program lie potentials for cognitive functioning, understanding, death, and rebirth. Receptiveness, affiliation, healthy dependency, embodied sexuality, empathy, and intimacy are all potentials characteristic of the Lover program.

All of these programs must be adequately accessed, then balanced one against another in a healthy dynamic tension,

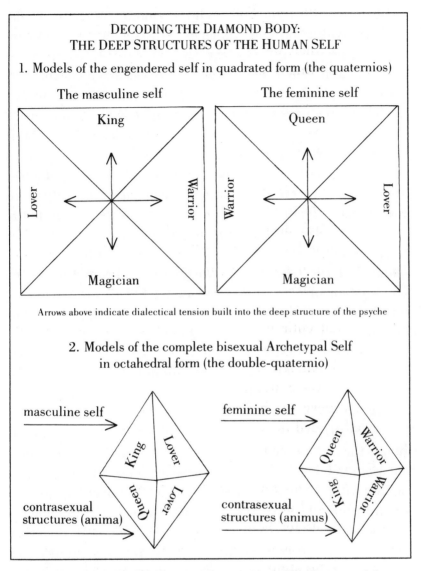

DECODING THE DIAMOND BODY:
THE DEEP STRUCTURES OF THE HUMAN SELF

1. Models of the engendered self in quadrated form (the quaternios)

The masculine self   The feminine self

King   Queen

Lover   Warrior   Warrior   Lover

Magician   Magician

Arrows above indicate dialectical tension built into the deep structure of the psyche

2. Models of the complete bisexual Archetypal Self
in octahedral form (the double-quaternio)

masculine self   feminine self

King Lover   Queen Warrior
Queen Lover   King Warrior

contrasexual   contrasexual
structures (anima)   structures (animus)

Figure 4: Adapted with permission from Robert L. Moore, *The Magician and the Analyst: Ritual, Sacred Space, and Psychotherapy.* (Chicago: Center for the Scientific Study of Religion, 1992).

analogous to the tension of a well-functioning human musculature. Individuation and wholeness are not just esoteric concepts. The psyche has clear and discernible components
available to it, which require deliberate sustained efforts to be
attained, consolidated, and maintained. On the basis of our
model, individuation requires development along four axes.
This development counteracts the dialectical tensions built
into psychic structure.

We chose the pyramid for our model because it most
graphically illustrates the struggle involved in individuation.
Individuation in this sense is the Ego's struggle to reunite the
archetypal polar opposites at the base of each of the faces of
the pyramid. (See pages 25 to 27 in Chapter 2.) *Wholeness is
imaged in the capstone of the pyramid.* From the eye of
illumination printed on our one-dollar bill to the temple on
top of the Maya pyramids, we have noticed the support mythological traditions give to our intuited model of the goal of
psychological and spiritual quest. *We believe we have been
privileged to stumble, in the course of our research, across the
actual encoded psychological structure underlying these
mythic images.*

While the relation of the four foundational archetypes to
Jung's theory of typology has yet to be researched, there does
not seem to be any one-to-one correspondence. It seems likely
that we will find sensation and feeling in the Lover's quadrant,
and intuition and thinking in the Magician's—but typological
theory neglects the other two quarters. Jung's insistence that
Shadow work precede deep work on the Anima/Animus is, we
think, clearly imaged in our model. Here the contrasexual is
a realm as rich and diverse as that of the engendered Ego—yet
deeper in the psyche and more difficult to understand.

Finally, we think our model helps make sense of the way
in which male and female developmental challenges are similar—in the four powers there are to be accessed and inte-

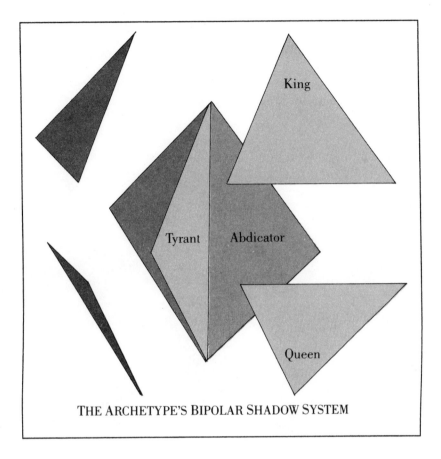

THE ARCHETYPE'S BIPOLAR SHADOW SYSTEM

grated—and different—in their structural organization. This structural asymmetry will, we conjecture, help us understand gender differences in developmental trajectories, psychopathology distributions, and perceptual and communication styles. In short, it seems that Jung did in fact intuit the biomorphic form of the psyche's deep structures. We believe our model is a decoding of that structure, enabling us to relate research data from many different sources, and confirming Jung's assumption that the psyche is structured as an octahedral double quaternio.

APPENDIX B

ARCHETYPES AND THE LIMBIC SYSTEM

ACCORDING TO A NUMBER OF BRAIN RESEARCH-
ers, most notably Paul MacLean, the limbic system (aug-
menting the more basic instincts of the underlying R-complex, or reptilian brain) is the seat of mammalian and
species-typical instincts for all primates, including humans.
Located in the paleocortical area, the limbic system consists of
the fornix, hippocampus, cingulate cortex, anterior thalamic
nucleus, amygdala, septum, the mammillary bodies, and associated hypothalamic areas. The paleocortex (as the term's
Greek roots suggest) is the older brain, a region we share with

other mammals. Ours is genetically configured particularly like the paleocortices of other primates.

Because the mechanism of evolution serves to develop new structures gradually, based upon older ones, there remain in our bodies any number of archaic structures that continue to fulfill their more primitive functions. One familiar vestigial organ, the appendix, no longer serves any apparent function (it is believed to have once aided the digestion of grasses) and because of this is now a frequent site of infection. The limbic system, however, continues in its inherited functions, and suggestively seems to be the locus for foundational archetypal structures—suggestively because this would appear to link human archetypes with the instinctive patterns of other species.

Paul Broca, in 1878, was the first to identify a large convolution common to the brains of all mammals as the "great limbic lobe."[1] In 1937 James Papez realized that this limbic system was the seat of the experience and expression of emotion.[2] Paul MacLean later developed the full concept of the limbic system.[3] MacLean came to believe the system was not only the center for emotion but also the integration center for correlating "every form of internal and external perception." It has, he claims, "many strong connections with the hypothalamus for discharging its impression."[4] While some researchers do not accept this notion, there appears to be no other neurological system available to play such an integrative role.

Within the limbic system are three primary subsystems:

1. the affiliative/attachment subsystem[5]
2. the autonomy/aggression subsystem[6]
3. the integrative/inhibition subsystem[7]

The affiliation/attachment subsystem, as the name implies, is almost certainly responsible for general mammalian tendencies to form social units characterized by nurturing, affection, and play. In humans and other primates these affiliative impulses may result in such complex psychological and social phenomena as reliance, dependence, and collaboration. The affiliative impulse seems to arise (along with each species's particular structures of affiliation) primarily in the cingulate gyrus.[8] MacLean has proposed that the concept of "family," for example, may be structured into the limbic system.[9]

Exploration, fear, defensive strategies, fighting, the acquisition of territory, the need for control (over the inner and outer worlds), and other self-definitive, self-preservative behaviors are a result of the autonomy/aggression instinct. This impulse enables humans to form cohesive selves through adversity. It may also give rise to the instinct to order society hierarchically.[10] The autonomy/aggression subsystem appears to be located in the amygdaloid complex.[11] There is evidence that in primates the amygdala plays a hierarchically ordering role for our societies.[12]

The third major limbic subsystem mediates the integration/inhibition instinct and is apparently located in the hippocampus and the septum.[13] MacLean believes this subsystem is the integrative center for the entire nervous system.[14] The hippocampus can be thought of as the gatekeeper of the limbic system, which system is the capital of the nervous system as a whole. Teamed with the neocortex (which brings cognitive functions into play), the hippocampus "gate mechanism" seems to be responsible for regulating, arranging, prioritizing, and modulating data from nearly every aspect of the nervous system. The hippocampus regulates alternating affiliative/attachment and autonomous/aggressive behaviors. When properly operating, this system regulates these competing drives to appropriately interact with any set of environmental stimuli, both inner and outer.

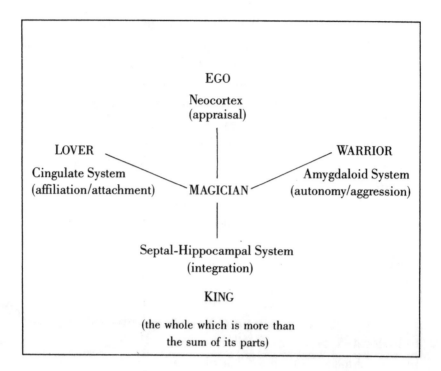

We believe that the four foundational archetypes we present in this series arise in the limbic system and are then elaborated and refined as they pass upward through the neocortex. This elaboration may be primarily achieved either by the Left Brain's rational, logical functions, or by the Right Brain's intuitive, holistic mode. They may be given "humane" form especially in the frontal lobes, which seem to be responsible for empathetic and altruistic emotions as well as for refined cognitive processes. In order for the Ego to know and access any of the four major archetypes, it must experience a particular archetype as an asymmetrical composite of each of the others. In light of the brain research we've cited, a provocative correspondence suggests itself between the archetypal and the limbic systems.

It seems clear that what we call the Lover arises originally in the affiliative/attachment subsystem, and our Warrior arises in the autonomy/aggression subsystem. The Magician (which some other psychologies mistake as the Ego) arises in the integration/inhibition subsystem at its interface with the neo-cortical structures. We'd locate the Ego within the neocortex proper. This maintains the Ego's status as the apparent center of waking consciousness. Here it is separate from the Magician but initially at least more closely related to this archetype than it is to the Lover or the Warrior.

The King manifests as the integrated, mature functioning of all the neocortical and limbic subsystems. Though it seems to arise in the septal-hippocampal subsystem, it transcends this subsystem's gatekeeping functions. More than a regula-tor, the King embraces the Warrior, Magician, and Lover in an integrated, constituitive manner.

On page 228 we have provided an elaboration of George Everly's diagram of the limbic system, including with it our four archetypes of mature masculinity.

APPENDIX C

ARCHETYPES AND THE ANIMA

I N THIS APPENDIX WE WILL SKETCH OUT SOME OF the structures and dynamics of the feminine psyche. Our particular interest will be in the Anima, the inner feminine element of the masculine psyche. We follow Jung in emphasizing that Shadow integration must precede serious work with the contra-sexual Anima or Animus. Implicit in Jung's approach is his understanding that integration of the personal Shadow solidifies the integrity of the Ego, and its achievement of a healthy psychosexual identity. Without a cohesive nuclear self, work with inner contrasexual structures can be confusing at best, and dangerous at worst.

We add to Jung's insights a description of the actual structural configurations of the contra-sexual Anima. The structure is similar for the feminine Animus (the inner masculine subpersonality in a woman), as we will make plain. As we've argued, the Shadow system involves both a personal Shadow and the bipolar Shadow of each of the four archetypes. After attending to the initiatory and integrative processes involved in mastering this Shadow system, a man can safely turn his attention to his Anima.

The aim of a relationship with the contra-sexual should not be to develop androgyny. Androgynous personalities entertain grandiose fantasies of "completeness within the Self." While there may be some genuinely biologically based androgynous personalities, as some brain research seems to suggest, for most men and women, androgyny is a masturbatory narcissistic stance, a kind of psychological hermaphroditism. For most people, any attempt to join the contra-sexual to the Ego results in a regressive merger rather than a mature complementary relationship. A merger with the Anima renders a man incapable of forming a mature relationship with his inner feminine energies, as surely as it skews his outer-world relationships with women. Jung believed that as a man's Ego grows stronger, his awareness of the contra-sexual as truly "other" will increase, until finally he can initiate what should become a lifelong relationship with his personified Anima through dreamwork, active imagination, and any other techniques he finds useful.

Contrary to what some contemporary Jungians claim, we believe the Anima is not an amorphous, ethereal "mood." The Anima has a dynamic structure that mirrors that of the masculine archetypes. As our diagram on page 234 (explicated in Appendix A) illustrates, the Anima is the feminine inverse of the four-faceted masculine archetypal pyramid. Turned upside down, the model becomes that of a feminine psyche. A woman's pyramid is composed of Queen, Lover, Warrior, and Magician archetypal facets, and her inverse pyramid is the masculine structure we've delineated. This masculine structure is her Animus.

Just as the masculine psyche demonstrates genetically determined archetypal patternings, the feminine psyche has its own distinct coloring. These masculine and feminine psychic systems each retain their distinct characteristics when operating as contra-sexual subsystems. Because of this we will quickly examine the deep structures of the feminine psyche, as they are the same as those in place in the male Anima.

Years ago Toni Wolff, a Zurich-trained Jungian analyst, described in *Structural Forms of the Feminine Psyche* four foundational personality types in women. These "forms" she called the Mother, the Amazon, the Medial woman, and the Hetaira. These forms parallel rather closely our concept of the four feminine archetypes, and by extension, the Anima. (See Appendix A.)

Wolff seems to us to have been very close to decoding the feminine psyche. However, her work includes a number of missteps which kept her from finally succeeding. Her first error was in focusing on the form of the Mother instead of the Queen. While it can be argued that the Mother (like the Father) is an archetype, the maternal and paternal forms are less inclusive than the King and Queen, and are more properly *aspects* of the royal archetypes than archetypes themselves.

The Queen is a numinous, mature structure, including and *exceeding* the Mother. The Great Goddess imagery of the ancient religions issues from the Queen's impact on the psyche. The Mother's focus, per se, is on a single family, where she is especially concerned with the needs of the infant human. The Mother is therefore less inclusively fertile than the Queen, from whom the earth itself derives its fecundity; and she is less inclusively nurturing, because the Queen nur-

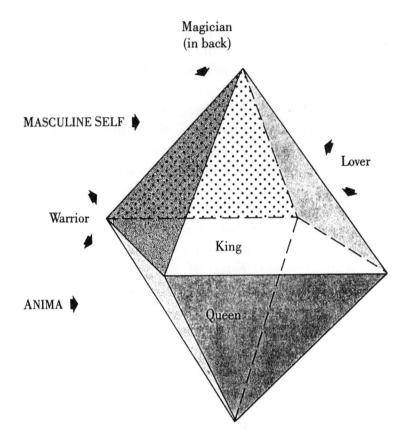

Magician
(in back)

MASCULINE SELF

Lover

Warrior

King

ANIMA

Queen

tures *the planet* she engenders, and not only children. And like the fully expressed King, the Queen encompasses each of the other three archetypes. Wolff excludes her other three forms from the Mother's influence.

Others might argue that the Mother does, in fact, integrate the feminine Warrior, Magician, and Lover. But to the extent that she does so she is approaching identity with the Queen. Though the Mother archetype provides a strong image of nurturing and blessing, she offers to a somewhat lesser degree an image of teaching and discipline (the Magician and Warrior) and, as Mother, no image at all of erotic love (the

Lover). The Queen, however, provides images of all of these traits.

Wolff's second mistake is to weight the feminine Warrior with the culturally compromised image of the Amazon. In our system, the feminine Warrior is clearly related to Wolff's Amazon, but the legendary Greek form she's chosen often misdirects the aggressive energy that is this archetype's domain. Instead of using this energy in the service of the royal couple, supporting and extending the created cosmos, the Amazon of the myths all too frequently uses her aggression against males, even to the point of exiling her sons.

The fully expressed feminine Warrior helps a woman consolidate an independent Self by defining and defending legitimate psychological boundaries. The Warrior enables a woman to achieve other difficult tasks through strategic thinking, self-discipline, and hard work. But the feminine Warrior is not in any sense antimale. The Warrior does not misinterpret the battles she must fight as narrow tribal disputes, except in the legitimate defense of a woman's offspring. Where her children are threatened, a woman accessing her Warrior is programmed to react with swift and relentless ruthlessness. Otherwise, the woman in an axis with her Warrior correctly sees her battles as primarily personal efforts to establish a Self, and as transpersonal efforts to defend creation.

But by using the largely negative image of the Amazon, Wolff ends up really examining primarily the Shadow Warrior, in her sadistic expression. Possessed by the Sadist, a woman's fury is directed not only against men in general but against other women as well, and even against her own children.[1] A woman who allows the Amazonian Sadist to act for her in her life misses the potential benefits of the full expression of the feminine Warrior.

We hope the resources of the feminine Warrior will be

accepted more fully into our culture. We would then see women engaged in a more active psychological and physical defense of themselves and their mates, as well as a fuller participation in the struggle against communal and global forces of destruction. There is evidence that our culture is increasingly learning to steward this energy—especially in the arenas of social and environmental reform.

The Hetaira is, like the Amazon, a culture-bound term. In ancient Greece the hetaira functioned much as the more familiar geisha did in Japanese culture—as a well-educated female companion and prostitute. But a prostitute is a manifestation of the Shadow Lover, no matter how well-educated. In Wolff's system the Hetaira displays both aspects of the Lover's bipolar Shadow, the Addict and the Impotent Lover. The Addict is operative in Wolff's claim that women under the influence of the Hetaira have a tendency to go from one man to another. The Impotent Lover is disclosed by the knowledge that psychologically a prostitute is often engaged in a fruitless repetition of her unsuccessful childhood attempt to gain her father's admiration and love.

The Hetaira seems to be a second-generation archetype, composed of fragments of more basic ones. She includes both poles of the Magician's Shadow—as a Manipulator she causes a woman to use men for their money and her own narrow interests, and as the Innocent One she lures a woman into displaying her naïveté about relationships. The Sadist manifests in a woman's underlying anger toward men. The Warrior's other Shadow pole, the Masochist, appears in her willingness to place herself in harm's way.

To the extent Wolff's final type, the Medial, approaches the concept of the shaman, it is an appropriate and full expression of the archetype of the Magician. It is Wolff's least limiting term.

Despite any other shortcomings, it is striking that Wolff's

conceptualization of the archetypal dynamics of the *feminine* psyche agrees so closely with our own system of thought concerning the *male* psyche. We interpret this as a verification of our instinct to extend the concept of the quadrated psyche from the masculine to the feminine Self, and to the Anima and Animus.

To our way of thinking then, a woman's quadrated psyche functions just as does a man's. She balances the energies of four foundational archetypes—the Queen, Warrior, Magician, and Lover. The Queen guides a woman toward a centered calm, a sense of inner order she can extend into the outer world. She becomes gifted with the capacity to bless and join in fructifying union with the other members of her "realm." The Warrior guides a woman in self-discipline and self-defense, as well as in the defense of others. Her achievements are encouraged by the Warrior, and her sense of service to a Transpersonal Other reinforced. The Magician provides a capacity to introspect, to raise and contain power, to heal and to act as a mediator between the human and the divine spheres. Drawing on the Magician's powers, a woman may serve as a spiritual guide to others, especially in the task of initiating younger women into the mysteries of adult responsibilities and joys. And the Lover empowers a woman to be passionately and creatively engaged with all things, to be uninhibited sexually (playing and displaying) and profoundly spiritual.

Of course, the relationship between the masculine and feminine aspects of the Self are often problematic. For the Anima is a whole structure, and no man experiences it simply piece by piece, pair by pair. Just as he balances the energies of *his* four foundational archetypes, he must balance the four different signals that reach him from his Anima. It can be useful to separate out the different sources of these signals in order to distinguish their characteristics, so long as we remember that they operate as a whole.

The feminine energies beside each of the male archetypes give them depth and definition. But when a man is caught in one or more of the bipolar Shadow systems of the masculine archetype, he encounters *all* of the Anima's complementary Shadow energies too. At the Warrior's *active* Sadist pole, for example, he will meet with the *passive* poles of the Shadow Anima, the Weakling/Abdicator, the Innocent One, the Impotent Lover, and especially with the Masochist. If he is Ego-identified instead with the Masochist, he will be confronted by the feminine Tyrant, the Manipulator, the Addict, and especially with the woman Warrior at her Sadist pole.

Relations between the masculine and feminine Warriors can be particularly strained. The only really successful mode for a relationship between them is as comrades-in-arms.[2] Otherwise the aggressive/aversive energies they each channel can be directed against the other, causing empathic breaks in man-woman relationships that are difficult to repair. A Warrior needs an enemy, and too often the masculine and feminine Warriors make enemies of each other.

A man who does not access the fully expressed Warrior (whose feminine counterpart is his comrade-in-arms) will tend to experience his Anima, and all the women in his life, in a split and shadowy way. He will see one aspect of the feminine as the Tyrant Queen—his sophomorically idealized and "virginal" mother. Women who are not like her he sees as whores, and we've seen what a complex mixture of Shadow elements a prostitute carries. The Tyrant Queen sends this man to his death to defend her. He, in turn, "fucks" a whore (rather than "making love" with her) in an act of revenge against his mother, overcoming "her" resistance with brutality. Here is the power issue the rapist fails to manage. He wants power over what he sees as an inordinately powerful, abusive woman. Perhaps his mother was physically or verbally abusive to him, or perhaps she was neglectful and uninterested. Such a man is of course not accessing his Warrior appropriately. Instead, he is a psychotic boy without any experience of his legitimate power.

Until a man becomes secure in his masculine identity, he will remain a sadomasochist in his relationships with women. If he is not secure he feels that he is risking invasion by his Anima. He has yet to learn to respect his own legitimate territories as well as those of the feminine psyche, both within and without. The maturing male learns there is a space within him he can never invade, and that will never be "his." He must approach his Anima with respect. Once he learns to deal with this "other" with discipline and respect, he has the prerequisite knowledge necessary to deal respectfully with any "other," including the women he loves, other men, other species, and finally the Transpersonal Other we all need to serve.

The octahedral Self we diagrammed in Appendix A gives a good visual model for imagining these Anima dynamics. While it does not portray the vital interpenetration of the masculine and feminine structures, it does show how the contra-sexual system is contained *within* the total structure, and is in no way external to it. The two structures together form the "diamond body" of the great Self. Though it is in some sense merely a pictorial construct, it is an appropriately suggestive and allusive one. Like the implicit structure of a crystal, we each have a perfect diamond Self within, waiting the chance to form. We are gifted then with an inner vision of the possible human which has the clarity, radiance, and perfection of a jewel.

NOTES

Complete bibliographical information on works cited in these notes will be found in the Bibliography that follows.

CHAPTER 1: GENDER IDENTITY, GENDER ASYMMETRY, AND THE SEXUAL IMBALANCE OF POWER

1. By "radical androgyny" we refer to the claims made by some feminists, whether male or female, that there are no differences between the sexes (except what they regard as incidental biological divergences). When it comes to assigning blame, however, particularly for

aggressive behavior and fear of intimacy, some feminists draw very clear distinctions between the sexes, always at the expense of the male. One would think from their claims that women have no Shadow. A woman's only weakness seems to be that she "loves men too much." It is impossible to love someone too much. What *is* possible is to become so addicted to another that personal responsibilities are relinquished. However, shadowy business of this kind is common to both sexes. The idealization of androgyny is against nature and scientific evidence; it is also hypocritical. For related discussion, see Robert Ardrey, in toto but especially *African Genesis*, pp. 143 ff. (in Bibliography under Anthropology); James Ashbrook, *The Human Mind and the Mind of God*, pp. 57–59, 96–97, 105, 322ff., 324–327, 339 (in Bibliography under Brain Research); Sam Keen, *Fire in the Belly*, pp. 195ff. (in Bibliography under Other Psychologies); Anne Moir and David Jessel, *Brain Sex: The Real Difference Between Men and Women* (in Bibliography under Brain Research); Anthony Stevens, *Archetypes: A Natural History of the Self*, pp. 23ff., 48ff., 81–84, 174ff. (in Bibliography under Jungian Thought); Edward O. Wilson, in toto but especially *On Human Nature*, pp. 16, 18–21, 121ff. (in Bibliography under Anthropology).

2. An example of this phenomenon is Riane Eisler, *The Chalice and the Blade: Our History, Our Future* (in Bibliography under Anthropology). Although Ms. Eisler purports to demonstrate a "partnership" model of male/female relationships, she provides a stereotypic negative metaphor of the "Blade" to designate male qualities. Her central image of partnership is of a mother Goddess nurturing her child, by implication her son—hardly a relationship between equals. Also see Mary Daley, *Beyond God the Father and Gyn/Ecology;* and Rosemary Ruether, *Sexism and God-Talk: Toward a Feminist Theology*, pp. 104ff. (both in Bibliography under Theology and Philosophy).

3. Alice Miller, *The Drama of the Gifted Child, For Your Own Good*, and *Thou Shalt Not Be Aware* (in Bibliography under Other Psychologies).

4. Research in this area clearly links the development of high civilization (beyond the "high culture" of the late Neolithic) with the advent of sacral kingships and the attendant assemblage of larger nation-states. For an extensive record of sources, see the Bibliography's Kingship listing. See there especially Basham; Emery; Frankfort, *The Birth of Civilization in the Near East;* Kwanten; Schele and

Freidel; and Wales. See also Julian Jaynes, *The Origin of Conscious-ness in the Breakdown of the Bicameral Mind* (in Bibliography under Brain Research); John Weir Perry, *Lord of the Four Quarters* (in Bibliography under Mythology and Religion); and Wilson, pp. 89–90.

5. Carl Jung, *Aion* in *The Portable Jung*, pp. 148 ff.; Jolande Jacobi, *The Psychology of C. G. Jung*, pp. 5, 114ff., 120–121; Jung, *Man and His Symbols*, pp. 186ff., and *Mysterium Coniunctionis*; Loren Pedersen, *Dark Hearts*; John Sanford, *The Invisible Partners*; and Stevens, pp. 174ff., 193–194 (all in Bibliography under Jungian Thought).

6. Moir and Jessel, p. 31.

7. Stevens, pp. 79–80; and Wilson, pp. 132–137.

8. See Bibliography under Brain Research.

9. David Gilmore, *Man in the Making: Cultural Concepts of Masculinity*, "Work" in the index (in Bibliography under Anthropology).

10. Don Browning, *Generative Man*, p. 145ff. (in Bibliography under Other Psychologies).

11. Niebuhr isn't always as frank about his distrust of power as Lord Acton was when he said, "Power corrupts, absolute power corrupts absolutely." He does frequently, however, cast the desire for power, and its achievement and uses, in an exaggeratedly negative light. He assumes (as liberal Christians have for centuries, and some feminists do today) that the quest for power is inherently mistaken, and that its achievement is invariably destructive for principal and subordinate alike. Writers such as Keen, Ruether, Eisler, and Daley betray an unconscious utopianism in their works—and as Stevens notes in *Archetypes* (p. 139), utopianism will always fail.

12. Gérard Lauzun, *Sigmund Freud: The Man and His Theories*, pp. 64–65 (in Bibliography under Other Psychologies); and Reinhold Niebuhr, *The Nature and Destiny of Man*, pp. 44, 192 (in Bibliography under Theology and Philosophy).

13. Anthony Stevens, *The Roots of War*, pp. 36–38 (in Bibliography under Jungian Thought); and Anthony Storr, in toto and especially *Human Destructiveness*, pp. 11, 21, 23, 34, 42 (in Bibliography under Other Psychologies). Even Gilmore affirms the almost universal necessity for aggressive male behaviors, as channeled into the culturally defined roles of protector, provider, and procreator. Keen finds himself (pp. 112ff.) endorsing "fierce gentlemen" as if they were vital

to the survival of the species. This comes after his emphatic rejection of sociobiological claims and the notion of an aggressive instinct, and despite his embrasure of the romantic socialization model of gender definition.

14. Cultures have seldom celebrated initiation ceremonies for their girls. By and large girls have been considered naturally initiated by their first menstruation. Boys have been, in contrast, forcibly taken through initiation rituals designed to awaken in them an awareness of their risk-taking and self-sacrificial responsibilities. This may also reflect a widespread human awareness that innate masculine aggressive potentials require extremely careful containment and channeling if they are not to become dangerous to the human community in the behavior of irresponsible, immature, "monster boy" males. See the Bibliography under Ritual and Initiation; see also Mircea Eliade, *Rites and Symbols of Initiation* (in Bibliography under Mythology and Religion); Gilmore; Joseph Henderson, *Thresholds of Initiation* (in Bibliography under Mythology and Religion); Keen, pp. 27–33; Victor Turner, *The Ritual Process: Structure and Anti-Structure* (in Bibliography under Anthropology); and Hutton Webster, *Primitive Secret Societies* (in Bibliography under Anthropology).

CHAPTER 2: DECODING THE MALE PSYCHE

1. See Bibliography under Jungian Thought.

2. Carl Jung, "The Relations of the Ego and the Unconscious," in *The Portable Jung*, p. 75; Jolande Jacobi, *The Psychology of C. G. Jung*, p. 1; Aniela Jaffé, *The Myth of Meaning: Jung and the Expansion of Consciousness*, pp. 40–42; Carl Jung, *Psychology and Alchemy*, p. 215; and Anthony Stevens, *Archetypes: A Natural History of the Self*, pp. 43–47 (all in Bibliography under Jungian Thought).

3. Jacobi, p. 1; and Stevens, pp. 43–47.

4. Joseph Campbell, *The Hero with a Thousand Faces*, pp. 3ff. (in Bibliography under Mythology and Religion); and Jacobi, "Mythology/Myths" in the index.

5. Campbell, p. 258.

6. Mircea Eliade, *Cosmos and History: The Myth of the Eternal Return*, p. 3 (in Bibliography under Mythology and Religion); Jacobi, pp. 5–10; see the first two chapters on the nature of consciousness in

Julian Jaynes, *The Origin of Consciousness in the Breakdown of the Bicameral Mind* (in Bibliography under Brain Research); and Henri Frankfort, *Kingship and the Gods*, pp. 27–29 (in Bibliography under Kingship).

7. Carl Jung, "Aion," in *Psyche and Symbol*, pp. 1–6 (in Bibliography under Jungian Thought).

8. John O. Beahrs, *Unity and Multiplicy*, especially chs. 1 and 4 (in Bibliography under Other Psychologies).

9. Nearly every school of psychology acknowledges this, in one way or another. The Jungian approach to the Shadow, the work of developmental psychologists with the inner Child (see especially Alice Miller), and the work of hypnotherapists like Dr. John Beahrs with multiple-personality disorders all are particularly relevant.

10. Carl Jung, "The Structure and Dynamics of the Psyche," in *The Portable Jung*, especially p. 52; and Stevens, especially pp. 26, 40, 51ff.

11. Carl Jung, "The Concept of the Collective Unconscious," in *The Portable Jung*, pp. 59–69.

12. Bruno Bettleheim, *Freud and Man's Soul*, pp. 53–64; and Gérard Lauzun, *Sigmund Freud: The Man and His Theories*, "Id" in the index (both in Bibliography under Other Psychologies).

13. Don Browning, *Generative Man: Psychoanalytic Perspectives*, p. 158 (in Bibliography under Other Psychologies).

14. Ibid.

15. Ibid., p. 159.

16. Ibid., pp. 145–147, 158, 159; Jacobi, "Libido" in the index; and Lauzun, "Libido" in the index.

17. See Bibliography. Although Jean Bolen does not do this, she tends to identify the Gods and Goddesses with human personality types. Bolen's Gods and Goddesses do parallel cognition, feeling, and behavioral styles observable in men and women. *But no human being is an archetype, and neither is any God or Goddess.* Bolen's work describes complex configurations of archetypes (our foundational four from the psyches of men and women, as well as countless others that determine our modes of perception) as expressed through different Ego identities, personal complexes, cultural and Superego conditioning, etc. Her Gods and Goddesses are simpler than human personalities, and so on this level they approach the archetypes more nearly than all but the most dysfunctional human personalities. But we believe the

Libido takes form at the most basic levels of drive as either a King (or Queen), Warrior, Magician, or Lover, and then after progressive explication and diversification presents itself in complex manifestations. These foundational four are the node around which collect the culture-specific ideals, parental introjects, and other family myths that provide so many layers of archetypal functioning.

18. Jacobi, pp. 1–9ff.

19. Marie Louise von Franz, *Projection and Reflection in Jungian Psychology* (in Bibliography under Jungian Thought). See Index under Shadow, Projection of.

20. Individuation is a matter, for Jungians, of bringing into Ego consciousness (1) what has been otherwise split off and repressed, as well as (2) awakening insights that have never been conscious. For the distinction between complexes and archetypes, and their relation to the two categories above, see Jolande Jacobi's *Complex, Archetype, Symbol in the Psychology of C. G. Jung.*

21. See Theodore Millon's excellent work with the concept of bipolarity in *Modern Psychopathology* (in Bibliography under Other Psychologies).

22. Theodore Millon, *Disorders of Personality: DSM-III: Axis II,* in toto but especially p. 58 (in Bibliography under Other Psychologies).

23. James Hillman et al., *Puer Papers,* especially Hillman's chapter "Senex and Puer: An Aspect of the Historical and Psychological Present" (in Bibliography under Jungian Thought).

24. Paul Tillich, *Systematic Theology,* vol. 3, especially ch. 1 and "The Kingdom of God as the End of History" (in Bibliography under Theology and Philosophy).

25. Ibid., "Hegel" in the index; also see Sean Kelly, *Individuation and the Absolute: Hegel, Jung, and the Path Toward Wholeness,* in press.

26. See Bibliography under Theology and Philosophy; see also Alfred North Whitehead, *Process and Reality* (in Bibliography under Theology and Philosophy).

27. Jung, *Psychology and Alchemy,* "Coniunctio" in the index.

28. In Greek mythology and legend, the Symplegades were two great rocks in the middle of the ocean. When a ship tried to pass between them, they would rush together and destroy the ship.

29. Stevens, pp. 259–275.

30. Ibid., pp. 260, 264. For the relevance of the limbic system to the four foundational archetypes, see Appendix B.

31. Rudolf Otto, *The Idea of the Holy*, in toto but especially pp. 12ff., 25 (in Bibliography under Mythology and Religion).

32. Eliade, *Cosmos and History*, pp. 12ff., and *Patterns in Comparative Religion*, "Temple," "Tree, Cosmic," "Palace," "Mountain, Cosmic" in the index.

33. Ibid., "Kings," "Rulers," in the index. The literature on sacral kingship, and the king's mediation of the sacred and profane worlds, is vast. See also the Bibliography under Kingship.

34. See Bibliography under Kingship. Also see James Frazer, *The Golden Bough*, "King," "Queen," in the index (in Bibliography under Mythology and Religion); and John Weir Perry, *Lord of the Four Quarters*, p. 32 (in Bibliography under Mythology and Religion).

35. Jane Goodall, *In the Shadow of Man*, p. 284 (in Bibliography under Primate Ethology).

36. Jane Goodall, *Through a Window*, p. 13 (in Bibliography under Primate Ethology).

37. See Bibliography under Primate Ethology. Also see Frans de Waal, *Chimpanzee Politics* (in Bibliography under Primate Ethology); Goodall, *Through a Window* and *In the Shadow of Man;* and Michael MacKinnon, *The Ape Within Us* (in Bibliography under Anthropology).

38. Geoffrey Bourne, *Primate Odyssey*, pp. 321ff. (in Bibliography under Primate Ethology).

39. de Waal: See Index under Alpha Male; Goodall, *In the Shadow of Man*, pp. 112ff.

40. de Waal, pp. 109–110, 200, 204–205.

41. Goodall, *In the Shadow of Man*, pp. 73–74; MacKinnon, p. 85.

CHAPTER 3: THE KILLER APE

1. See Bibliography under Primate Ethology and Anthropology. Note especially Robert Ardrey, *African Genesis;* Edward O. Wilson, *On Human Nature*, ch. 5; de Waal, *Chimpanzee Politics: Power and Sex Among Apes*, and *Peacemaking Among Primates;* and Michael MacKinnon, *The Ape Within Us.* For divergent views of hominid

evolution, see Helen E. Fisher, *The Sex Contract;* and Elaine Morgan, *The Descent of Woman.* Also see Anthony Stevens, *The Roots of War: A Jungian Perspective,* especially ch. 3 (in Bibliography under Jungian Thought).

2. Note especially, Anthony Stevens, *Archetypes: A Natural History of the Self,* pp. 259–275 (in Bibliography under Jungian Thought).

3. See Anne Moir and David Jessel, *Brain Sex: The Real Difference Between Men and Women,* especially chs. 1–3 and epilogue to the American edition (in Bibliography under Brain Research).

4. See Bibliography under Other Psychologies and Alice Miller there.

5. "Aggression," as the British psychiatrist Anthony Storr and others use the term, is synonymous with "self-affirmation" and "self-recognition." In his book *Human Destructiveness* (in Bibliography under Other Psychologies), Storr lays out a well-reasoned series of definitions of innate human aggression and what factors in the environment lead to aggression's turning into rageful violence. See especially pp. 3–33 and 10–12.

6. For comparison, see Stevens, *The Roots of War,* especially chs. 1–3 and 6. See also Ronald R. Lee and J. Colby Martin, *Psychotherapy After Kohut;* and Ernest Wolf, *Treating the Self* (both in Bibliography under Other Psychologies). "Fragmentation" and "Fragmented Self" in the index.

7. Stevens, *Archetypes,* pp. 180ff.; and Moir and Jessel, "Childhood Differences" in the index.

8. See Heinz L. Ansbacher and Rowena R. Ansbacher, *The Individual Psychology of Alfred Adler* (New York: Harper & Row, 1964), pp. 111–112.

9. See note 7 this chapter.

10. See Gérard Lauzun, *Sigmund Freud: The Man and His Theories,* "Id" in the index; and Bruno Bettelheim, *Freud and Man's Soul,* pp. 53ff. (both in Bibliography under Other Psychologies).

11. See Moir and Jessel, especially ch. 3 and epilogue to the American edition.

12. Ibid., pp. 103ff.

13. The ancient hunter is evidenced in the caves of south and central France and in other cave sites and possible dwellings throughout the Near East and Asia. In addition, very early evidence dates from

over 1 mya at sites in Africa. See Richard G. Klein, *The Human Career: Human Biological and Cultural Origins*, "Hunting" in the index (in Bibliography under Anthropology). As we use the concept of the Warrior, the Hunter is a specialized form of this more basic program for aversive behavior. See Appendix B.

14. In his televised lecture series *The Transformation of Myths Through Time*.

15. See Joseph Campbell, *The Mythic Image* (in Bibliography under Mythology and Religion).

16. The literature on this theme of the differing developmental tasks of boys and girls is growing rapidly. For a representative sample, see Lillian Rubin, *Intimate Strangers: Men and Women Together*, especially chs. 3 and 4 (in Bibliography under Other Psychologies); and David D. Gilmore, *Manhood in the Making: Cultural Concepts of Masculinity*, especially pp. 26–29 (in Bibliography under Anthropology).

17. The role of the father in the son's development is imaged differently in different psychologies. See Arthur Colman and Libby Colman, *Earth Father/Sky Father: The Changing Concept of Fathering* (Englewood Cliffs, N.J.: Prentice-Hall, Inc., 1981). Compare Jay R. Greenberg and Stephen A. Mitchell, *Object Relations in Psychoanalytic Theory* (Cambridge: Harvard University Press, 1983).

18. See Andrew Bard Schmookler, *Out of Weakness: Healing the Wounds That Drive Us to War*, "Scarcity: and Chosenness" in the index and ch. 1 (in Bibliography under Other Psychologies).

CHAPTER 4:
HISTORICAL IMAGES OF THE WARRIOR

1. For example, see Robert Ardrey, *African Genesis: A Personal Investigation into the Animal Origins and Nature of Man*, pp. 23, 69, 147, 225 (in Bibliography under Anthropology).

2. See, for example, Richard G. Klein, *The Human Career: Human Biological and Cultural Origins*, p. 162 (in Bibliography under Anthropology). Also, see his general discussion of human origins in ch. 3.

3. Ibid., ch. 3, especially p. 170.

4. See Jane Goodall, *Through a Window: My Thirty Years with*

the Chimpanzees of Gombe, p. 13 (in Bibliography under Primate Ethology).

5. Klein, p. 47.

6. See Bibliography under Primate Ethology, especially Frans de Waal, *Chimpanzee Politics* and *Peacemaking Among Primates;* and Jane Goodall, *In the Shadow of Man.*

7. See chapter 2 of Robert Moore and Douglas Gillette, *The King Within: Accessing the King in the Male Psyche*, a companion volume to this series, for a relevant discussion.

8. See de Waal, *Peacemaking Among Primates*, for the most comprehensive discussion of these behaviors, not only among chimpanzees but also among other primates.

9. See in Bibliography under Primate Ethology, "Baboons" in the index.

10. See Goodall, *In the Shadow of Man*, p. 54; Goodall, *Through a Window*, "Charging Displays" in the index; de Waal, *Chimpanzee Politics*, "Display Behaviour" in the index.

11. Among such God images in patriarchal religions are the Canaanite Ba'al, the Indian Indra, the Greek Zeus, and the Hebrew Yahweh, to name a few.

12. Shakespeare, *King Lear*, act 3, sc. 2.

13. In Freudian terms, the "pleasure principle" is traded for the so-called reality principle.

14. See Smithsonian Editors, *Man and Beast: Comparative Social Behavior*, especially E. O. Wilson's chapter, "Competitive and Aggressive Behavior" (in Bibliography under Anthropology). Also there, see E. O. Wilson, *On Human Nature*, p. 104.

15. See Anthony Stevens, *The Roots of War: A Jungian Perspective*, "Pseudospeciation" in the index (in Bibliography under Jungian Thought), for a fuller discussion.

16. For the most up-to-date analysis of this, see Klein, chs. 4–7.

17. The literature in this area is vast. For the most recent analysis, see Klein, ch. 3.

18. The literature in this area of investigation is enormous. For a relatively concise documentation of this discussion, and the importance of the warrior elites in civilization building, see the Bibliography under Kingship. Note especially A. L. Basham, *The Wonder That Was India;* W. B. Emery, *Archaic Egypt:* Kwanten, *Imperial Nomads: A History of Central Asia;* Henri Frankfort, *The Birth of Civilization*

in the Near East; Julian Jaynes, *The Origin of Consciousness in the Breakdown of the Bi-Cameral Mind;* John Weir Perry, *Lord of the Four Quarters: The Mythology of Kingship;* Linda Schele and David A. Freidel, *A Forest of Kings: The Untold Story of the Ancient Maya;* and H. G. Wales, *The Mountain of God: A Study in Early Religion and Kingship.*

19. See Moore and Gillette, ch. 3.

20. Ibid.

21. See note 18 this chapter.

22. Among these latter God images were the Persian Ahura Mazda, the Hebrew Yahweh, the Egyptian Ra, and the Aztec Tonatiu.

23. See Jaynes, ch. 4.

24. The research into Persian influence on other religions is enormous. For a sampling, see Neil Forsyth, *The Old Enemy: Satan and the Combat Myth,* "Zoroastrianism" in the index (in Bibliography under Mythology and Religion). See also works by Mircea Eliade, and William W. Malandra, *An Introduction to Ancient Iranian Religion* (in Bibliography under Mythology and Religion).

25. See, for example, Joscelyn Godwin, *Mystery Religions in the Ancient World,* "The Path of the Warrior" and "Mithraism" and "Mithras" in the index (in Bibliography under Mythology and Religion). See also Franz Cumont, *The Mysteries of Mithra* (in Bibliography under Mythology and Religion).

26. See Stephen R. Turnbull, *The Book of the Samurai: The Warrior Class of Japan* (in Bibliography under History), for a thorough discussion of the samurai tradition. Also see Rick Feilds, *The Code of the Warrior in History, Myth, and Everyday Life,* "Samurai" in the index (in Bibliography under Anthropology).

27. See Peter Berger, *Facing up to Modernity: Excursions in Society, Politics, and Religions* (in Bibliography under History).

28. See Carl Jung, *Modern Man in Search of a Soul,* ch. 10 (in Bibliography under Jungian Thought).

29. Carl Jung quoted in Barbara Hannah, *Jung: His Life and Work* (Boston: Shambhala, 1991), pp. 209–213.

30. Carl Jung, *Civilization in Transition,* part 4, para. 574–5 (in Bibliography under Jungian Thought).

CHAPTER 5: MYTHIC IMAGES OF THE WARRIOR:
THE COSMIC COMBAT

1. The literature on the Myth of the Cosmic Combat is enormous. For a few representative samples, see in the Bibliography under Mythology and Religion the works of Mircea Eliade, and Neil Forsyth, *The Old Enemy: Satan and the Combat Myth.*

2. See note 1. This is a general intuition of all religious traditions and also an assumption in one way or another of the various schools of psychology. For interesting reflections upon this theme, see the writings of C. S. Lewis, including his fiction, especially the *Perelandra* trilogy, as well as such motion picture explorations as the *Star Wars* saga.

3. See the theologian Paul Tillich, *Systematic Theology,* as well as collections of his sermons and essays and other works, for example, *The Eternal Now* (both in Bibliography under Theology and Philosophy).

4. Linda Schele and David A. Freidel, *A Forest of Kings: The Untold Story of the Ancient Maya,* "War, Sacred" and "War Captives" in the index (in Bibliography under Kingship).

5. See Irwin Blacker, *Cortes and the Aztec Conquest,* pp. 109–111 (in Bibliography under History).

6. 1 Sam. 17:23–58.

7. See Henri Frankfort, *Kingship and the Gods: A Study of Ancient Near Eastern Religion as the Integration of Society and Nature,* "Seth," "Osiris," and "Horus" in the index (in Bibliography under Kingship).

8. See Mircea Eliade, *Cosmos and History: The Myth of the Eternal Return,* pp. 55ff. (in Bibliography under Mythology and Religion). Also see Frankfort, "Creation (Mesopotamian)" and "Creation, Babylonian Epic of" in the index. Note as well Samuel N. Kramer, *Sumerian Mythology: A Study of Spiritual and Literary Achievement in the Third Millennium B.C.* (in Bibliography under Mythology and Religion).

9. See A. L. Basham, *The Wonder That Was India,* pp. 240–241 (in Bibliography under Kingship). Also see Walter Krickeberg et al., *Pre-Columbian American Religions;* and John Weir Perry, *Lord of*

the Four Quarters, pp. 194, 201, 195–199 (both in Bibliography under Mythology and Religion). In addition, see works there by Mircea Eliade and Joseph Campbell.

10. 1 Cor. 15:51–55.

11. Note Eliade, pp. 54, 56, 62.

12. Ibid., pp. 56–59.

13. See G. S. Kirk and J. E. Raven, *The Presocratic Philosophers*, "Heraclitus of Ephesus" in the index (in Bibliography under Theology and Philosophy).

14. For a sampling of this vast eschatological literature, see Joseph Campbell, *The Masks of God: Occidental Mythology*, "Zoroastrianism" in the index and pp. 200–212 (in Bibliography under Mythology and Religion). See also Rev. 21:1–7.

15. Rev. 19:11–20:15.

16. The psychological literature on the phenomenon of projection is enormous. Virtually all schools of psychology acknowledge and seek to understand how it is that we project our own repressed and unacknowledged wishes, motives, and talents upon others. For a representative sampling in this area, see Richard I. Evans, *Jung on Elementary Psychology: A Discussion Between C. G. Jung and Richard I. Evans;* Carl Jung, *Man and His Symbols*, pp. 72–75; and Marie Louise Von Franz, *Projection and Recollection in Jungian Psychology* (all in Bibliography under Jungian Thought). For the perspectives of other schools, see David Shapiro, *Neurotic Styles;* and Ronald R. Lee and J. Colby Martin, *Psychology After Kohut*, "Projection" and "Projective Identification" in the index (in Bibliography under Other Psychologies).

CHAPTER 6: THE WAY OF THE WARRIOR

1. See, for example, Anthony Storr, *Human Destructiveness*, ch. 1 (in Bibliography under Other Psychologies). Also see Ronald R. Lee and J. Colby Martin, *Psychotherapy After Kohut*, ch. 14 (in Bibliography under Other Psychologies). In addition, see Robert Moore and Douglas Gillette, *King, Warrior, Magician, Lover: Rediscovering the Archetypes of the Mature Masculine* (in Bibliography under Jungian Thought).

2. See Lee and Martin, "False Self" in the index.

3. The Jungian literature on the Anima is vast. For a sampling, see Joseph Campbell, ed., *The Portable Jung*, pp. 148ff.; Jolande Jacobi, *The Psychology of C. G. Jung*, pp. 5, 114ff., 120–1; Carl Jung, *Man and His Symbols*; Carl Jung, *Mysterium Coniunctionis: An Inquiry into the Separation and Synthesis of Psychic Opposites in Alchemy*; Loren E. Pedersen, *Dark Hearts: The Unconscious Forces That Shape Men's Lives*; John A. Sanford, *The Invisible Partners: How the Male and Female in Each of Us Affects Our Relationships*; and Anthony Stevens, *Archetypes: A Natural History of the Self* (all in Bibliography under Jungian Thought).

4. An interesting myth that speaks of this fear is the "Myth of the Tapir Woman" of the Mehinaku Native Americans of Central Brazil. David D. Gilmore, in *Manhood in the Making: Cultural Concepts of Masculinity*, pp. 96–98 (in Bibliography under Anthropology).

5. It also entails a necessary idealization of the masculine qualities of the father and later of the male peer group.

6. From Judah Goldin's version of "The Wisdom of the Fathers," Judah Goldman, *The Living Talmud*, p. 105 (in Bibliography under Theology and Philosophy).

7. See Don S. Browning, *Generative Man: Psychoanalytic Perspectives*, chs. 6 and 7, especially p. 192 (in Bibliography under Other Psychologies).

8. The Warrior as an archetype is in the service of the masculine Self, what we have called the King archetype. Brain structure research, we believe, shows that the Warrior arises in the aversive/aggressive subsystem of the Limbic System, and that the King is the totality of masculine brain functions, of which the Warrior is a vital part. (See Appendix B.) In terms of the psychology that emanates from the "wiring" of the male brain, the Warrior, when properly integrated into the whole, is on a self-affirmative, world-building mission. When the Warrior becomes detached from the hegemony of the King, or when the Warrior possesses the Ego, a man becomes either sadistic or masochistic. Unintegrated Warrior energy either crashes like a loose canon through acting-out behaviors in the external world (the Sadist), or turns inward and eats a man alive (the Masochist). The King, and ultimately a "divine" Reality, identical to Jung's cogendered King/Queen Self, is the highest form of the Transpersonal Other that the Warrior can serve.

9. That is, we will project upon them our own idealizations and infinite longings for mirroring, for confirmation, for pleasure, etc., instead of transferring such idealizations and longings to the only adequate image capable of holding them, what religions have called "God." For a treatment of this idea in the arena of romantic love, see Robert Johnson, *We: Understanding the Psychology of Romantic Love* (in Bibliography under Jungian Thought).

10. From the "Villa of the Mysteries," Pompeii, late first century B.C.

11. Castaneda, Carlos. *Journey to Ixtlan: The Lessons of Don Juan*, pp. 84–85 (in Bibliography under Theology and Philosophy).

12. This is contained in, for example, the Hindu image of the god Shiva, dancing the dance of universal destruction, destroying Maya and the misleading works of the spaciotemporal world. We also know, from our own lives, that sometimes, perhaps most often, change and growth are a gradual process of almost microscopically small "bites" of new learning. But sometimes we come to a moment when the only thing that will serve is a sudden, dramatic "slaying" of our past ways of thinking, feeling, and acting. Then, and only then, are we ready for renewal. Often, without any intention on our part, the old ways rapidly stale, and we feel that something has died inside us. Unless we are chronically depressed, this experience of "death" is temporary and serves as preparation for the coming of new life. Of course, the idea that the old must die in order for the new to be born is ubiquitous throughout nature and the human experience. The Creation Myths throughout the world, as well as myths of Death and Resurrection, reflect this deep understanding.

CHAPTER 7:
THE MASOCHIST: A DISHONEST WARRIOR

1. See Theodore Millon's comprehensive work with the concept of bipolarity in his *Modern Psychopathology: A Biosocial Approach to Maladaptive Learning and Functioning*; also see his *Disorders of Personality: DSM–III: Axis II*, especially p. 58 (both in Bibliography under Other Psychologies). In addition, see James Hillman et al., *Puer Papers*, "Senes and Puer: An Aspect of the Historical and Psychological Present" (in Bibliography under Jungian Thought).

2. For a fuller discussion of this concept, see Murray Stein, ed., *Jungian Analysis*, ch. 16 (in Bibliography under Jungian Thought).

3. See Millon, *Disorders of Personality*, ch. 4.

4. Ibid., ch. 9.

CHAPTER 8: THE SADIST: POSSESSION BY THE WARRIOR WITHIN

1. See D. W. Winnicott, *The Maturational Processes and the Facilitating Environment* (London: Hogarth Press, 1965); and D. W. Winnicott, *Playing and Reality* (New York: Penguin Books, 1980).

2. Actual childhood experiences of humiliation and shaming constellate the primordial Sadist in the psyche. Originally, our rage is a defense thrown up by the Libido to keep us alive, to mobilize us to fight back against the toxic effects on the budding self structures of these humiliating and shaming (in the language of Self-psychology, "fragmenting") experiences.

3. Their humanity would awaken not only their empathy for others, but more important, their empathy for themselves. To experience themselves empathically would be to experience just how violated they had been, how betrayed, how attacked. The realization that we have been brutalized even as very small infants by those once-all-powerful adults whom we were compelled by need (actual physical need as well as archetypally motived idealizations) to love, adore, and trust is intolerable to most people because it is too painful, and because it reminds us of our *ongoing* vulnerability in the face of the inevitability of our own deaths.

4. See Ann Ulanov and Barry Ulanov, *Cinderella and Her Sisters: The Envied and the Envying* (in Bibliography under Other Psychologies), for an in-depth discussion of the dynamics of envy.

5. See Theodore Millon, *Disorders of Personality* ch. 7 (in Bibliography under Other Psychologies).

6. For example, see Millon's discussion of this phenomenon, pp. 212–13, ibid., 396.

7. Ibid., p. 396. Here he discusses this same dynamic as it appears in the paranoid personality.

8. See Appendix C.

9. Women become objects for the gratification of power needs

primarily, and secondarily, for the relief of genitally confined sexual arousal. The Warrior in his sadistic Shadow pole is coldly detached from any kind of relatedness. The old boot camp chant, "This is my rifle and this is my gun; this is for shooting and this is for fun!" sums up the Shadow Warrior's violation of a woman's personhood.

10. See Gérard Lauzun, *Sigmund Freud: The Man and His Theories*, p. 154 (in Bibliography under Other Psychologies). Also see Herbert Marcus, *Eros and Civilization: A Philosophical Inquiry into Freud*, "Sublimation" in the index (in Bibliography under Other Psychologies).

CHAPTER 9: DRAWING THE SWORD: THE CHALLENGE OF INITIATION

1. This may seem unlikely at first glance. But two points need to be noted. The first is that the vast majority of the men who participate in various facets of the men's movement share the general complaint that they feel disempowered, unable to set and maintain legitimate boundaries in interpersonal relationships and in relationship to their work, and unable to live out their own deep feelings about who they really are—in their personal lives and professionally. The second point is that the incidence of young male violence—primarily against other young males, secondarily against women, children, the elderly, and others—is on the rise. Violent acting out is an indication not of centered empowerment but of a profound sense of impotence, frustration, inadequate avenues for legitimate self-affirmation and appropriate aggression, and a general blockade of Libido.

2. See Carl Jung, *Aion: Researches into the Phenomenology of the Self*, "Androgyny," "Quaternio/Quaternity," "Self," and "Syzygy" in the index; see also Carl Jung, *Mysterium Coniunctionis: An Inquiry into the Separation and Synthesis of Psychic Opposites in Alchemy*, "Androgyne/Androgeny" and "Self" in the index (both in Bibliography under Jungian Thought). In addition, see Appendices A and C.

3. The literature of family systems theory repeatedly emphasizes that children are forced to live out the unlived lives of their parents. See, for example, Lynn Hoffman, *Foundations of Family Therapy* (New York: Basic Books, 1981).

4. While Self-psychologists do not usually talk in the so-called mechanistic language of the Freudians, i.e., "super-ego," they use similar, though more processual, concepts for describing this phenomenon. See Ronald R. Lee and J. Colby Martin, *Psychotherapy After Kohut*, ch. 15 (in Bibliography under Other Psychologies).

5. This pervasive prejudice in our Christian heritage, still a powerful subterranean influence on our contemporary secular culture, probably originates in Jesus' own admonitions to "turn the other cheek," and to not resist evil. It also stems from a misunderstanding of the nature of his sacrifice on the Cross, the propensity to see him as a suffering martyr instead of as a man who consciously chose to embrace evil and "swallow up" death in victory, as St. Paul says. The "meek and mild" ideal, with its injunction even against feeling anger (Matt. 5:21–22), has resulted in the demonization of legitimate self-affirmation and aggression. Much of modern psychotherapeutic process is an attempt to free people from the toxic effects of repressing their need to be self-affirming.

6. Men need to feel *em*powered. That is, they need to feel a deep and living connection with (a) their own feelings, whatever those feelings are, and (b) their instincts, whatever those instincts are. Men need permission to feel sad, angry, hurt, fearful, depressed, exuberant, wild, lonely. And they need permission to honor their animal instincts, which include instincts for aggression and sexuality. Becoming *empowered* is not the same thing as seeking external forms of power. In fact, the two tend in opposite directions, at least initially. Often, the quest for power in the form of dominance is a dysfunctional substitute for real connectedness with our authentic selves. On the other hand, if we begin acting from a sense of *inner* power, power of the external variety may fall into our hands as well. Then our task is to steward our "realms" so that others too will be enabled to live their lives more authentically. Empowered men are not a threat. Genuinely empowered men are a blessing.

7. We are using the term the "mysteries of the sword" as a way of describing the path of the warrior that includes the vital tasks of personal empowerment and public mission. These tasks inevitably entail the facing of life-and-death issues—perhaps physical life-and-death issues, but even more fundamentally, the issues surrounding psychological/spiritual life and death, the life or death of the Soul.

8. Men have, or more realistically *are had by*, both penis and

phallus. If "penis" is used as a symbol for softness and tenderness, fine. But if the soft penis is used as a comprehensive and defining symbol for masculinity, then those who so use it are cutting men off from their Libido and from connection with their firmness, their decisiveness, and their phallic joy.

9. See Eugene Monick, *Phallos: Sacred Image of the Masculine* (in Bibliography under Jungian Thought).

10. This is common knowledge among biologists. For an interesting look at the genetic impulse for old age and death, see Robert A. Wallace, *The Genesis Factor*, ch. 7 (in Bibliography under Anthropology).

11. For example, Matt. 26:30–56.

12. Robert Bly, *Iron John: A Book About Men*, p. 151 (in Bibliography under Literature).

13. See, for example, Jolande Jacobi, *The Psychology of C. G. Jung*, pp. 60ff., 124ff. (in Bibliography under Jungian Thought). See also Carl Jung, *The Structure and Dynamics of the Psyche*, vol. 8 of *Collected Works* (New York: Princeton University Press, 1960), pp. 314–315.

14. For example, see Ad de Vries's excellent *Dictionary of Symbols and Imagery*, "Lake," "Ocean," and "Water" in the index (in Bibliography under Jungian Thought).

15. There are numerous references in the literature of depth psychology to stones as symbols of the masculine Self. For example, see Carl Jung, *Psychology and Religion: West and East*, "Philosophers' Stone" in the index and especially p. 314 (in Bibliography under Jungian Thought).

16. See Robert Moore and Douglas Gillette, *The King Within: Accessing the King in the Male Psyche*, pp. 215–216 (in Bibliography under Jungian Thought).

17. While there are different interpretations of these images, past and present, the interpretation we offer here is informed by our psychoanalytic understanding of the trajectory of initiation into maturity in each of the four masculine powers. In our view the process of initiation moves from denial and projection of a power (or libidinal energy), encounter with the power in the self, initial inflation and grandiose acting out, acceptance of mentorship, attainment of mastery with humility, and finally stewardship of the power in service of mature selfhood and human community. This initiation/maturation process

will be discussed in *The Magician Within*, a forthcoming volume in this series.

CHAPTER 10: THE APPRENTICE KNIGHT: ACCESSING AND MASTERING WARRIOR ENERGY

1. See Appendix B.

2. For an extensive introduction to the various techniques of active imagination, see Robert Moore and Douglas Gillette, *The King Within: Accessing the King in the Male Psyche*, ch. 9 (in Bibliography under Jungian Thought), a companion volume to this series.

3. George R. Bach, *Creative Aggression: The AA of Assertive Living* (New York: NAL/Dutton), 1989.

4. Ambrose Hollingworth Redmoon, "No Peaceful Warriors: How Can You Call Yourself a Warrior If You Won't Fight?" *Gnosis Magazine* (Fall 1991):40–44.

APPENDIX B: ARCHETYPES AND THE LIMBIC SYSTEM

The argument of this appendix owes a great debt to George S. Everly, Jr.'s synthesis of the most recent work of a number of brain researchers in his paper "The Biological Bases of Personality: The Contribution of Paleocortical Anatomy and Physiology to Personality and Personality Disorders." He presented this paper at the First International Congress on Disorders of Personality, in Copenhagen, Denmark, in August 1988.

1. Paul D. MacLean, *The Triune Brain in Evolution: Role in Paleocerebral Functions*, p. 257 (in Bibliography under Brain Research).

2. Ibid., p. 264.

3. Ibid., in toto.

4. Everly, p. 5.

5. Ibid., p. 5.

6. Ibid., p. 5.

7. Ibid., p. 5.

8. Ibid., p. 6.

9. MacLean, ch. 21.

10. Everly, p. 7.

11. Everly, p. 8; and MacLean, ch. 19.

12. MacLean, pp. 322ff.

13. Everly, p. 9; and MacLean, chs. 18–27.

14. MacLean, pp. 497, 498, ch. 27.

APPENDIX C: ARCHETYPES AND THE ANIMA

1. See Alice Miller's discussion of "poisonous pedagogy" and the role of the mother in destroying her children's sense of Self (in Bibliography under Other Psychologies).

2. An example of this can be found in the Canaanite Baʻal cycle of myths. In them Baʻal, king of the created world, has two enemies to defeat—chaos (Yamm) and death (Mot). He succeeds against Yamm, but is slain by Mot. His sister and his queen, Anath, kills Baʻal and resurrects Baʻal. Anath further proves herself to be Baʻal's comrade-in-arms when she summons his enemies to a banquet, locks the doors, and kills them all.

BIBLIOGRAPHY

1. ANTHROPOLOGY

Ardrey, Robert. *African Genesis: A Personal Investigation into the Animal Origins and Nature of Man.* New York: Dell, 1963.
———. *The Social Contract: A Personal Inquiry into the Evolutionary Sources of Order and Disorder.* New York: Dell, 1971.
Clemente, C. D., and D. B. Lindsley, eds. *Aggression and Defense: Neural Mechanisms and Social Patterns.* Vol. 5. Berkeley: University of California Press, 1967.
Dart, Raymond A. "The Predatory Transition from Ape to Man." *International Anthropological and Linguistic Review* 1 (1953): 201–219.

Eisler, Riane. *The Chalice and the Blade: Our History, Our Future.* San Francisco: Harper & Row, 1988.

Feilds, Rick. *The Code of the Warrior in History, Myth, and Everyday Life.* New York: HarperCollins, 1991.

Fisher, Helen E. *The Sex Contract: The Evolution of Human Behavior.* New York: Quill, 1983.

Gillette, Douglas. "Men and Intimacy." *Wingspan: A Journal of the Male Spirit* (September 1990): 9.

———. Review of Gilmore, *Manhood in the Making. Wingspan: A Journal of the Male Spirit* (Spring, 1991): 12.

Gilmore, David. *Manhood in the Making: Cultural Concepts of Masculinity.* New Haven: Yale University Press, 1990.

Herdt, Gilbert H., ed. *Rituals of Manhood: Male Initiation in Papua New Guinea.* Berkeley: University of California Press, 1982.

Johnson, Roger N. *Aggression in Man and Animals.* Philadelphia: Saunders, 1972.

Klein, Richard G. *The Human Career: Human Biological and Cultural Origins.* Chicago: University of Chicago Press, 1989.

Laughlin, William S. "Hunting: An Integrating Biobehavior System and Its Evolutionary Importance." In *Man the Hunter,* edited by Richard B. Lee and Irven DeVore. Chicago: Aldine, 1966.

Leakey, Louis S. B. "Development of Aggression as a Factor in Early Human and Pre-Human Evolution." In *Aggression and Defense,* edited by Clemente and Lindsley. Berkeley: University of California Press, 1967.

Lopez, Barry Holstrum. *Of Wolves and Men.* New York: Charles Scribner's Sons, 1978.

MacKinnon, Michael. *The Ape Within Us.* New York: Holt, Rinehart and Winston, 1978.

Montagu, Ashley, ed. *Man and Aggression.* New York: Stein and Day, 1973.

Morgan, Elaine. *The Descent of Woman.* New York: Stein and Day, 1972.

Morris, Desmond. *Intimate Behavior.* New York: Random House, 1971.

———. *The Naked Ape: A Zoologist's Study of the Human Animal.* New York: McGraw-Hill, 1967.

Rappaport, R. A. "The Sacred in Human Evolution." *Annual Review of Ecology and Systematics* 2 (1971): 23–44.

Roper, M. K. "A Survey of the Evidence for Intrahuman Killing in the Pleistocene." *Current Anthropology* 10 (1989): 427–459.

Scott, J. P. "Biological Basis of Human Warfare: An Interdisciplinary Problem." In *Interdisciplinary Relationships in the Social Sciences,* edited by M. Sherif and C. Sherif. Chicago: Aldine, 1969.

Smithsonian Editors. *Man and Beast: Comparative Social Behavior.* Smithsonian Annual III. Washington, D.C.: Smithsonian Institution Press, 1971.

Tierney, Patrick. *The Highest Altar: Unveiling the Mystery of Human Sacrifice.* New York: Penguin Books, 1989.

Turner, Victor. *The Ritual Process: Structure and Anti-Structure.* Ithaca: Cornell University Press, 1969.

Wallace, Robert A. *The Genesis Factor.* New York: William Morrow, 1979.

Webster, Hutton. *Primitive Secret Societies.* New York: Macmillan, 1932.

Wilson, Edward. O. *On Human Nature.* Cambridge: Harvard University Press, 1978.

———. *Sociobiology: The Abridged Edition.* Cambridge: Harvard University Press, 1980.

———. *Sociobiology: The New Synthesis.* Cambridge: Harvard University Press, 1975.

Zillman, Dolf. *Hostility and Aggression.* Hillsdale, N.J.: Halsted Press, 1979.

2. BRAIN RESEARCH

Ashbrook, James B. *The Human Mind and the Mind of God: Theological Promise in Brain Research.* Lanham, Md.: University Press of America, 1984.

Harth, Erich. *Windows on the Mind: Reflections on the Physical Basis of Consciousness.* New York: Quill, 1983.

Jaynes, Julian. *The Origin of Consciousness in the Breakdown of the Bicameral Mind.* Boston: Houghton Mifflin, 1976.

MacLean, Paul D. *The Triune Brain in Evolution: Role in Paleocerebral Functions.* New York: Plenum Press, 1990.

Moir, Anne, and David Jessel. *Brain Sex: The Real Difference Be-*

tween Men and Women. New York: Carol Publishing Group, 1991.

Restak, Richard M. *The Brain*. New York: Bantam Books, 1984.

3. COMMAND

Brewer, William B. *Operation Torch*. New York: St. Martin's Press, 1985.

Essame, H. *Patton: A Study in Command*. New York: Charles Scribner's Sons, 1976.

Gabriel, Richard A., and Paul Savage. *Crisis in Command: Misman- agement in the Army*. New York: Hill & Wang, 1978.

Keegan, John. *The Mask of Command*. New York: Penguin, 1987.

MacArthur, Douglas. *Reminiscences*. New York: McGraw-Hill, 1964.

Manchester, William. *American Caesar: Douglas MacArthur, 1880– 1964*. Boston: Little, Brown, 1978.

Mosley, Leonard. *Marshall: Hero for Our Times*. New York: Hearst Books, 1982.

Phillips, T. R., ed. *Roots of Strategy*. Harrisburg, Pa.: Stackpole Books, 1985.

———. *Roots of Strategy*. Book Two. Harrisburg, Pa.: Stackpole Books, 1987.

Sharon, Ariel. *Warrior: An Autobiography*. New York: Simon & Schuster, 1989.

Wallace, Brenton. *Patton and His Third Army*. Nashville: Battery Press, 1981.

Warren, Bennis G., and Burt Names. *Leaders*. New York: Harper & Row, 1985.

Yeager, Chuck. *Yeager: An Autobiography*. New York: Bantam Books, 1985.

4. COURTESY AND COURTLY LOVE

Baron, Francis Xavier. *Amour Courtois, The Medieval Ideal of Love: A Bibliography*. Louisville: University of Louisville Press, 1973.

Boase, Roger. *The Origin and Meaning of Courtly Love*. Totowa, N.J.: Rowman and Littlefield, 1977.

Bornstein, Diane. *Mirror of Courtesy*. Hamden, Conn.: Archon Books, 1975. Interface of ceremony, the ideal, and social action.

Cross, Tom Peete. *Lancelot and Guinevere: A Study of the Origins of Courtly Love*. Chicago: University of Chicago Press, 1930.

Ferrante, Joan M. *In Pursuit of Perfection: Courtly Love in Medieval Literature*. Port Washington, N.Y.: Kennikat Press, 1975.

Goldin, Frederic. *The Mirror of Narcissus in the Courtly Love Lyric*. Ithaca: Cornell University Press, 1967.

Kaum Blumstein, Andree. *Misogyny and Idealization in the Courtly Romance*. Bonn: Bouvier, 1977.

Leclercq, Jean. *Monks and Love in 12th Century France: Psycho-Historical Essays*. New York: Oxford University Press, 1979. See Chapter 5, "Aggressiveness or Repression in St. Bernard and His Monks."

Newman, Francis X., ed. *The Meaning of Courtly Love*. Albany: State University of New York Press, 1969.

Owen, Douglas David Roy. *Noble Lovers*. New York: New York University Press, 1975.

Rougemont, Denis de. *Passion and Society*. Translated by Montgomery Belgion. London: Faber & Faber, 1941.

Salomon, Louis Bernard. *The Devil Take Her: A Study of the Rebellious Lover in English Poetry*. Philadelphia: University of Pennsylvania Press, 1931.

Topsfield, L. T. *Troubadors and Love*. London: Cambridge University Press, 1975.

5. HISTORY

Albright, William F. *The Archeology of Palestine*. New York: Penguin Books, 1949.

Aldred, Cyril. *Akhenaten, Pharaoh of Egypt: A New Study*. London: Thames & Hudson, 1968; London: Sphere Books, Abacus edition, 1972.

"Andean Civilization." *Encyclopedia Britannica*. Chicago, 1967. Vol. 1, pp. 889–891.

Barnett, R. D., and Werner Forman. *Assyrian Palace Reliefs and Their Influence on the Sculptures of Babylon and Persia*. London: Batchworth Press.

Barr, Stringfellow. *The Will of Zeus: A History of Greece.* New York: Dell, 1965.

Berger, Peter. *Facing Up to Modernity: Excursions in Society, Politics, and Religions.* New York: Basic Books, 1977.

Blacker, Irwin R., and *Horizon* Magazine Editors. *Cortes and the Aztec Conquest.* New York: American Heritage, 1965.

Browning, Robert. *The Emperor Julian.* Berkeley: University of California Press, 1976.

Cristofani, Mauro. *The Etruscans.* New York: Galahad Books, 1979.

Edwards, I. E. S. *The Pyramids of Egypt.* Harmondsworth, Middlesex, Eng.: Penguin Books, 1947.

Gernet, Jacques. *A History of Chinese Civilization.* New York: Cambridge University Press, 1982. Originally published in French as *Le Monde chinois.* Paris: Librairie Armand Colin, 1972.

Gimbutas, Marija. *The Goddesses and Gods of Old Europe: Myths and Cult Images.* Berkeley: University of California Press, 1982.

Gurney, O. R. *The Hittites.* New York: Penguin Books, 1952.

Morley, Sylvanus G., George W. Brainerd, and Robert J. Sharer. *The Ancient Maya.* 4th ed. Stanford: Stanford University Press, 1983.

National Geographic Editors. *The Age of Chivalry.* Washington, D.C.: National Geographic Society, 1969.

Peterson, Frederick. *Ancient Mexico: An Introduction to the Pre-Hispanic Cultures.* 1959. Reprint. Toms River, N.J.: Capricorn Books, 1962.

Steindorff, George, and Keith C. Seele. *When Egypt Ruled the East.* Chicago: University of Chicago Press, 1942.

Thompson, J. Eric S. *The Rise and Fall of Maya Civilization.* Norman: University of Oklahoma Press, 1954. Especially Chapter 2.

Time Editors. *The Epic of Man.* New York: Time, 1961. Especially Chapter 7.

Time-Life Books Editors. *The Age of the God-Kings, 3000–1500 B.C.* New York: Time-Life Books, 1990.

Turnbull, Stephen R. *The Book of the Samurai: The Warrior Class of Japan.* New York: W. H. Smith Publishers, 1982.

6. JUNGIAN THOUGHT

Andrews, Valerie, Robert Bosnak, and Karen Walter Goodwin, eds. *Facing Apocalypse*. Dallas: Spring Publications, 1987.

Corneau, Guy. *Absent Fathers, Lost Sons: The Search for Masculine Identity*. Boston: Shambhala, 1991.

de Castillejo, Irene Claremont Day. *Knowing Woman: A Feminine Psychology*. New York: G. P. Putnam's Sons, 1973; New York: Harper & Row, 1974.

De Vries, Ad. *Dictionary of Symbols and Imagery*. Amsterdam: North-Holland Publishing Co., 1984.

Edinger, Edward. *The Creation of Consciousness: Jung's Myth for Modern Man*. Toronto: Inner City Books, 1984.

———. *Ego and Archetype*. New York: G. P. Putnam's Sons, 1972; New York: Penguin Books, 1974.

Evans, Richard I. *Jung on Elementary Psychology: A Discussion Between C. G. Jung and Richard I. Evans*. New York: E. P. Dutton, 1976.

Garrison, Jim. *The Darkness of God: Theology after Hiroshima*. Grand Rapids, Mich.: William B. Eerdmans, 1982.

Hannah, Barbara. *Encounters with the Soul: Active Imagination as Developed by C. G. Jung*. Boston: Sigo Press, 1981.

Hillman, James et al. *Puer Papers*. Dallas: Spring Publications, 1979. Especially the chapter by Hillman, "Senex and Puer: An Aspect of the Historical and Psychological Present."

Jacobi, Jolande. *Complex, Archetype, Symbol in the Psychology of C. G. Jung*. Princeton: Princeton University Press, 1959. Originally published as *Komplex/Archetypus/Symbol in der Psychologie C. G. Jungs*. Zurich and Stuttgart: Rascher Verlag, 1957.

———. *The Psychology of C. G. Jung*. London: Routledge & Kegan Paul, 1942; New Haven: Yale University Press, 1973.

Jaffé, Aniela. *The Myth of Meaning: Jung and the Expansion of Consciousness*. New York: Penguin Books, 1975.

Johnson, Robert. *We: Understanding the Psychology of Romantic Love*. San Francisco: Harper & Row, 1983.

Jung, Carl G. *Aion. Researches into the Phenomenology of the Self*.

Vol. 9 of *The Collected Works of C. G. Jung*. Princeton: Princeton University Press, 1959.

——. *Civilization in Transition*. Vol. 10 of *The Collected Works of C. G. Jung*. Princeton: Princeton University Press, 1970.

——. *Man and His Symbols*. New York: Dell, 1964; London: Aldus Books, 1964.

——. *Modern Man in Search of a Soul*. New York: Harcourt Brace Jovanovich, 1933.

——. *Mysterium Coniunctionis: An Inquiry into the Separation and Synthesis of Psychic Opposites in Alchemy*. 2d ed. Princeton: Princeton University Press, 1970.

——. *The Portable Jung*. Edited by Joseph Campbell. New York: Penguin Books, 1971. Reprint of Jung's work in *Aion*, pp. 148ff.

——. *Psyche and Symbol: A Selection from the Writings of C. G. Jung*. Edited by Violet deLaszlo. Garden City, N.Y.: Doubleday, 1958.

——. *Psychology and Alchemy*. 2d ed. 1953. Reprint. Princeton: Princeton University Press, 1980.

——. *Psychology and Religion: West and East*. Vol. 11 of *The Collected Works of C. G. Jung*. 2d ed. Princeton: Princeton University Press, 1958.

Layard, John. *A Celtic Quest: Sexuality and Soul in Individuation*. Dallas: Spring Publications, 1975.

Monich, Eugene. *Phallos: Sacred Image of the Masculine*. Toronto: Inner City Books, 1987.

Moore, Robert, ed. *Carl Jung and Christian Spirituality*. Mahwah, N.J.: Paulist Press, 1988.

——. *The Magician and the Analyst: Ritual, Sacred Space, and Psychotherapy*. Chicago: Center for the Scientific Study of Religion, 1992.

——, and Forrest Craven. "Dancing the Four Quarters: Visions of Grassroots Masculine Leadership in the 1990's." North American Masculine Mysteries School, 1991.

——, and Douglas Gillette. *King, Warrior, Magician, Lover: Rediscovering the Archetypes of Mature Masculinity*. San Francisco: HarperCollins, 1990.

——, and Michael Meade. *The Great Self Within: Men and the Quest for Significance*. St. Paul: Alley Press, 1990.

——, and Daniel Meckel, eds. *Jung and Christianity in Dialogue:*

Faith Feminism, and Hermeneutics. Mahwah, N.J.: Paulist Press, 1991.

Neumann, Erich. *Art and the Creative Unconscious.* Princeton: Princeton University Press, 1959.

Pedersen, Loren E. *Dark Hearts: The Unconscious Forces That Shape Men's Lives.* Boston: Shambhala, 1991.

Perry, John Weir. *Roots of Renewal in Myth and Madness: The Meaning of Psychotic Episodes.* San Francisco: Jossey-Bass, 1976.

Sanford, John A. *Dreams: God's Forgotten Language.* New York: J. B. Lippincott, 1968.

———. *Evil: The Shadow Side of Reality.* New York: Crossroad, 1981.

———. *The Invisible Partners: How the Male and Female in Each of Us Affects Our Relationships.* New York: Paulist Press, 1980.

Stein, Murray, ed. *Jungian Analysis.* Boulder: Shambhala, 1984.

Stevens, Anthony. *Archetypes: A Natural History of the Self.* New York: Quill, 1983. Originally published as *Archetype: A Natural History of the Self.* London: Routledge & Kegan, 1982.

———. *The Roots of War: A Jungian Perspective.* New York: Paragon House, 1989.

Von Franz, Marie Louise. *Projection and Recollection in Jungian Psychology.* Peru, Ill.: Open Court, 1980. Originally published as *Spiegelungen der Seele: Projektion und innere Sammlung.* Stuttgart: Kreuz Verlag, 1978.

———. *Shadow and Evil in Fairytales.* Dallas: Spring Publications, 1974.

Wolff, Toni. "Structural Forms of the Feminine Psyche." Privately printed for the Students Association, C. G. Jung Institute, Zurich, July 1956.

7. KINGSHIP

Basham, A. L. *The Wonder That Was India.* 1954. Reprint. New York: Grove Press, 1959.

Bricker, Victoria Reifler. *The Indian Christ, the Indian King: The Historical Substrate of Maya Myth and Ritual.* Austin: University of Texas Press, 1981.

Chaney, William A. *The Cult of Kingship in Anglo-Saxon England.* Berkeley: University of California Press, 1970.

Emery, Walter B. *Archaic Egypt.* Harmondsworth, Middlesex, Eng.: Penguin Books, 1961.

Engnell, Ivan. *Studies in Divine Kingship in the Ancient Near East.* Uppsala: Almquist and Wiksells, 1943; Oxford: Basil Blackwell, 1967.

Evans-Pritchard, Edward E. *The Divine Kingship of the Shilluk of the Nilotic Sudan.* Cambridge, Eng.: Cambridge University Press, 1948.

Frankfort, Henri. *The Birth of Civilization in the Near East.* Garden City, N.Y.: Doubleday, 1956.

———. *Kingship and the Gods: A Study of Ancient Near Eastern Religion as the Integration of Society and Nature.* Chicago: University of Chicago Press, 1948.

Gadd, C. J. *Ideas of Divine Rule in the Ancient East.* Schweich Lectures on Biblical Archeology. London: British Academy, 1948.

Gonda, Jan. "Ancient Indian Kingship from the Religious Point of view." *Numen* 3 (1955): 36–71, 122–155; *Numen* 4 (1956): 4, 24–58, 127–164.

Grottanelli, Christiano. "Kingship in the Ancient Mediterranean World." *Encyclopedia of Religions* 8 (1987): 317–322.

Hadfield, Percival. *Traits of Divine Kingship in Africa.* Westport, Conn.: Greenwood Press, 1979.

Hocart, Arthur Maurice. *Kingship.* London: Oxford University Press, 1927.

Hooke, S. H. *Myth, Ritual, and Kingship: Essays on the Theory and Practice of Kingship in the Ancient Near East and in Israel.* Oxford: Clarendon Press, 1958.

Johnson, Aubrey R. *Sacral Kingship in Ancient Israel.* Cardiff: University of Wales Press, 1955.

Kantorowicz, Ernest H. *The King's Two Bodies: A Study in Medieval Political Theology.* Princeton: Princeton University Press, 1957.

Keightley, David N. "The Religious Commitment: Shang Theology and the Genesis of Chinese Political Culture." *History of Religions* 17, no. 2 (November 1977/February–May 1978): 211–225.

Kenik, Helen A. "Code of Conduct for a King: Psalm 101." *Journal of Biblical Literature* 95, no. 3 (1976): 391–403.

Kwanten. *Imperial Nomads: A History of Central Asia, 500–1500.* Philadelphia: University of Pennsylvania Press, 1979.

Malandra, William W. *An Introduction to Ancient Iranian Religion: Readings from the "Avesta" and "Achaemenid" Inscriptions.* Minneapolis: University of Minnesota Press, 1983.

Meyerowitz, Eva L. R. *The Divine Kingship in Ghana and Ancient Egypt.* London: Faber & Faber, 1940.

Moore, Robert, and Douglas Gillette. *The King Within: Accessing the King in the Male Psyche.* New York: William Morrow, 1992.

Mumford, Lewis. *The City in History: Its Origins, Transformations, and Prospects.* New York: Harcourt, Brace and World, 1968.

Murray, M. A. "Evidence for the Custom of Killing the King in Ancient Egypt." *Man* 14 (1914): 17–23. London: Royal Anthropological Institute, 1914.

Myers, Henry Allen. *Medieval Kingship.* Chicago: Nelson-Hall, 1982.

Parrinder, Edward G. "Divine Kingship in West Africa." *Numen* 3 (1956): 111–121.

Peters, Edward. *The Shadow King: Rex Inutilis in Medieval Law and Literature, 751–1327.* New Haven: Yale University Press, 1970.

Richards, J. W. "Sacral Kings of Iran." *Mankind Quarterly* 20, nos. 1–2 (1979): 143–160.

Ruttan, Karl. "The Evolution of the Kingship Archetype in the Old Testament." Thesis, Chicago Theological Seminary, 1975.

Schele, Linda, and David A. Freidel. *A Forest of Kings: The Untold Story of the Ancient Maya.* New York: William Morrow, 1990.

Seligman, C. G. *Egypt and Negro Africa: A Study in Divine Kingship.* London: G. Routledge and Sons, 1934.

Tucci, Giuseppe. "The Secret Characters of the Kings of Ancient Tibet." *East and West* 6, no. 3 (October 1955): 197–205.

Valeri, Valerio. *Kingship and Sacrifice: Ritual and Society in Ancient Hawaii.* Translated from Hawaiian by Paula Wissing. Chicago: University of Chicago Press, 1985.

Waida, Manabu. "Notes on Sacred Kingship in Central Asia." *Numen* 23 (December 1976): 179–190.

———. "Sacred Kingship in Early Japan." Ph.D. diss., University of Chicago, 1974.

———. "Sacred Kingship in Early Japan: A Historical Introduction." *History of Religions* 15, no. 4 (May 1976): 319–342.

———. "Symbolism of 'Descent' in Tibetan Sacred Kingship and Some East Asian Parallels." *Numen* 20 (April 1973): 60–78.

Wales, H. G. *The Mountain of God: A Study in Early Religion and Kingship.* London: Bernard Quaritch, 1953.

Wilson, John A. *The Culture of Ancient Egypt.* Chicago: University of Chicago Press, 1956. Originally published as *The Burden of Egypt.*

Zuidema, R. Tom. "The Lion in the City: Royal Symbols of Transition in Cuzco." *Journal of Latin American Lore* 9, no. 1 (Summer 1983): 39–100.

8. LITERATURE

Aeschylus. *Agamemnon.* In *Greek Literature in Translation,* edited by Whitney Oates and Charles Murphey. New York: David McKay, 1944.

Bly, Robert. *Iron John: A Book About Men.* New York: Vintage Books, 1992.

Euripides. *The Bachae.* In *Euripedes V,* edited by David Grene and Richmond Lattimore. New York: Washington Square Press, 1968.

Herbert, Frank. *Dune.* New York: Putnam, 1984.

Hesse, Hermann. *The Journey to the East.* Translated by Hilda Rosner. New York: Farrar, Straus & Giroux, 1956.

Lacy, Norris J., ed. *The Arthurian Encyclopedia.* New York: Garland, 1986.

Lewis, C. S. *'Til We Have Faces.* New York: Harcourt, Brace and World, 1956.

Sophocles. In *Sophocles I,* edited by David Grene and Richmond Lattimore. Chicago: University of Chicago Press, 1954.

Tennyson, Alfred. *Idylls of the King.* Edited by J. M. Gray. New Haven: Yale University Press, 1983.

Tolkien, J.R.R. *The Return of the King.* New York: Ballantine Books, 1965.

White, T. H. *The Once and Future King.* London: Collins, 1958.

9. MARTIAL ARTS

Aiki News. Bilingual magazine of Aikido. Tokyo: Demeure Saito #201, Daikyo-cho, 3-banchi, Shinjuku-ku.

Dobson, Terry, and Victor Miller. *Giving In to Get Your Way*. New York: Delacorte Press, 1978.

Draeger, Donn F. *Classical Budo*. New York: Weatherhill, 1973.

———. *Modern Bujutsu and Budo*. New York: Weatherhill, 1974.

Heckler, Richard Strozzi, ed. *Aikido and the New Warrior*. Berkeley: North Atlantic Books, 1985.

———. *The Anatomy of Change*. Boulder: Shambhala, 1984.

Klickstein, Bruce. *Living Aikido*. Berkeley: North Atlantic Books, 1987.

Leonard, George. *The Silent Pulse*. New York: E. P. Dutton, 1978.

———. *The Ultimate Athlete*. New York: Viking, 1975.

Saito, Morihiro. *Traditional Aikido*. Vols. 1–5. Tokyo: Minato, 1976.

Stevens, John. *Aikido: The Way of Harmony*. Boulder: Shambhala, 1984.

Tohei, Koichi. *Book of Ki: Co-ordinating Mind and Body in Daily Life*. Tokyo: Japan Publications, 1976.

Uyeshiba, Kisshomaru. *The Spirit of Aikido*. Translated from Japanese by Tartetsu Unno. New York, San Francisco, and Tokyo: Kodansha International, 1984. Paperback edition, 1988.

Uyeshiba, Morihei, and Kissomaru Uyeshiba. *Aikido*. New York: Japan Publications, 1985.

Westbrook, A., and O. Ratti. *Aikido and the Dynamic Sphere*. Rutland, Vt.: Charles E. Tuttle, 1970.

10. MEDIEVAL KNIGHTHOOD, CHIVALRY, AND SPIRITUALITY

Barber, Richard William. *The Knight and Chivalry*. London: Longman, 1970.

———. *The Reign of Chivalry*.

Bernard of Clairvaux. *Bernard of Clairvaux: Selected Works*. Edited by Gillian R. Evans. In *Classics of Western Spirituality* series.

New York: Paulist Press, 1987. See especially "Sermon on the Song of Songs."

Boemer, H. *The Jesuits*. Philadelphia: Castle Press, 1928.

Bradford, Ernle. *The Shield and the Sword: The Knights of St. John, Jerusalem, Rhodes and Malta*. New York: E. P. Dutton, 1973.

Carlson, David. "Religious Writers and Church Councils on Chivalry." In *The Study of Chivalry: Resources and Approaches*, edited by Howell Chickering and Thomas Seiler. Kalamazoo, Mich.: Board of the Medieval Institute, 1988. Includes Bernard of Clairvaux's *"De Laude Novae Militiae"* (In Praise of the New Chivalry).

Cheyette, Frederic L., ed. *Lordship and Community in Medieval Europe*. 1968. Reprint. Melbourne, Fla: Krieger, 1975. See especially the essay by Arno Bornst, "Knighthood in the High Middle Ages."

Duby, Georges. *The Three Orders: Feudal Society Imagined*. Translated by Arthur Goldhammer. Chicago: University of Chicago Press, 1982.

Gautier, Leon. *Chivalry*. Edited by Jacques Levron. Translated by D. C. Dunning. New York: Barnes and Noble, 1965. See especially Chapter 5 on ritual admission to chivalry.

Harper-Bill, Christopher, and Ruth Harvey, eds. *The Ideals and Practice of Medieval Knighthood II*. Papers from the Third Strawberry Hill Conference on Medieval Knighthood. Wolfeboro, N.H.: Boydell Press, 1988.

Kauffman, Christopher J. *Faith and Fraternalism: The History of the Knights of Columbus*. New York: Harper & Row, 1982.

Keen, Maurice. *Chivalry*. New Haven: Yale University Press, 1984. Definitive historical study.

Liu, Jo-yu. *The Chinese Knight-Errant*. Chicago: University of Chicago Press, 1967.

Shakleford, H. K. *The Knight's Armor: A History of the Early Origin of the Order of Knights of Pythias*. New Haven: J. H. Benham, 1869.

Woodhouse, F. C. *The Military Religious Orders of the Middle Ages*. New York: Pott, Young, 1879.

11. MYTHOLOGY AND RELIGION

Albright, William F. *Yahweh and the Gods of Canaan: A Historical Analysis of Two Contrasting Faiths.* Garden City, N.Y.: Doubleday, 1968.

Barnstone, Willis, ed. *The Other Bible.* San Francisco: Harper & Row, 1984.

Breasted, James H. *The Dawn of Conscience: The Sources of Our Moral Heritage in the Ancient World.* New York: Charles Scribner's Sons, 1933.

Campbell, Joseph. *The Hero with a Thousand Faces.* Rev. ed. Princeton: Princeton University Press, 1968.

———. *The Masks of God: Creative Mythology.* New York: Penguin, 1970.

———. *The Masks of God: Occidental Mythology.* New York: Viking Press, 1964; New York: Penguin, 1976.

———. *The Mythic Image.* Princeton: Princeton University Press, 1974.

———. *The Power of Myth.* Garden City, N.Y.: Doubleday, 1988.

Carrasco, David. *Quetzalcoatl and the Irony of Empire: Myths and Prophecies in the Aztec Tradition.* Chicago: University of Chicago Press, 1982.

Cohn-Haft, Louis. *Source Readings in Ancient History: The Ancient Near East.* New York: Thomas Y. Crowell, 1965.

Cumont, Franz. *The Mysteries of Mithra.* 1903. Reprint. New York: Dover Publications, 1956.

Dodds, E. R. *Pagan and Christian in an Age of Anxiety: Some Aspects of Religious Experience from Marcus Aurelius to Constantine.* New York: W. W. Norton, 1965.

Eliade, Mircea. *Cosmos and History: The Myth of the Eternal Return.* Princeton: Bollingen Foundation, 1954; New York: Harper & Row, 1959.

———. *Patterns in Comparative Religion.* New York: World Publishing, 1963. Originally published as *Traite d'histoire des religions.* Paris: Éditions Payot.

———. *Rites and Symbols of Initiation: The Mysteries of Birth and Rebirth.* New York: Harper & Row, 1958.

————. *The Sacred and the Profane: The Nature of Religion: The Significance of Religious Myth, Symbolism, and Ritual Within Life and Culture.* New York: Harcourt, Brace and World, 1959. Originally published in German. Reinbek: Rowohlt Taschenbuch Verlag, 1957.

Forsyth, Neil. *The Old Enemy: Satan and the Combat Myth.* Princeton: Princeton University Press, 1987.

Frankfort, Henri. *Ancient Egyptian Religion.* New York: Columbia University Press, 1948; New York: Harper & Row, 1961.

Frazer, James G. *The Golden Bough: A Study in Magic and Religion.* 12 vols. 3d ed. 1915. Reprint. New York: Macmillan, 1922. Paperback edition, 1963.

Gaer, Joseph. *How the Great Religions Began.* 1929. Reprint. New York: New American Library/Signet Books, 1954.

Godwin, Joscelyn. *Mystery Religions in the Ancient World.* San Francisco: Harper & Row, 1981; London: Thames & Hudson, 1981.

Graves, Robert. *The Greek Myths.* 2 vols. Harmondsworth, Middlesex, Eng.: Penguin Books, 1955.

Hadas, Moses. *The Apocrypha: An American Translation.* New York: Alfred A. Knopf and Random House, 1959.

Hamilton, Edith. *Mythology: Timeless Tales of Gods and Heroes.* New York: New American Library, 1940.

Henderson, Joseph L. *Thresholds of Initiation.* Middletown, Conn.: Wesleyan University Press, 1967.

Hooke, S. H. *Middle Eastern Mythology.* New York: Penguin Books, 1963.

James, William. *The Varieties of Religious Experience.* New York: New American Library, 1958.

Jobes, Gertrude. *Dictionary of Mythology, Folklore, and Symbols.* Metuchen, N.J.: Scarecrow Press, 1962.

Kramer, Samuel Noah. *Sumerian Mythology: A Study of Spiritual and Literary Achievement in the Third Millennium B.C.* New York: Harper & Row, 1961.

Krickenberg, Walter et al. *Pre-Columbian American Religions.* New York: Holt, Rinehart and Winston, 1968.

Lind, Millard C. *Yahweh Is a Warrior: The Theology of Warfare in Ancient Israel.* Scottdale, Pa.: Herald Press, 1980.

MacCana, Proinsias. *Celtic Mythology*. London: Hamlyn, 1970.

Miller, Patrick D. *The Divine Warrior in Early Israel*. Cambridge: Harvard University Press, 1973.

Moody, Raymond. *Life After Life*. New York: Bantam Books, 1975.

Mylonas, George E. *Eleusis and the Eleusinian Mysteries*. Princeton: Princeton University Press, 1961.

Oikonomides, A. N. *Mithraic Art: A Search for Unpublished and Unidentified Monuments*. Chicago: Ares, 1975.

Otto, Rudolf. *The Idea of the Holy*. New York: Oxford University Press, 1923.

Pagels, Elaine. *The Gnostic Gospels*. New York: Random House/Vintage Books, 1979.

Perowne, Stewart. *Roman Mythology*. London: Hamlyn, 1969.

Perry, John Weir. *Lord of the Four Quarters: The Mythology of Kingship*. Mahwah, N.J.: Paulist Press, 1991.

———. *Lord of the Four Quarters: Myths of the Royal Father*. New York: G. Braziller, 1966; New York: Macmillan/Collier Books, 1970.

Pritchard, James B., ed. *An Anthology of Texts and Pictures*. Vol. 1 of *The Ancient Near East*. Princeton: Princeton University Press, 1958.

Reichel-Dolmatoff, Gerardo. *Amazonian Cosmos: The Sexual and Religious Symbolism of the Tukano Indians*. Translated from Spanish by Gerardo Reichel-Dolmatoff. Chicago: University of Chicago Press, 1971.

Robinson, James M., ed. *The Nag Hammadi Library*. San Francisco: Harper & Row, 1977.

Scholem, Gershom. *Major Trends in Jewish Mysticism*. New York: Schocken Books, 1946.

———. *Origins of the Kaballah*. Edited by R. J. Werblowsky. Translated by Allan Arkush. Princeton: Princeton University Press (for the Jewish Publication Society), 1987. Originally published as *Ursprung und Anfänge der Kabbala*. Berlin: Walter de Gruyter, 1962.

Seltman, Charles T. *The Twelve Olympians*. New York: Thomas Y. Crowell, 1960.

Smith, Huston. *The Religions of Man*. New York: Harper & Row, 1965.

Smith, Morton. *Jesus the Magician*. San Francisco: Harper & Row, 1978.

Sullivan, Lawrence, ed. *Healing and Restoring: Health and Medicine in the World's Religious Traditions*. New York: Macmillan, 1988.

Thomas, D. Winton, ed. *Documents from Old Testament Times*. New York: Harper & Row, 1961.

Thompson, Brian. *The Story of Prince Rama*. Harmondsworth, Middlesex, Eng.: Penguin Books, 1980.

Underhill, Evelyn. *Mysticism*. New York: E. P. Dutton, 1911.

Walker, J.B.R. *The Comprehensive Concordance to the Holy Scriptures*. 1929. Reprint. New York: Macmillan, 1948.

Watts, Alan, and Eliot Elisofan. *Erotic Spirituality: The Vision of Konarak*. New York: Macmillan/Collier Books, 1971.

Weston, Jesse L. *From Ritual to Romance: An Account of the Holy Grail from Ancient Ritual to Christian Symbol*. Cambridge: Cambridge University Press, 1920; Garden City, N.Y.: Doubleday, 1957.

Wheatley, Paul. *The Pivot of the Four Quarters*. Chicago: Aldine Publishing, 1971.

12. OTHER PSYCHOLOGIES

Ansbacher, Heinz L., and Rowena R. Ansbacher. *The Individual Psychology of Alfred Adler*. New York: Harper & Row, 1964.

Beahrs, John O. *Unity and Multiplicity: Multilevel Consciousness of Self in Hypnosis, Psychiatric Disorder and Mental Health*. New York: Brunner/Mazel, 1981.

Bettelheim, Bruno. *Freud and Man's Soul*. New York: Alfred A. Knopf, 1983.

Bowlby, John. *Separation: Anxiety and Anger*. New York: Basic Books, 1973.

Browning, Don. *Generative Man: Psychoanalytic Perspectives*. Philadelphia: Westminster Press, 1973; New York: Dell, 1975.

Freud, Sigmund. *Moses and Monotheism*. New York: Alfred A. Knopf, 1939.

———. *Totem and Taboo*. New York: W. W. Norton, 1950; London: Routledge & Kegan Paul, 1950.

Hendrix, Harville. *Getting the Love You Want*. New York: Henry Holt, 1988.

Keen, Sam. *Fire in the Belly: On Being a Man*. New York: Bantam, 1991.

Lauzun, Gérard. *Sigmund Freud: The Man and His Theories*. Greenwich, Conn.: Fawcett, 1962; Paris: Pierre Seghers, 1962.

Lee, Ronald R., and J. Colby Martin. *Psychotherapy After Kohut: A Textbook of Self Psychology*. Hillsdale, N.J.: Analytic Press, 1991.

Marcuse, Herbert. *Eros and Civilization: A Philosophical Inquiry into Freud*. Boston: Beacon Press, 1955.

Miller, Alice. *The Drama of the Gifted Child: How Narcissistic Parents Form and Deform the Emotional Lives of their Talented Children*. New York: Basic Books, 1981. Originally published as *Das Drama des begabten Kindes*. Frankfurt am Main: Suhrkamp, 1979.

———. *For Your Own Good: Hidden Cruelty in Child-Rearing and the Roots of Violence*. New York: Farrar Straus Giroux, 1984. Originally published as *Am Anfang war Erziehung*. Frankfurt am Main: Suhrkamp, 1980.

———. *Thou Shalt Not Be Aware: Society's Betrayal of the Child*. New York: Farrar Straus Giroux, 1984. Originally published as *Du sollst nicht merken*. Frankfurt am Main: Suhrkamp, 1981.

Millon, Theodore. *Disorders of Personality: DSM-III: Axis II*. New York: John Wiley & Sons, 1981.

———. *Modern Psychopathology: A Biosocial Approach to Maladaptive Learning and Functioning*. Prospect Heights, Ill.: Waveland Press, 1983.

Peck, M. Scott. *People of the Lie: The Hope for Healing Human Evil*. New York: Simon & Schuster, 1983.

———. *The Road Less Traveled: A New Psychology of Love, Traditional Values and Spiritual Growth*. New York: Simon & Schuster, 1978.

Rizzuto, Ana-Maria. *The Birth of the Living God: A Psychoanalytic Study*. Chicago: University of Chicago Press, 1979.

Rogers, David J. *Fighting to Win: Samurai Techniques for Your Work and Life*. Garden City, N.Y.: Doubleday, 1984.

Schmookler, Andrew Bard. *Out of Weakness: Healing the Wounds That Lead Us to War*. Toronto: Bantam Books, 1988.

Shapiro, David. *Neurotic Styles.* New York: Basic Books, 1965.

Spencer, Laura J. *Winning Through Participation.* Dubuque, Iowa: Kendall Hunt (under the auspices of the Institute for Cultural Affairs), 1989.

Storr, Anthony. *Human Aggression.* New York: Bantam Books, 1968.

———. *Human Destructiveness.* New York: Grove Weidenfeld, 1991.

———. *The Integrity of the Personality.* New York: Random House, 1992.

Ulanov, Ann, and Barry Ulanov. *Cinderella and Her Sisters: The Envied and the Envying.* Philadelphia: Westminster Press, 1983.

Winnicott, D. W. *Home Is Where We Start From.* New York: W. W. Norton, 1986.

Wolf, Ernest S. *Treating the Self: Elements of Clinical Self Psychology.* New York: Guilford Press, 1988.

13. PHYSICS AND COSMOLOGY

Editors of Time-Life Books. *Voyage Through the Universe: The Cosmos.* Alexandria, Va.: Time-Life Books, 1988.

Ferris, Timothy. *The Red Limit: The Search for the Edge of the Universe.* New York: William Morrow, 1977; New York: Bantam Books, 1977.

Morris, Richard. *Time's Arrows: Scientific Attitudes Toward Time.* New York: Simon & Schuster, 1984.

14. PRIMATE ETHOLOGY

Barnett, S. A. "Attack and Defense in Animal Societies." In *Aggression and Defense,* edited by Clemente and Lindsley. Berkeley: University of California Press, 1967.

Bourne, Geoffrey H. *Primate Odyssey.* New York: G. P. Putnam's Sons, 1974.

Davis, D. E. "The Physiological Analysis of Aggressive Behavior." In *Social Behavior and Organization Among Vertebrates,* edited by William Etkin. Chicago: University of Chicago Press, 1964.

Desmond, Adrian J. *The Ape's Reflection.* New York: Dial Press/James Wade, 1979.

de Waal, Frans. *Chimpanzee Politics: Power and Sex Among Apes.* New York: Harper & Row, 1982.

———. *Peacemaking Among Primates.* Cambridge: Harvard University Press, 1989.

Eibl-Eibesfeldt, I. *Biology of Peace and War.*

———. "The Fighting Behavior of Animals." *Scientific American* 205 (1961): 112–122.

Fossy, Dian. *Gorillas in the Mist.* Boston: Houghton Mifflin, 1983.

Goodall, Jane. *In the Shadow of Man.* Boston: Houghton Mifflin, 1971.

———. *Through a Window: My Thirty Years with the Chimpanzees of Gombe.* Boston: Houghton Mifflin, 1990.

Heltne, Paul G., and Linda A. Marquardt. *Understanding Chimpanzees.* Cambridge: Harvard University Press, 1989.

Shaw, C. E. "The Male Combat Dance of Crotalid Snakes." *Herpetologia* 4 (1948): 137–145.

Tinbergen, N. "Fighting and Threat in Animals." *New Biology* 14 (1953): 9–24.

15. RITUAL AND INITIATION

Almond, Richard. *The Healing Community: Dynamics of the Therapeutic Milieu.* Stanford: Stanford University Press, 1974.

Bellak, L., M. Hurvich, and H. Gediman. *Ego Functions in Schizophrenics, Neurotics, and Normals.* New York: John Wiley & Sons, 1973.

Benedict, Ruth. "Ritual." *Encyclopaedia of the Social Sciences* 13 (1934): 396–398.

Bossard, James A. S., and Eleanor S. Bell. "Ritual in Family Living." *American Sociological Review* 14 (1949): 463–469.

Davis, Madeleine, and David Wallbridge. *Boundary and Space: An Introduction to the Work of D. W. Winnicott.* New York: Brunner/Mazel, 1981.

Eliade, Mircea. *Rites and Symbols of Initiation: The Mysteries of Birth and Rebirth.* New York: Harper & Row, 1958.

Erikson, Erik. "The Ontogeny of Ritualization." In *Psychoanalysis—A General Psychology,* edited by Loewenstein et al. New York: International Universities Press, 1966.

Frank, Jerome D. *Persuasion and Healing: A Comparative Study of Psychotherapy.* New York: Schocken Books, 1963.

Gay, Volney P. "Psychopathology and Ritual: Freud's Essay 'Obsessive Actions and Religious Practises.' " *Psychoanalytic Review* 62 (1975): 493–507.

———. "Ritual and Self-Esteem in Victor Turner and Heinz Kohut." *Zygon* 18 (September 1983): 271–282.

Goodheart, William B. "Theory of Analytical Interaction." *San Francisco Jung Institute Library Journal* 1, no. 4 (1980): 2–39.

Grimes, Ronald. "Ritual Studies: Two Models." *Religious Studies Review* 2 (1976): 13–25.

Groesbeck, C. Jess. "The Archetypal Image of the Wounded Healer." *The Journal of Analytical Psychology* 20 (1975): 122–145.

Grolnick, Simon A., and Leonard Barkin, eds. *Between Reality and Fantasy: Transitional Objects and Phenomena.* New York: Jason Aronson, 1978.

Guggenbuhl-Craig, Adolf. *Power in the Helping Professions.* Irving, Tex.: Spring, 1971.

Harrison, Jane. *Ancient Art and Ritual.* London: Williams & Norgate, 1913.

———. *Themis: A Study of the Social Origins of Greek Religion.* Cambridge: Cambridge University Press, 1912.

Hart, Onno van der. *Rituals in Psychotherapy: Transition and Continuity.* New York: Irvington Publishers, 1983.

Langs, Robert. *The Bipersonal Field.* New York: Jason Aronson, 1976.

———. *Interactions.* New York: Jason Aronson, 1980.

———. *Technique in Transition.* New York: Jason Aronson, 1978.

———. *The Therapeutic Environment.* New York: Jason Aronson, 1979.

Leach, E. R. "Ritual." *International Encyclopaedia of the Social Sciences* 13:520–526.

McCurdy, Alexander III. "Establishing and Maintaining the Analytical Structure." In *Jungian Analysis,* edited by Murray Stein. Lasalle, Ill.: Open Court, 1982.

Moore, Robert L. "Contemporary Psychotherapy as Ritual Process: An Initial Reconnaissance." *Zygon* 18 (September 1983): 283–294.

———. "Ritual Process, Initiation, and Contemporary Religion." In

Jung's Challenge to Contemporary Religion, edited by Murray Stein and Robert L. Moore. Wilmette, Ill.: Chiron Press, 1987.

Moore, Robert L., Ralph W. Burhoe, and Philip J. Hefner, eds. "Ritual in Human Adaptation." Symposium reported in *Zygon* 18 (September 1983): 209–325.

Perry, John Weir *Roots of Renewal in Myth and Madness*. San Francisco: Jossey-Bass, 1976.

Posinsky, S. H. "Ritual, Neurotic and Social." *American Imago* 19 (1962): 375–390.

Reik, Theodor. *Ritual: Psychoanalytic Studies*. London: Hogarth Press, 1931.

Turner, Victor. *The Drums of Affliction*. Oxford: Clarendon Press, 1968.

———. *From Ritual to Theatre*. New York: Performing Arts Journal Publications, 1982.

———. *Process, Performance and Pilgrimage: A Study in Comparative Symbology*. New Delhi: Concept Publishing Co., 1979.

———. *The Ritual Process: Structure and Anti-Structure*. Chicago: Aldine, 1969; Ithaca: Cornell University Press, 1969.

Turner, Victor, and Edith Turner. *Image and Pilgrimage in Christian Culture*. New York: Columbia University Press, 1978.

van Gennep, Arnold. *The Rites of Passage*. 1908. Reprint. Chicago: University of Chicago Press, 1960.

16. THEOLOGY AND PHILOSOPHY

Castaneda, Carlos. *Journey to Ixtlan: The Lessons of Don Juan*. New York: Simon & Schuster, 1972; New York: Pocket Books, 1974.

Daley, Mary. *Beyond God the Father: Toward a Philosophy of Women's Liberation*. Boston: Beacon Press, 1973.

———. *Gyn/Ecology: The Metaethics of Radical Feminism*. Boston: Beacon Press, 1979.

de Chardin, Teilhard. *The Phenomenon of Man*. New York: Harper & Row, 1959.

Evans-Wentz, W. Y., ed. *The Tibetan Book of the Dead*, 3d ed. New York: Oxford University Press, 1960.

Goldin, Judah. *The Living Talmud*. New Haven: Yale University Press, 1955; New York: New American Library, 1957.

Greenleaf, Robert K. *Servant Leadership: A Journey into the Nature of Legitimate Power and Greatness.* New York: Paulist Press, 1977.

Kelly, J. N. *Early Christian Doctrines.* New York: Harper & Row, 1960.

Kelly, Sean. *Individuation and the Absolute: Hegel, Jung, and the Path Toward Wholeness.* New York: Paulist Press, forthcoming.

Kirk, G. F., and J. E. Raven. *The Presocratic Philosophers.* New York: Cambridge University Press, 1957.

Loye, David. *The Sphinx and the Rainbow: Brain, Mind, and Future Vision.* Boston: Shambhala, 1983.

Nicholas of Cusa. *The Vision of God.* Translated by Gurney. Edited by Evelyn Underhill. New York: Ungar, 1960.

Niebuhr, Reinhold. *The Nature and Destiny of Man.* Vol. 1. New York: Charles Scribner's Sons, 1964.

Nikhilananda, Swami. *The Upanishads.* New York: Ramakrishna-Vivekananda Center, 1949.

Nilsson, Martin P. *Greek Piety.* New York: W. W. Norton, 1969.

Norris, Richard A., Jr., and William G. Rusch, eds. *The Christological Controversy.* Translated by Richard A. Norris. Philadelphia: Fortress Press, 1980.

Plato. "Apology," "Phaedo," and "Republic." In *Plato,* edited by Benjamin Jowett and Louise Loomis. Roslyn, N.Y.: Walter J. Black, 1942.

Prabhupada. *Bhagavad-Gita As It Is.* Bhaktivedanta Book Trust, 1968.

Ruether, Rosemary R. *Sexism and God-Talk: Toward a Feminist Theology.* Boston: Beacon Press, 1973.

Tillich, Paul. *The Courage to Be.* New Haven: Yale University Press, 1952.

——. *The Eternal Now.* New York: Charles Scribner's Sons, 1963.

——. *Systematic Theology.* Vol. 3. Chicago: University of Chicago Press, 1963. Especially Chapter 1, and "The Kingdom of God as the End of History."

Wei, Henry. *The Guiding Light of Lao Tze.* Wheaton, Ill.: Theosophical Publishing House, 1982.

Whitehead, Alfred North. *Adventures of Ideas.* New York: Macmillan, 1933; New York: Free Press, 1967.

————. *Process and Reality*. New York: Macmillan Publishing Co., 1978.

17. WAR AND WEAPONS

Anderson, J. K. *Military Theory and Practice in the Age of Xenophon*. Berkeley: University of California Press, 1970.

Bailey, Ronald H. *The Air War in Europe*. Alexandria, Va.: Time-Life, 1979.

Barker, Thomas M. *The Military Intellectual and Battle: Montecuccoali and the Thirty Years War*. Albany: State University of New York Press, 1975.

Beeler, John. *Warfare in Feudal Europe: 730–1200*. Ithaca: Cornell University Press, 1971.

Bohannan, P., ed. *Law and Warfare: Studies in the Anthropology of Conflict*. Austin: University of Texas Press, 1967.

Bracken, P. *Command and Control of Nuclear Forces*. New Haven: Yale University Press, 1983.

Bramson, Leon, and G. Goethals. *War: Studies from Psychology, Sociology and Anthropology*. New York: Basic Books, 1964.

Brodie, Bernard, and Fawn Brodie. *From Crossbow to H-Bomb*. Bloomington: University of Indiana Press, 1972.

Chandler, David G. *The Campaigns of Napoleon: The Mind and Method of History's Greatest Soldier*. New York: Macmillan, 1973.

Clausewitz, Karl von. *On War*. Edited by Michael Howard and Peter Paret. Princeton: Princeton University Press, 1976.

Contamine, Philippe. *War in the Middle Ages*. Translated by Michael Jones. London: Oxford University Press, 1984. Paperback Edition, Oxford: Basil Blackwell, 1986.

Corvisier, A. *Armies and Societies in Europe*. Bloomington: Indiana University Press, 1979.

Creveld, M. van. *Command in War*. Cambridge: Harvard University Press, 1985.

Delbruck, Hans. *History of the Art of War: Within the Framework of Political History*. Vol. 4. Westport, Conn.: Greenwood, 1975.

Depuy, Trevor. *The Evolution of Weapons and Warfare.* Fairfax, Va.: 1984.

Divale, William. *Warfare in Primitive Societies.* Oxford and Santa Barbara: AB-Clio, 1973.

Dixon, N. *On the Psychology of Military Incompetence.* London: 1976; New York: Basic Books, 1984.

Dower, John W. *War Without Mercy: Race and Power in the Pacific War.* New York: Pantheon, 1986.

Erickson, John. *The Soviet High Command: A Military Political History.* Boulder: Westview, 1984.

Ferguson, R. Brian, ed. *Warfare, Culture and Environment.* London and Orlando: Academic Press, 1984.

Geissler, Erhard. *Biological and Toxin Weapons Today.* Oxford: Oxford University Press, 1986.

Greenhalgh, P.A.C. *Early Greek Warfare: Horsemen and Chariots in the Homeric and Archaic Ages.* Cambridge, Eng.: Cambridge University Press, 1973.

Heath, E. G. *Archery: A Military History.* London: 1980.

Hersh, Seymour M. *Chemical and Biological Warfare: America's Hidden Arsenal.* Indianapolis: Bobbs-Merrill, 1968.

Hittle, J. *The Military Staff.* Harrisburg: Stackpole, 1961.

Howard, Michael. *War in European History.* London: Oxford University Press, 1976.

Howe, Russell W. *Weapons: The International Game of Arms, Money, and Diplomacy.* Garden City, N.Y.: Doubleday, 1980.

Hurley, Vic. *Arrows Against Steel: The History of the Bow.* New York: Mason Charter, 1975.

Jackel, Eberhard. *Hitler's Weltanschauung: A Blueprint for Power.* Middletown, Conn.: Wesleyan University Press, 1972.

Jomini, Baron de. *The Art of War.* Translated by G. H. Mendell. Westport, Conn.: Greenwood, 1971.

Keegan, John. *The Face of Battle.* New York: 1976. Paperback edition, New York: Penguin, 1983.

Keppie, Lawrence. *The Making of the Roman Army: From Republic to Empire.* Totowa, N.J.: B & N Imports, 1984.

Luttwak, E. *The Grand Strategy of the Roman Empire.* Baltimore: Johns Hopkins University Press, 1978.

MacNeill, W. H. *The Pursuit of Power: Technology, Armed Force, and Society Since A.D. 1000.* Chicago: University of Chicago Press, 1982.

Mahan, Alfred Thayer. *The Influence of Sea Power upon History, 1660–1783.* Boston: Little, Brown, 1974.

Mallett, M. *Mercenaries and Their Masters.* London and Totowa, N. J.: Rowman, 1974.

Nef, John U. *War and Human Progress: An Essay on the Rise of Industrial Civilization.* New York: Norton, 1968.

O'Connell, Robert L. *Of Arms and Men: A History of War, Weapons, and Aggression.* New York: Oxford University Press, 1989.

Polisensky, J. V. *War and Society in Europe, 1618–1848.* Cambridge: Cambridge University Press, 1978.

Pruitt, D., and R. Snyder, eds. *Theory and Research on the Causes of Wars.* Englewood Cliffs, N.J.: Prentice-Hall, 1969.

Ropp, Theodore. *War in the Modern World.* Durham, N.C.: Duke University Press, 1959.

Singer, Charles, E. J. Holmyard, and A. R. Hall, eds. *A History of Technology.* Oxford: Oxford University Press, 1954.

Spector, Ronald H. *Eagle Against the Sun: The American War with Japan.* New York: Free Press, 1985.

Turney-High, H. *Primitive War.* Columbia, S.C.: 1949.

Tzu, Sun. *The Art of War.* New York: Oxford University Press, 1971.

Verbruggen, J. *The Art of Warfare in Western Europe During the Middle Ages.* Amsterdam and New York: Elsevier, 1977.

Wedgewood, C. W. *The Thirty Years War.* New Haven: Yale University Press, 1939.

Wood, Charles T. *The Age of Chivalry.* New York: Universe, 1970.

Wright, Quincy. *A Study of War.* Chicago: University of Chicago Press, 1942.

18. AUDIOTAPES

Books and audiotapes by Robert Moore and Douglas Gillette may be ordered directly from: The Bookstore, C. G. Jung Institute of Chicago, 1567 Maple, Evanston, IL 60201.

Moore, Robert
  Archetypal Images of the King and Warrior
  Archetypal Images of the Magician and Lover

The Ego and Its Relations with the Unconscious, 2 tapes
The Four Couples Within: The Structure of the Self and the Dynamics of Relationship, 3 tapes
Healing the Masculine
Jihad: The Archetype of Spiritual Warfare
Jungian Psychology and Human Spirituality: Liberation from Tribalism in Religious Life, 5 tapes
The King Within: A Study in Masculine Psychology, 7 tapes
The Liminoid and the Liminal
The Lover Within: A Study in Masculine Psychology, 8 tapes
The Magician Within: A Study in Masculine Psychology, 4 tapes
Masculine Power: Archetypal Potential and Planetary Challenge
The Meaning of Sacred Space in Transformation
Narcissism and Human Evil
The Nature of Sacred Space
Portraits of Crisis: Experience and Theory, 2 tapes
The Psychology of Satan: Encountering the Dark Side of the Self, 8 tapes
Rediscovering Masculine Potentials, 4 tapes
Rediscovering the Mature Masculine: Resources from Archetypal Psychology, 3 tapes
Ritual, Initiation, and Contemporary Religion
The Trickster Archetype: Potential and Pathology, 3 tapes
The Vessel of Analysis
The Warrior Within: A Study in Masculine Psychology, 5 tapes

Robert Moore and Forrest Craver
Dancing the Four Quarters: Visions of Grassroots Masculine Leadership in the 1990's

Robert Moore and Douglas Gillette
King, Warrior, Magician, Lover: Rediscovering the Archetypes of the Mature Masculine

Robert Moore and Michael Meade
The Great Self Within: Men and the Quest for Significance

Robert Moore and Caroline Stevens
The One and the Two: Gender, Identity and Relationship, 8 tapes

INDEX

INDEX

INDEX

Grateful acknowledgment is made to the following individuals and publishers for permission to reproduce material used in creating the figures in this book. Every effort has been made to locate the copyright holders of material used here. Omissions brought to our attention will be corrected in future editions.

p. 4: Atsina Warriors, photograph by Edward S. Curtis, 1908. Published by AZUSA, courtesy of the Denver Public Library, Western History Department.

p. 31: The Jung Foundation (reproduced from Edward Edinger, *Ego and Archetype* [New York: Penguin Books, 1974]).

p. 32(top): Dr. Pedro Rojas (reproduced from *The Art and Architecture of Mexico from 10000 B.C. to the Present Day*).

p. 33(top): British Museum, Honolulu (reproduced from Joseph Campbell, *The Mythic Image* [Princeton: Princeton University Press, 1974]); (bottom): University of Chicago Press.

p. 39: Baron Hugo Van Lawick.

p. 40: Baron Hugo Van Lawick.

p. 46: Houghton Mifflin Co., Boston, for the photo by Hugo Van Lawick in *In the Shadow of Man* (1988) by Jane Goodall.

p. 55: Henri Frankfort, *Kingship and the Gods* (Chicago: University of Chicago Press, 1948), fig. 10, courtesy the Oriental Institute of the University of Chicago.

p. 56(top): Richard G. Klein, *The Human Career* (Chicago: University of Chicago Press, 1989), fig. 4.13; (bottom): HarperCollins, New York, for the photo on p. 4, South African Bushmen, photo no. N32618, cat. no. H 11406, Peabody Museum, Harvard University, Cambridge, Massachusetts, in *The Code of the Warrior in History, Myth, and Everyday Life* by Rick Fields.

p. 63: American Heritage Press, New York, for the picture on p. 276 of Short Bull in *Indian Wars* by Robert M. Utley and Wilcomb E. Washburn.

p. 68: Paulist Press, New York, and Institute for World Spirituality, Chicago, for pl. 15, Ba'al of Lightning, reproduced by permission of Claude F. A. Schaeffer in *Lord of the Four Quarters: The Mythology of Kingship* (1991) by John Weir Perry.

p. 72: Negative no. 324834, courtesy Department of Library Services, American Museum of Natural History, New York.

p. 75: Henri Frankfort, *Kingship and the Gods* (Chicago: University of Chicago Press, 1948), fig. 3, the Narmer palette, from Hierakonpolis; after a cast in the Oriental Institute, University of Chicago.

p. 77(top): HarperCollins, New York, p. 36, courtesy of the Bettmann Archive, New York, in *The Code of the Warrior in History, Myth, and Everyday Life* (1991) by Rick Fields; (bottom): Galahad Books, New York, p. 106, small bronze votive figure of a warrior; first half of the fifth century B.C.E.; Museo Archeologico, Florence, in *The Etruscans* by Mauro Cristofani.

p. 78: Grove Press, New York, pl. LLIb, memorial to a Chieftan, Dumad, Baroda, C.E. 1298, in *The Wonder That Was India* (1954) by A. L. Basham.

p. 79: London: Batchworth Press, cover image, illustrations photographed by Werner Forman, in *Assyrian Palace Reliefs and Their Influence on the Sculptures of Babylon and Persia*, by R. D. Barnett.

p. 80: Berkeley: University of California Press, fig. 6, a Persian king hunting wild boar, silver bowl, Freer Gallery of Art, Washington, D.C., in *The Emperor Julian* (1976) by Robert Browning.

p. 82: Feltham, Middlesex, England: Hamlyn Publishing, p. 102, in *Roman Mythology* (1969) by Stewart Perowne.

p. 83: New York: W. H. Smith, p. 129, a proud samurai, in *The Book of the Samurai: The Warrior Class of Japan* (1982) by Stephen R. Turnbull.

p. 90: New York: Grove Press, p. 130, fig. 10, royal warriors (after a terra-cotta plaque from Ahicchatra, U.P., circa 6th century A.D.), in *The Wonder That Was India* (1954) by A. L. Basham.

p. 94: New York: Coward, McCann and Geoghegan, p. 154, in full plate armor, the Red Cross Knight from Spenser's *Faerie Queene*, courtesy of RTH, Radio Times Hulton Picture Library, London, in *The Mystery of King Arthur* (1975) by Elizabeth Jenkins.

p. 99: New York: Time, p. 56, massive stone statue of a Toltec warrior, Tula, valley of

Mexico, courtesy of Giselle Freund, in *Ancient America* (1967) by Jonathan Norton Leonard and Editors of Time-Life Books.

p. 103: New York: Perennial Library/Harper & Row, p. 92, pl. 193, a portion of the vast underground tomb for the Chinese emperor Qin Shi Huang, Xi'an, Shaanxi Province, in *Historical Atlas of World Mythology, Vol. 2: The Way of the Seeded Earth: Part I: The Sacrifice* (1988) by Joseph Campbell.

p. 111: New York: Coward, McCann and Geoghegan, pp. 112–113, M.S. 805 f. 262, fourteenth century, in *The Mystery of King Arthur* (1975) by Elizabeth Jenkins.

p. 112: New York: Time, p. 53, Amitabha Buddha, Kamakura, Japan, photo by K. Tateishi, in *The World's Great Religions* (1957) by Editors of Time-Life Books.

p. 117: Jack Holland and John Monroe, *Empires: Their Rise and Fall: The Order of Rome: Imperium Romanum: Charlemagne and the Holy Roman Empire* (Boston: Boston Publishing, 1986), p. 104, Otto I, Saxon king of the Germans, picture researcher, Janet Adams.

p. 133: London: Batchworth Press, pl. 40, King Tiglath-pileser leading the storming of the city, probably in Babylonia; prisoners beheaded and impaled (Nimrud, Central Palace), British Museum, no. 118903, in *Assyrian Palace Reliefs and Their Influence on the Sculptures of Babylon and Persia* by R. D. Barnett.

p. 136: New York: Doubleday, p. 111, Kayan party in longhouse, in *The Power of Myth* (1988) by Joseph Campbell, with Bill Moyers, ed. Betty Sue Flowers.

p. 144: Bollingen Series XCVII: 2, Princeton University Press, p. 165, a young Masai, in *C. G. Jung: Word and Image* (1979) by Aniela Jaffe, ed.

p. 147: Minneapolis: Dillon Press, p. 60, Akseli Gallen-Kallela took inspiration from the Kalevala, Finland's folk epic; here the artist depicts the witch Louhi attacking Väinämöinen and his faithful followers, in *Of Finnish Ways* (1981) by Aini Rajanen.

p. 153: New York: Time, p. 268, New Guinean with ritual ax, photo by Eliot Elisofon, from set 28703, in *The Epic of Man* (1961) by Editors of Life.

p. 156: Beverly Hills, Calif.: A and M Records, illustration on back cover of the record album *Rick Wakeman: The Myths and Legends of King Arthur and the Knights of the Round Table.*

p. 158: New York: Coward, McCann and Geoghegan, p. 198, Arthur's knights accoutred by their ladies before going into battle, detail of a tapestry by Edward Burne-Jones and William Morris, City Museums and Art Gallery, Birmingham, England, in *The Mystery of King Arthur* (1975) by Elizabeth Jenkins.

p. 167: New York: Time-Life, p. 38, special issue of *Life*, Fall 1990, "Ernest Hemingway," in *The One Hundred Most Important Americans of the 20th Century.*

p. 169: Boston: Houghton Mifflin, p. 194, Churchill in his constituency, at the opening of a fifty-acre recreation area, October 14, 1937; medals include Northwest Frontier of India, 1887; Battle of Omdurman, 1898; Boer War, 1899–1901, in *Winston Churchill: The Wilderness Years* (1982) by Martin Gilbert.

p. 170: New York: HarperCollins, p. 98, portrait of the Imperial Bodyguard Huerh-chia, Ch'ing Dynasty, dated 1769, the Dillon Fund Gift, courtesy the Metropolitan Museum of Art, New York, in *The Code of the Warrior in History, Myth, and Everyday Life* (1991) by Rick Fields.

p. 196: New York: Charles Scribner's Sons, p. 103, family cohesiveness, the key to life in hunting families, credit to John Bangress, in *Of Wolves and Men* (1978) by Barry Holstum Lopez.

Color photo 1: New York: Time, pp. 37–38, a bear hunters' ritual, painting by Rudolf F. Zallinger-Romain Robert, in *The Epic of Man* (1961) by Editors of Life.

Color photo 2: New York: Time, p. 30, military standard, a mosaic made for display in royal processions, details a successful campaign by troops of the powerful city-state of Ur around 2500 B.C.E.; Trustees of the British Museum, London, in *The Age of God-Kings: Time-Frame 300–1500 B.C.* (1987) by Editors of Time-Life Books.

Color photo 3: New York: Viking Penguin, pl. 20, Nubian soldiers with bows and arrows, painted wooden model from the tomb of the nomarch Mesehti at Asyut, Middle Kingdom, Eleventh Dynasty, approximately 2000 B.C.E.; Egyptian Museum, Cairo, in *The Art of Egypt: The Time of the Pharaohs* (1980) by Irmgard Woldering.

Color photo 4: New York: Viking Penguin, p. 59, *The Last Battle*, painting by Jeroo Roy, in *The Story of Prince Rama* (1980) by Brian Thompson.

Color photo 5: Editors of Life, *The Epic of Man* (New York: Time, 1961), p. 160, the head of a warrior bespeaks many of the qualities of the Etruscans: strength, intelligence, and martial prowess, Dmitri Kessel, courtesy Villa Giulia Museum; originally appeared in *Life*, February 13, 1956, p. 58.

Color photo 6: New York: W. H. Smith, cover image, no attribution, in *The Book of the Samurai: The Warrior Class of Japan* (1982) by Stephen R. Turnbull.

Color photo 7: New York: Time, p. 72, guardian image, Dmitri Kessel, from set 20713, in *The World's Great Religions* (1957) by Editors of Time-Life Books.

Color photo 8: Feltham, Middlesex, England: Hamlyn House, pl. 111, *Simon Bolivar the Liberator*, by Fernando Leal, 1932, Escuela Nacional Preparatoria, Mexico, D.F., in *The Art and Architecture of Mexico* (1986) by Pedro Rojas.

Color photo 9: New York: Nonesuch Records, record album, *The Wild Bull*, by Morton Subotnick.

Color photo 10: New York: W. H. Smith, p. 170, a Samurai giving a cup of water to a wounded comrade, from Yoshitoshi's *Kwaidai Higaku Senso*, in *The Book of the Samurai: The Warrior Class of Japan* (1982) by Stephen R. Turnbull.

Color photo 11: Gemini Smith, distributed by Doubleday, Garden City, New York, p. 135, Mixtec Warriors from *Mexico: A History in Art* by Bradley Smith.